Cockfight

A Fable of Failure

Kier-La Janisse

For Jimmy

Table of Contents

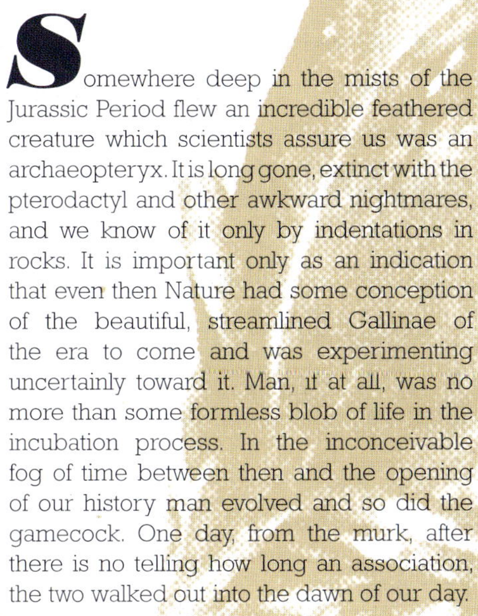

Tim Pridgen,
Courage: The Story of Modern Cockfighting

Somewhere deep in the mists of the Jurassic Period flew an incredible feathered creature which scientists assure us was an archaeopteryx. It is long gone, extinct with the pterodactyl and other awkward nightmares, and we know of it only by indentations in rocks. It is important only as an indication that even then Nature had some conception of the beautiful, streamlined Gallinae of the era to come and was experimenting uncertainly toward it. Man, if at all, was no more than some formless blob of life in the incubation process. In the inconceivable fog of time between then and the opening of our history man evolved and so did the gamecock. One day, from the murk, after there is no telling how long an association, the two walked out into the dawn of our day.

Intro~duction

WELC
MANSF

Mansfield, Georgia looks much the same as it did in 1974, when New World Pictures descended on the tiny town of less than 400 people to shoot a film whose main character shared the hamlet's name. Many storefronts in the sleepy town square sit vacant, some lost to fire or succumbed to various forms of decrepitude over the years, while a new roadside diner called Rooster's finds itself — rather fittingly in this context — the locus of social activity. The bus station where cocker Frank Mansfield disembarks, driven back home penniless after losing everything in a match, is now a lot that sells cars and ornate backyard sheds, but one can cross the street to where the railroad tracks once were - they were ripped up in 2016 — and see the town pretty much as Warren Oates did when he played the complex anti-hero of Monte Hellman's controversial film *Cockfighter*.

Frank Mansfield (Warren Oates) is a solitary cockfighter who, after shooting his mouth off, loses his prize cock in a late night drunken hack, immediately before he is poised to win a decisive tournament. As a result, he takes a vow of silence until he can win the Cockfighter of the Year Award. He teams up with former Madison Avenue ad man Omar Baradinsky, who dropped out to raise fighting cocks, and they make a partnership for the season, hustling their way through the cockfighting circuit in the hopes of being invited to the prestigious Southern Conference Tournament in Milledgeville, where Frank will get his long-awaited second chance at winning the medal.

In addition to constantly fielding the question of "why *Cockfighter*?" the typical trajectory when I bring it up is for the conversation to be hijacked by a discussion of *Two-Lane Blacktop*. Even Monte Hellman himself deflected the conversation in such a way. Now, *Two-Lane Blacktop* is a great film. It is a canonical film. There are books about it. But this is a book about *Cockfighter*.

Furthermore, it's not just a book about the film *Cockfighter*, nor is it just a book about the book *Cockfighter*, although it does delve into the production history of both. But it is also a book about work, about ideals, about stubbornness — and perhaps most of all it's about what happens when you break a promise to yourself. That said, this is not the True Story of *Cockfighter*. All the people who could tell that story are dead. This is *my* story of *Cockfighter*, with all the layers of meaning and mythology that it has shown me.

I first saw *Cockfighter* when Anchor Bay re-issued it in 2001. My friend Norm Hill — I

worked at Black Dog Video in Vancouver, he worked at Scarecrow in Seattle, so we were cross-border video store buddies — had been working with Bill Lustig for Anchor Bay producing releases for the then-burgeoning format of DVDs, and he was a big champion of Monte Hellman. Up to that point I'd only seen *Two-Lane Blacktop*, and that too was due to Anchor Bay's highly-anticipated release of the film in 1999. Anchor Bay was the first (and practically the only) sponsor of my film festival CineMuerte (1999-2005) and next to the mail-order bootlegs I voraciously devoured, their releases of forgotten cult and Euro-Horror films were my lifeblood at that time.

Though I respected *Two-Lane Blacktop*, I connected with *Cockfighter* more profoundly — even though the two films are plumbing similar themes. Both films feature protagonists who are not big on words who specialise in an illegal subculture and navigate their worlds with an internally-codified brand of integrity and no resources, yet are determined to be the best in their field — and to be acknowledged as such. Neither have much use for women. In fact, Frank Mansfield thinks there's nothing more beautiful in the world than an ace cock in the morning sun.

There were many reasons this particular film resonated as it did, chief among them the protagonist's undeterred vision to achieve something that society at large deems alternately ridiculous and barbaric. His work ethic is evident. His values are clear

MANSFIELD
BAR B Q
DRINK
Coca-Cola
WELCOME TO
MANSFIELD, GA
BLACKWELL
GROCERY
Fresh Meats
Produce
POTATOES 20LBS

and consistent. He is not swayed in the least by sexual possibilities. Even the chickens themselves — though they're unanimously considered stupid animals — are born fighters and they fight to win. It's not hard to see why Frank Mansfield's competitive impulse would lead him to this particular animal. And why human relationships take a back seat. He's never met the human version of a dead game chicken.

I could relate to Frank's wilful solitude and his skepticism of any brand of companionship, the criticism he tolerates for wanting to be alone. And boy, could I ever relate to his devotion to a type of work that brands him a fool.

Also, there's always been a bit of backwoods culture in me; I associate it with my own longtime transience, which draws me to stories of roving survivalists, but it was likely birthed in the 1970s when Outlaw Country infiltrated the airwaves, and stoked through my late teens as fiscal necessity partnered me with the motley crews of maker-culture: people who make their own food (tip: don't make bannock out of drywall), fix their own machines, and play half-strung guitars late into the night. There remains little distinction in these communities between cowboys, bikers and hippies — people who come together with nothing in common but their lack of resources and a love of John Prine. Sometimes it's enough.

That's the milieu that fertilised my appreciation for *Cockfighter*. But it's an appreciation that would also cause me to face some uncomfortable personal contradictions, both in terms of my "culturally subjective" tolerance for violence, and of the obsolete, binary views of gender definition that I seem to cling to.

My previous book *House of Psychotic Women* (2012) explores depictions of female neurosis onscreen in horror and exploitation films, and was touted by many as a profoundly feminist work. Critics of the book, however, identified a deep-seated misogyny in my readings of the films that they saw as fueled by a tenuous grasp of psychoanalysis and a reliance on outdated texts that were inherently patriarchal. I was grateful for these readings, and frankly surprised they weren't more common. While my personal experiences with women have changed significantly since *House of Psychotic Women* — I would argue *because* of it — I found it odd that after the book's publication I was constantly invited to speak about women's issues. My trepidation to be a spokesperson for such things derived from the fact that while I *related* to the characters in the films I was discussing — destructive women who often sabotaged their own happiness due to unresolved trauma — I didn't want to *be* them. I wanted to be Charles Bronson in *The Mechanic*. Kris Kristofferson in *Cisco Pike*. Roy Scheider in *The Seven-Ups*. Robert Culp in *Hickey & Boggs*. Warren Oates in *Cockfighter*. Characters who embodied a combination of machismo and phlegmatic cool — the very cultural monolith that the characters in *House of Psychotic Women* are always battling against.

But of all these films, *Cockfighter* was the one I circled again and again. Perhaps because its protagonist's pastime is so grim, and yet the documentary minutiae of the film not only *normalises cockfighting*, it imbues it with a sense of craft

AUTOSALES.COM
678·342·7000
GABUILDINGS.COM
BUY OR RENT-TO-OWN
EAGLE CARPORTS
CARPORTS, BARNS, GARAGES & MORE
LOW PRICES!
FREE INSTALLATION!

and nobility. The film doesn't condemn its characters, and if director Monte Hellman had reservations about the sport (he did), that judgement doesn't show up onscreen.

Hellman wasn't the only one with misgivings about *Cockfighter*; its few champions among the cast and crew have died, and those still left to talk about it have baggage related to its financial constraints and ultimate box office failure — if they indeed remember anything about it at all, beyond treasuring the opportunity to work alongside the beloved rascal Warren Oates. Added to which, the film remains unreleased in several countries (due to animal cruelty prohibitions related to its lengthy cockfighting sequences), so canonical status is elusive. Americans are much happier being represented by the gearhead culture in *Two-Lane Blacktop* than acknowledging the millions generated annually by the (now illegal in 50 states) cockfighting industry.

But this sport's history, in America and elsewhere, runs deep. Claims that the country was founded by cockfighters have persisted over the centuries[1], and the methodology and language of cockfighting has been transferred over the years to governmental applications the world over. Most people might be surprised to learn that when chickens were first domesticated, it wasn't for food. And though both author Charles Willeford and director Monte Hellman always maintained that the story is not "about" cockfighting, there are peculiarities to this subculture that ooze out of every frame of the film, and every facial expression and every hand gesture Frank Mansfield communicates with. So this book is also — to the chagrin of many, I'm sure — about cockfighting. Because the history of the sport itself is inseparable from the themes that permeate the story, from Frank's willful silence as a form of protest against

1 George Washington, Thomas Jefferson, John Adams, Abraham Lincoln and Andrew Jackson have all been touted by cockfighters as being active in the sport. Although minimal archival documentation exists to support these claims, this belief strongly contributes to the sense of entitlement concerning the sport's legal status.

himself, to the ritual space of the cockpit, the gothic grit and racial residue of Southern culture, and the mythological implications of the Great White Cock.

Given the sport's acutely ingrained foothold in the South, it's not surprising that producer Roger Corman saw it as ripe for exploitation in one of his drive-in pictures. Or that the artwork for the film — a painting by John Solie — would depict the salacious combination of the cowboy-outfitted Oates with a bottle in one hand and a wad of cash in the other, a kittenish blonde kneeling suggestively in cutoffs, and a frenzied fighting cock in mid-flight; a perfect trifecta of masculine fantasy projections. When I first considered this artwork, I found the twisted abstraction of the fighting cock in particular — more expressively rendered than his human counterparts — especially appealing. I resolved to get a tattoo of this fighting cock. Or rather, a pair of them.

Of course, I recognised the dilemma in that — I couldn't get a permanent body modification depicting a controversial bloodsport I'd only experienced through the distant lens of a Hollywood movie without first immersing myself into a real-world understanding of the pursuit itself; I didn't want to spend my life having to make excuses for it. And so began the adventure that eventually resulted in this book.

I went south, to Louisiana, where — until 2008 — cockfighting was a profuse and still-legal pastime. I visited cockpits ranging from multi-tiered stadiums to an obscure Cajun pit where I coveted a weird cocker's satin jacket, whose pair of beautifully-embroidered cocks battling on the back were crowned with the words, "Til Death do us Part." I held a fighting cock in my lap, watched the operatic flurry of blood and feathers, and saw bedraggled warriors die pecking in the drag, game til the very end. And most of all, I met the people, the generations of cockfighters who had devoted their lives to being good at something, even if it was something few could tolerate or even understand.

In the Anchor Bay commentary for *Cockfighter*, moderator Dennis Bartok notes that the film reminds him of Budd Boetticher's films about bullfighting. "Never had any single event made such an impression," said Boetticher of seeing his first bullfight. "Perhaps it was because the art of the bullring was so dangerous. Or perhaps it was because it was so medieval."

Chapter One.

Charles Willeford's Cockfighter

"The dedicated obsession of a fanatical sport. As in the bullring — to the death. Legal in Florida — illegal in the forty-nine other states. The iron will of a man, whose entire life was channeled into one supreme ambition!"

Original 1962 cover blurb

I assume most people reading about *Cockfighter*, have read *Cockfighter* (or have at least seen the 1974 film based on it), but if you need a refresher, here goes: Frank Mansfield is a professional cockfighter. At the start of the story Frank has not spoken for two years, having taken a vow of silence until he can win the Cockfighter of the Year Award. After betting everything on his prize chicken Sandspur, he loses his car, trailer, and female companion to fellow cocker Jack Burke. He plays guitar in a small dive bar to earn money while he plans his next move. There, he meets wealthy widow Berenice Hungerford who is fascinated by his ramblin', gamblin' lifestyle. Meanwhile his devoted sweetheart Mary Elizabeth is impatiently waiting for him to propose marriage back in the same small Georgia town where his brother Randall lives rent-free in the Mansfield family home — which Frank opts to sell out from under him in order to finance the upcoming cockfighting season. From there, Frank goes from town to town across the American South, accompanied by his new ace cock Icarus, his seasonal partner Omar Baradinsky and aided by multi-tasking farm hand Buford. Together this motley crew wagers in hacks and derbies with a colorful cast of characters who make their living the same way Frank does, all building up to the annual Milledgeville Southern Conference Tournament where he hopes to emerge triumphant. When both Berenice and Mary Elizabeth show up to the tournament — in seats Frank himself has reserved for them, each unbeknownst to the other — we will see which bird wins, in both senses of the word.

If you've only seen the film, you're probably wondering, *who the hell is Berenice?* Well, we'll get to that.

Before *Cockfighter* was a film by Monte Hellman, it was a novel by Charles Willeford. At the behest of producer Roger Corman, Willeford also wrote the film's script — an endeavour he undertook for the first and only time. Willeford is now best known as the writer of the Hoke Moseley detective novels (beginning with *Miami Blues* in 1984), through which he achieved a level of mainstream success that had always eluded his earlier work. But at the time of *Cockfighter*'s original publication in 1962 — or even its re-release in 1972 — he was not the marketable name he would become. Willeford was considered a pulp writer, but less tied to the trappings of any specific genre than he would be with the later advent of Hoke Moseley, whose creation planted Willeford firmly in the pantheon of the great crime writers.

Willeford referred to *Cockfighter* as "the most difficult novel I have ever written."

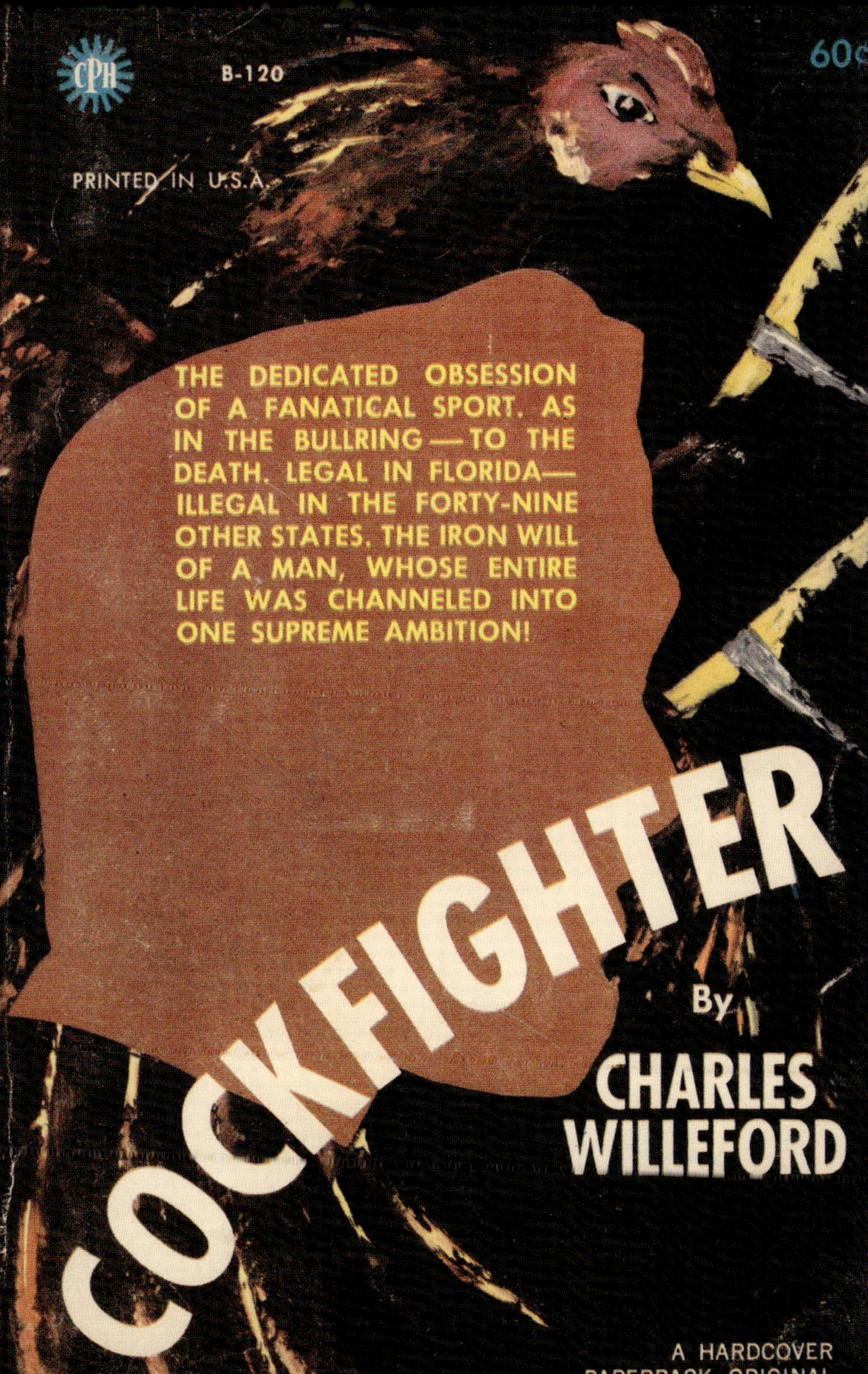
CPH
B-120
60¢
PRINTED IN U.S.A.
THE DEDICATED OBSESSION OF A FANATICAL SPORT. AS IN THE BULLRING — TO THE DEATH. LEGAL IN FLORIDA— ILLEGAL IN THE FORTY-NINE OTHER STATES. THE IRON WILL OF A MAN, WHOSE ENTIRE LIFE WAS CHANNELED INTO ONE SUPREME AMBITION!
COCKFIGHTER
By
CHARLES WILLEFORD
A HARDCOVER PAPERBACK ORIGINAL

But he also listed it as his favourite, alongside The *Burnt Orange Heresy*, which was released a year before *Cockfighter* went into its second printing in 1972. According to *Cockfighter Journal*, the limited-edition book he wrote documenting his experiences on the set of the film, he attended a cockfight in Palm Beach (slightly north of Fort Lauderdale) a decade before the book's first publication, and the experience convinced him it would be a great context for a novel.[2] In the journal, he claims it was his only firsthand experience with cockfighting until being on set for the shooting of Monte Hellman's film over a decade later. This isn't exactly true. He had to do extensive research — 18 months of it, in fact — and attended an International Cockfighting Tournament in Orlando as well as visiting with many cockfighters and breeders over that time. According to an interview in Don Herron's biography of Willeford, the latter also wrote separate articles on cockfighting in the Caribbean and Haiti. It would be an ongoing research project.

The novel *Cockfighter* took shape in a gradual, accumulative fashion, with Willeford crafting earlier short pieces that would feed into its characters and their abiding obsession with roosters. What would become Cockfighter had been percolating since at least 1959, as his short story "The Alectryomancer" can be seen as a clear precursor. Sometimes literally: "A chicken's brain is about the size of a BB," and "a gamecock is incapable of deceit," declare

2 ***Cockfighter Journal: The Story of a Shooting*** **was printed by Neville Publishing in 1989, limited to 300 numbered copies, plus an additional 26 lettered copies with a variant cover (my personal copy is number 23).**

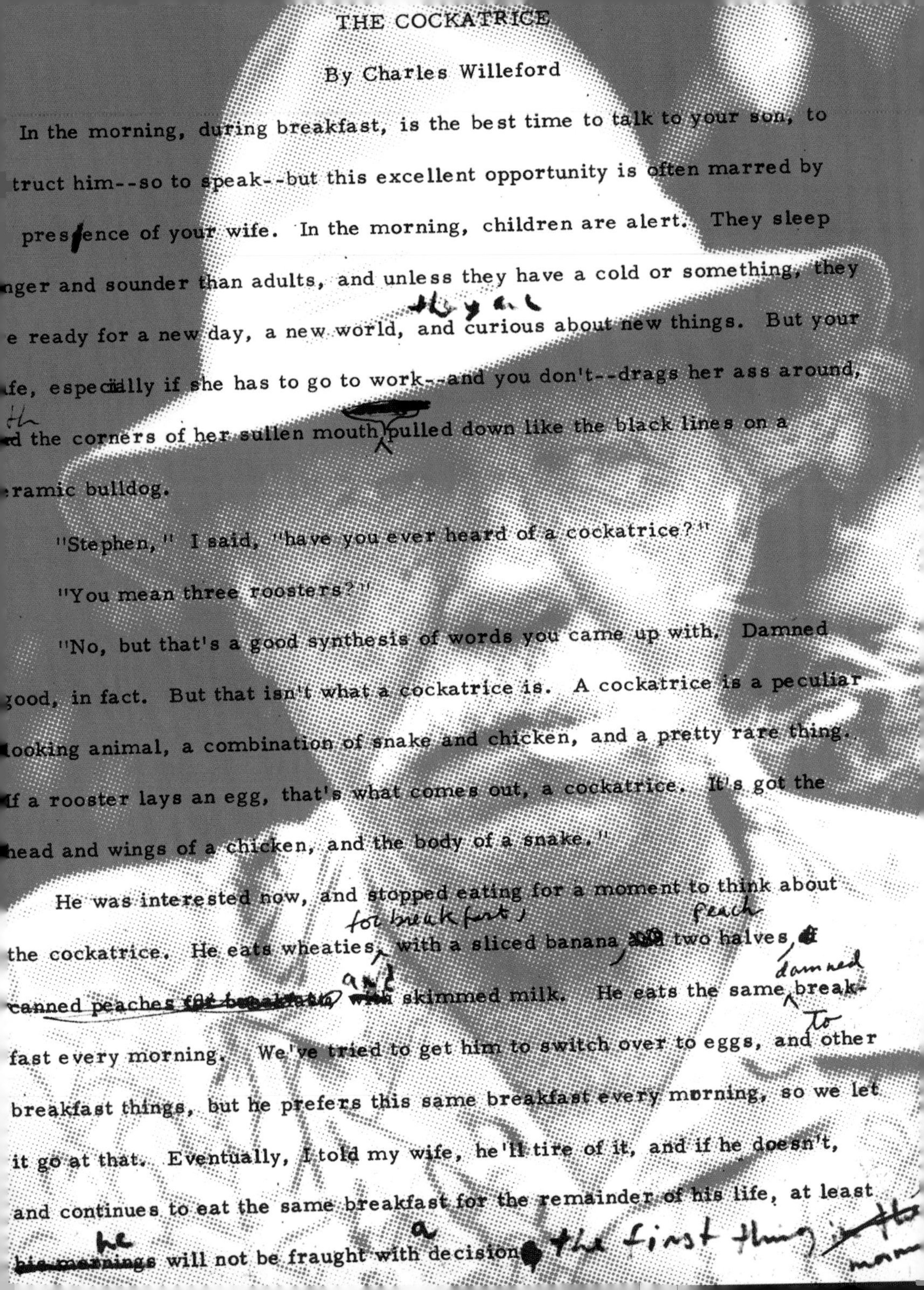

THE COCKATRICE

By Charles Willeford

In the morning, during breakfast, is the best time to talk to your son, to truct him--so to speak--but this excellent opportunity is often marred by presence of your wife. In the morning, children are alert. They sleep nger and sounder than adults, and unless they have a cold or something, they e ready for a new day, a new world, and curious about new things. But your fe, especially if she has to go to work--and you don't--drags her ass around, d the corners of her sullen mouth pulled down like the black lines on a ramic bulldog.

"Stephen," I said, "have you ever heard of a cockatrice?"

"You mean three roosters?"

"No, but that's a good synthesis of words you came up with. Damned good, in fact. But that isn't what a cockatrice is. A cockatrice is a peculiar looking animal, a combination of snake and chicken, and a pretty rare thing. If a rooster lays an egg, that's what comes out, a cockatrice. It's got the head and wings of a chicken, and the body of a snake."

He was interested now, and stopped eating for a moment to think about the cockatrice. He eats wheaties, for breakfast, with a sliced banana, peach two halves, canned peaches and skimmed milk. He eats the same damned breakfast every morning. We've tried to get him to switch over to eggs, and to other breakfast things, but he prefers this same breakfast every morning, so we let it go at that. Eventually, I told my wife, he'll tire of it, and if he doesn't, and continues to eat the same breakfast for the remainder of his life, at least he will not be fraught with a decision. the first thing in the morn

both texts, identically.[3] There are also earlier versions of Frank Mansfield in two other short stories, "The Gambler and the Guitar" (date unknown) and "Guitar Interlude" (date unknown), both of which focus on Frank's musical pursuits and gambling drive, but have not yet centred in on cockfighting as his particular vocation. Although it's unclear exactly when the two stories were written, Willeford's widow Betsy[4] places the date of the former at around 1963-64, but this would have been after *Cockfighter* was first published, and Willeford himself later conceded that he had "lived with" the character of Frank Mansfield for at least two years before writing the book, through earlier aborted projects.

In "The Gambler and the Guitar", Frank Mansfield is an addictive gambler whose vocal chords are fused together as the result of drinking prussic acid in a drunken suicide attempt, prompted by the fact that his addiction had cost him "his land in Georgia, a loss that forced the eviction of his brother Randall, and Randall's wife and children, from the farm that had been in the family for five generations." In this version of the character, Mansfield is nauseated with guilt at the thought of it, an aspect of the character that would be lost in the translation to *Cockfighter*. But curiously, chickens still force their way into the picture: he confesses he only likes to eat chicken salad sandwiches, and that his throat ailment requires him to throw his head back to swallow properly, "like a rooster drinking water."

Willeford would also return to the topic of chickens in his January 24, 1974 short story *The Cockatrice*, about an astrologer who tells his son that a cockatrice is a half snake/half rooster that materialises in the rare instance that a rooster lays an egg. The kid tells this tale around the schoolyard and is bullied for it, but the astrologer isn't concerned; he has given his son a knife and taught him how to fight with it. It's a fairly insignificant story, but it's interesting that the mystical aspects of "The Alectryomancer," the hard learned lessons of "The Cockatrice" and the centrality of fowl to both stories never quite left Willeford's brain. One could say he just liked chickens.

But though the context of Willeford's novel is the underground world of cockfighting, he insisted that it is not *about* cockfighting; As he writes in his set diary *Cockfighter Journal*, "... it is only incidental that Frank Mansfield is a cockfighter; he is a man with an obsession, and the novel could just as easily have been about an insurance salesman, or an account executive for an advertising firm." (I absolutely disagree with this, but more on that later).

Willeford's own attachment to his chosen material was evident in his unique manner of pitching the book. As his stepson Stephen Hooker — the son of Willeford's second wife, Mary Jo Norton, who was his wife at the time of *Cockfighter*'s conception through its adaptation to film — recalls:

> Back in '62, Dad decided to make a dramatic effort to sell *Cockfighter* to a publisher. He bought Little David, a three-time winning gamecock, recently retired. Little David had become difficult to match with an opponent due to his light weight. While he was with us in our little post-war suburban tract house, we tried to keep him from

3 "The Alectryomancer" will be discussed more thoroughly later in the book.
4 Betsy Willeford (nee Poller) was Willeford's third wife, married in 1981, though they had known each other professionally since the 1960s; Betsy was a longtime journalist for a variety of Miami area newspapers.

crowing throughout the night, city ordinances withstanding. Dad went to extreme lengths to fool the bird, without success. The next day our neighbors would ask about the crowing in the neighborhood. It went on like that until Dad left with one suitcase and a caged golden and red gamecock, complete with attached nameplate detailing the bird's championship status. I believe the trip was a success. Dad had some funny stories of sitting in publishers' waiting rooms with a crowing chicken, or worse, the bird in a crowded elevator. As for Little David, Dad said he donated him to a zoo after the trip. We all missed that bird.

The novel *Cockfighter* debuted via The Chicago Paperback House in 1962, but the publisher was hit by a car and killed soon after its release. The company folded shortly thereafter, and according to Jesse Pearson (who wrote the intro to the 2011 reissue) "over 20,000 copies of *Cockfighter* went straight into remaindersville." When Crown Publishers released *The Burnt Orange Heresy* in 1971, they offered to reprint *Cockfighter*, giving Willeford the rare chance to rewrite it. "I was able to put some more plot complications in and deepen the characterisations," he told biographer Don Herron, "I just had to polish it. I spent about three weeks on that." Although Herron maintained that the language in the reissue of *Cockfighter* is less "flowery" and "affected," I would just say it's more decisive. Ellipses and exclamation points are given the finality and matter-of-factness of a period. But Willeford didn't abandon "big words" when he required their nuance.

The revised version was released in hardcover from Crown Publishers in 1972 and excerpted in *Sports Illustrated* in May of that year, prefaced by a conciliatory note from the magazine's publisher ("Many readers will protest that it is not a sport at all… However well-written the novel may be, its theme is anathema to millions of Americans") which would prompt complaint letters to the magazine all the same. But Willeford was annoyed when someone bought up a whack of copies for the $6.95 retail price and was selling them in the cocker mags for 25 dollars, placing a small ad month after month. Willeford urged publisher Crown to place an official ad in the magazines to target that readership to no avail; it bothered him that this specialized demographic were being exploited by a scalper, who was presumably one of their own. Nevertheless, it would have been this 1972 edition of *Cockfighter* that the Cormans read, and which subsequently led to the motion picture deal.

Much of our understanding about what informs the character of Frank Mansfield — and the hyper-masculine world he occupies — can be gleaned from Willeford's pair of autobiographical works, *Something About a Soldier* (1986) and *I Was Looking for a Street* (1988, originally titled *Road Kid*), which outline the author's Depression-era childhood and experiences in the military. "As an enlisted man Charles suffered through a lot of longwinded and arbitrary pronouncements by half-bright officers and noticed a similar pattern in civilian life," explains Willeford's widow, Betsy. "Many of his books — notably, to me, *The Woman Chaser* — are peopled by men who believe they know all about everything." (This sentiment is directly echoed in *Cockfighter*, when Willeford describes Jack Burke's

Right and over: Original artwork by Wilson McLean for the May 22, 1972 issue of *Sports Illustrated*.

OUT TO MAKE

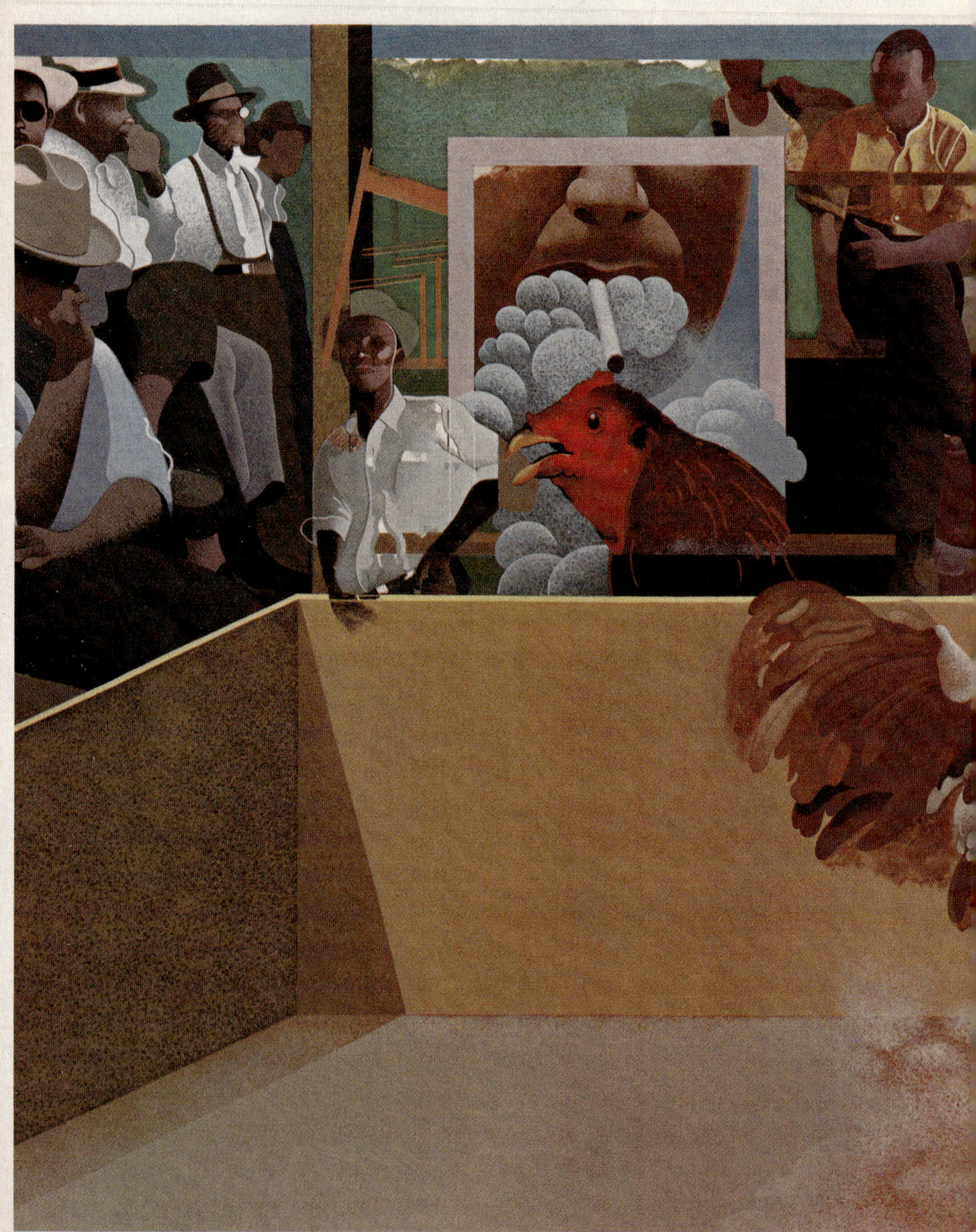

A KILLING

by CHARLES WILLEFORD

His money bird seemed razor-sharp, perhaps a hairline too sharp. But it was a risk he had to take. If the cock lost the match, they both would be dead

CONTINUED

ace cock as "as arrogant as a sergeant-major in the foreign legion") But as these autobiographical documents only appeared in his late career, most readers who knew his work had little idea of the wealth of life experience (and cultural education) Willeford brought to his books. And that was purely by design.

In his introduction to Charles Willeford's *Cockfighter Journal*, Southern writer James Lee Burke describes Willeford as "chivalric," noting that he never talked about himself and would play down his accomplishments; one would learn about his life only "from his work, and his friends." You wouldn't know from talking to him — and certainly not from his novels — that he'd been a soldier for 20 years (even faking his age to enlist early), retiring in 1956 with the rank of master sergeant, after having earned a purple heart in the Battle of the Bulge. Though he published his first novel in 1953, it took a further three decades for him to achieve commercial success — "tapping the decade's vogue for Miami crime stories," writer Nick Pinkerton points out (undoubtedly referring to things like the Miami-set crime novels of Elmore Leonard and Carl Hiaasen, the popularity of *Scarface* and *Miami Vice*, and Edna Buchanan's decade of Miami police beat reporting that won her a Pulitzer Prize) — not to mention the establishment of a series character in Hoke Moseley that gave publishers something to build on.

Julie Corman, Corman's wife and partner at New World Pictures, agrees with Burke's characterisation of Willeford as humble concerning his own exploits. "He was an unassuming guy whose wit and intelligence snuck up on you," says Julie. "Information about his many lives came up almost inadvertently. For instance: he was a tank commander under Patton in WWII in Europe. He fought at the Battle of the Bulge and merited a Silver Star, a Bronze Star for bravery and a Purple Heart. He studied art in Lima, Peru. After the war he ran the army radio station in Japan. He was a book critic for the *Miami Herald*. Most of all he was a poet. He was a regional original."

Stephen Hooker likewise holds that Willeford didn't show off his many accomplishments, and that it was only over time that Hooker was able to appreciate what a unique individual had been welcomed into his family. "I was about four or five when Charles and Mother married," Hooker remembers,

> He was a nice guy but seemed to be at a loss on how to interact with a little kid and left the child rearing to my mother. *I Was Looking For A Street* and *Something About A Soldier* may give some insight into his awkwardness as a dad. He was heavy set and balding, plus he was an enlisted soldier, not an officer, not my idea of a dad. Yes, at four I was a snob. My father, uncle and even my mother had been officers during the war, also we were Southerners from Birmingham with all that conjures about social standing and rank. At the wedding however, I was impressed with all his medals for bravery, and he did have a commanding presence, after all, a master sergeant is god among the troops and he had been a tank commander. Over the years I discovered his many fine traits, like family loyalty. He never corrected me in the presence of others, among other things. About the time of the wedding I was offered a chance to decide what to call him. "Dad" was uncomfortable but "Charles" was okay. Several years later, Charles wanted me to call him Dad or Pop, and I did off and on. As I matured he became warmer. He once said that as I grew older I became more interesting... By the time of his death we were very close.

Willeford's reticence in sharing unsolicited details about his own accomplishments helps illuminate the character development of Frank Mansfield, especially as the latter's value system is disrupted by his eventual realisation that he talks too damn much. Though Frank is presented as having always been a rogue of sorts, it's only with his vow of silence that he truly becomes A Man Apart. Not only does Frank's role as an observer mirror that of his creator, but the ease with which others accept his silence also highlights how little we actually need to share about ourselves to make our way through the world; there is a tacit acknowledgement of the general disinterest people have in each other.

Willeford's parents both died of TB in his youth, and their orphaned son lived with his wealthy grandmother in Topanga Canyon, who for a time sent him to the McKinlay Industrial School for Boys in the San Fernando Valley — where crime writer Eddie Bunker had also spent time as a child. When the Depression hit, his grandmother had a hard time caring for him and he struck out on his own, which, as Lucy Sante points out in the intro to the 2010 reprint of *I Was Looking for a Street*, was the fate of many teens of the era, as chronicled in William Wellman's *Wild Boys of the Road* (1933). As such, Sante likens Willeford's memoir to American tramping literature, a brand of writing born out of the mass worker migrations of 1870 and running through the Great Depression of the 1930s (more on this in a later chapter). Even Dody White, the teenaged girl Frank picks up and later offloads onto Jack Burke, comes from a family of fruit tramps in the book. As Willeford writes, "this constant exposure to the itinerant agricultural workers' lackadaisical code of living had made her wise beyond her age." In both the novel and original script there are references to "accordion-necked" fruit tramps in the audience for the fights.

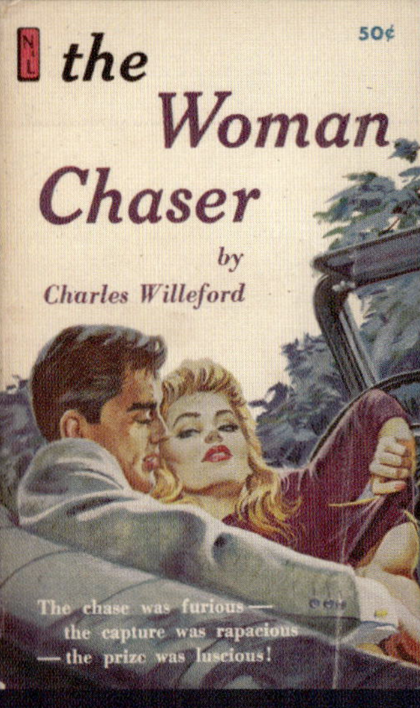
50¢
the
Woman
Chaser
by
Charles Willeford
The chase was furious—
the capture was rapacious
—the prize was luscious!

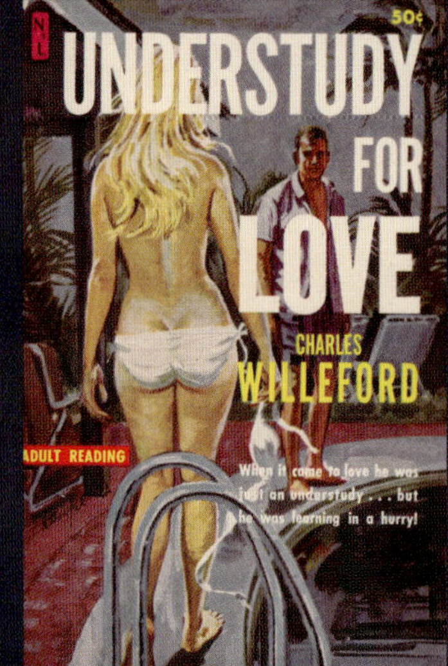
50¢
UNDERSTUDY
FOR
LOVE
CHARLES
WILLEFORD
ADULT READING
When it came to love he was
just an understudy . . . but
he was learning in a hurry!

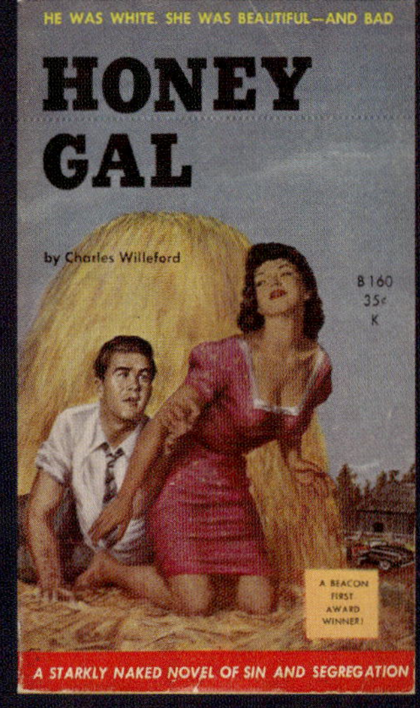
HE WAS WHITE. SHE WAS BEAUTIFUL—AND BAD
HONEY
GAL
by Charles Willeford
B 160
35¢
K
A BEACON
FIRST
AWARD
WINNER!
A STARKLY NAKED NOVEL OF SIN AND SEGREGATION

"No one writes a better crime novel than Charles Willeford."
—Elmore Leonard
PICK-UP
Charles Willeford
Any guy with the price of a drink could have her for the
night. . . Why did one man want her for a lifetime?

B1081S
75¢
K
Lust
is a
woman
CHARLES WILLEFORD
Millions share
her secret sexual
compulsion.
Only Maria didn't
fight it—
she *lived* it!

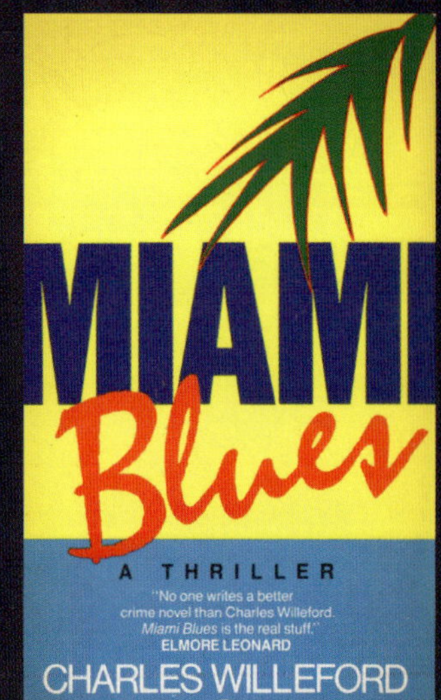
MIAMI
Blues
A THRILLER
"No one writes a better
crime novel than Charles Willeford.
Miami Blues is the real stuff."
ELMORE LEONARD
CHARLES WILLEFORD
Ballantine/Mystery/32016 (Canada $3.95) U.S. $2.95

There is no doubt that the male-dominated spaces of Willeford's time as a young drifter and soldier would inform the honour codes and work ethic of Frank Mansfield — not to mention the discipline needed to hold his tongue.

In his book *Neon Noir*, Woody Haut calls *Cockfighter* "one of Willeford's most devastating cultural critiques… in the tradition of low-life fiction" and (referring to its 1972 reissue) points out that its "excessive detail mirrors the discomforting images from Vietnam which, at the time, were appearing nightly on TV." He likens Frank's vow of silence to the creation of the "silent majority" and describes the book as investigating "the relationship between sport, chauvinism and war." Frank admits (through the book's internal monologue) that the worst part of his vow of silence is the passivity that accompanies it; he has no choice but to silently act as a receptacle for other people's confessions — an intolerable fate for a onetime loudmouth. Frank's silence will be discussed more in depth in a later chapter, but it is fascinating how silence invites so many different — and sometimes contradicting — interpretations.

In his on-set diary *Cockfighter Journal*, Willeford described the story as being loosely based on the Odyssey, with Frank as Odysseus, Omar as Telemachus, Ed Middleton as Nestor, Mary Elizabeth as Penelope and Tom Peeples as the Cyclops. "I lost the Circe and Siren chapters in the end," he joked, "but who would ever know except myself?" Of course, as Jesse Pearson also points out in his intro to the 2011 reissue, a side by side comparison of the two texts doesn't hold up as systematically as Willeford's claim would have us believe, though the archetype of the hero's journey is certainly there. Don Herron's biography of Willeford reveals an even earlier obsession with *The Odyssey*, as relayed through personal correspondence in the 1950s detailing his plans to write a book of the same name, "about a cowboy named Russell Haxby who, having read James Joyce's Ulysses, decides to go to Hollywood and do a movie with himself as screenwriter, star and director. The eighteen chapters will follow episodes of Ulysses, Telemachus, Nestor, etc." Willeford played with this idea through multiple aborted drafts with different titles, ultimately weaving elements into both *The Woman Chaser* and *Cockfighter*. The protagonist's name, Russell Haxby, would be repurposed for Willeford's first published novel, *High Priest of California* in 1953.

In her introduction to *I was Looking for a Street*, Lucy Sante notes that pulp writers had every bit of artistic ambition that "up-market" writers did, but they often didn't have the formal connections of University degrees and newspaper experience. Instead their experience came from the streets, the war, from prison and working in other industries. Willeford's work may have started out in the "pulp-fiction ghetto" as Nick Pinkerton has written, but his unique writing style — combining an adherence to genre touchstones with a meandering intricacy of character (his characters tend to rant and pontificate on any number of tangential subjects) in which the plot is really just a backdrop to the characters learning something about themselves — ultimately distinguished him as a writer worthy of serious academic appraisal. In the December 1988 issue of *Playboy* Harlan Ellison compared the comic *The Fish Police* to "Chandler and Willeford and the antic parts of Hammett." Positioned alongside Chandler and Hammett in this way, the implication was clear: Willeford had become canon.

Chapter Two.

The Solitary Believer:

Cockfighter, Southern Gothic & Grit Lit

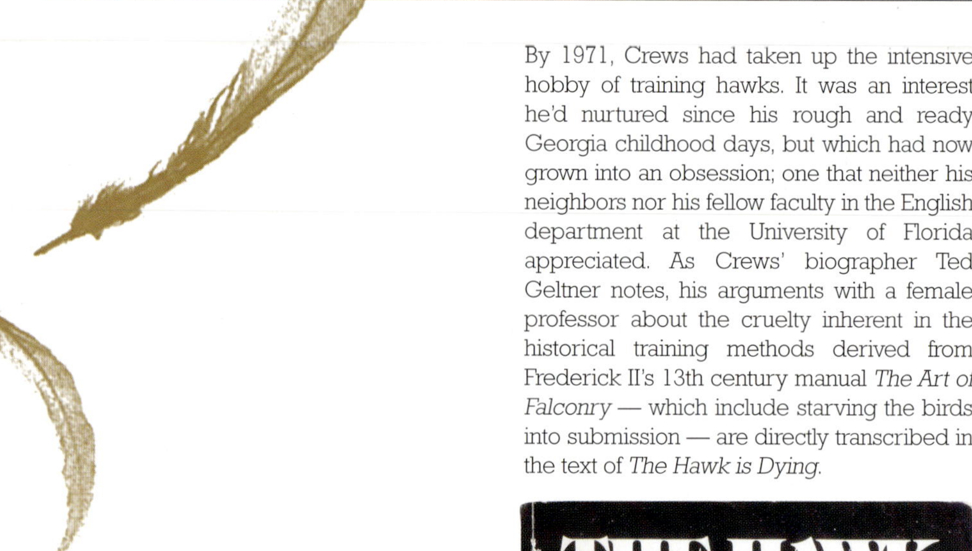

I said in the introduction to this book that whenever I bring up *Cockfighter* in conversation, the first thing somebody does is bring up *Two-Lane Blacktop*. Well, the second thing they bring up is Harry Crews.

Like Willeford, Crews was a Florida-based writer who had penned a highly visible experiential piece called "Cockfighting: An Unfashionable View," in the pages of *Esquire*, where he had a regular column called "Grits" over 14 issues from 1976-77. But he also released a semi-autobiographical novel the year before *Cockfighter*'s reissue called *The Hawk is Dying* (now out of print), about George Gattling, "a middle-aged, middle-class Gainesville suburbanite who, as his life is falling apart around him, devotes all his energy to the training of a red-tailed hawk."[5]

By 1971, Crews had taken up the intensive hobby of training hawks. It was an interest he'd nurtured since his rough and ready Georgia childhood days, but which had now grown into an obsession; one that neither his neighbors nor his fellow faculty in the English department at the University of Florida appreciated. As Crews' biographer Ted Geltner notes, his arguments with a female professor about the cruelty inherent in the historical training methods derived from Frederick II's 13th century manual *The Art of Falconry* — which include starving the birds into submission — are directly transcribed in the text of *The Hawk is Dying*.

5 Geltner, Ted. *Blood Bone and Marrow: A Biography of Harry Crews*. University of Georgia Press, 2016. Kindle edition Pg 156. Both *Cockfighter* and *The Hawk is Dying* would make for interesting comparisons with Barry Hines' *A Kestrel for a Knave* (1968), about an outcast Yorkshire boy named Billy Casper who befriends and trains a wild kestrel.

Right: Harry Crews, with illustration by George Ford from Daniel P. Mannix' *The Killers: The Story of a Fighting Cock and a Wild Hawk*.

The hobby would be abandoned as soon as Crews turned in his manuscript. But George Gattling's similarity to his creator was thinly-veiled in many ways: he is an outsider in a university milieu, has a 'son' who drowns, even the address of his house — 1800 NW Eighth Avenue in Gainesville — was Harry Crews' real home address at the time of writing the novel. And in the end it's George who questions whether *he's* the one being conditioned, and if the hawk is in fact teaching him how to be wild:

> George leaned back and closed his eyes. But in his darkened eyes soared a beautiful hawk, wheeling and turning in the blue fastness of a winter sky. The flying hawk was an extension of himself, was himself. But nobody looked. Nobody knew he was there. No matter what he did, no matter who had put him there, nobody ever knew or cared.

What's most interesting about a comparison of *The Hawk is Dying* and *Cockfighter* is that the differences between their respective protagonists directly reflect the differences in comportment between their two authors. There is desperation and deviance in Crews' George Gattling — both Crews and his protagonist take their birds along to inappropriate places, signifying disordered thoughts: a dive bar, a funeral parlor. Frank Mansfield does not share this shambolic quality; when Willeford's character fails, he does so gracefully. He doesn't agonise over his predicament, he just lets go of it and moves on.

And this is a great example of where we can see Willeford toying with the Southern tradition that *Cockfighter* is most assuredly situated in; the novel literally moves through the South according to a seasonal cockfighting conference timetable. There is a keen sense of place, an awareness that we are in the South, interacting with characters who have been raised within Southern families, Southern codes of behaviour, and often in a rural Southern landscape, with all the ghosts of an unsavoury past that entails. Frank Mansfield's movements systematically point to these things, and yet he remains *outside*. Not merely due to the practicality of his muteness, but because he rejects family without any residue, he lets go of property and possessions easily, and he stubbornly maintains his own peculiar system of ethics within the already closed ethical system of the cockfighting world. And yet I would still argue that Charles Willeford is a Southern writer, both by birth and by choice. "I don't know how Charles regarded his work," says Betsy Willeford. "It is safe, I believe, to say he considered himself a Southerner."

Plenty of scholars have attempted to define what Southern writing is, and who it includes. In its least debated form, Southern writing is written by people who were born and remain in the South, and write specifically about characters, events, landscape and culture in the South. Just as many have argued for the inclusion of writers who never lived in the South but whose writings are indelibly affected by their ancestral connections to the region, or those who only started writing after leaving the South and becoming established in a major Northern city, like Edgar Allan Poe, whose short story "The Fall of the House of Usher" is considered the Ur-text of Southern Gothic despite the fact that he never identified as a Southern writer, and the story predates the onset of the Civil War by over 20 years.[6]

For Willeford's part, he was born in Arkansas, moved to Greater Los Angeles at age three, had global adventures in the military and as a student of fine arts — even a stint in Newfoundland, which he hated — finally settling in Florida in 1958 when he was nearly 40 years old. By that time he had already published a book of poetry (*Proletarian Laughter*, 1948) and the novels *High Priest of California* (1953), *Pick-Up* (1955), and *Wild Wives* (1956), all set in San Francisco. *The Black Mass of Brother Springer* — released as *Honey Gal* on its first publication in 1958 — was his first novel to be written and published after relocating to the South, and is about a failed writer who ditches his wife and mounting debts to assume a false identity as the deacon of an all-Black church. So Willeford immediately drops himself into the thick of the region's racial preoccupations. Alongside a determination to institutionalise crime fiction through his university classes, his work would continue a throughline with the Southern tradition, both as a writer and as a teacher, recognising the dramatic value of its rich, troubled history.

"The 1920s assumptions about Southern religion, race, and general benightedness remained in force for the next half century," wrote Fred Hobson in his 1985 essay "The Savage South" — "The difference being that after the 1920s it was chiefly Southern writers, not Northern ones, who reinforced and popularised the image." He continues:

> After reading T.S. Stribling, Erskine Caldwell, and William Faulkner, Gerald Johnson announced in the *Virginia Quarterly Review* of January 1935 that he had witnessed a "Horrible South": 'These are the merchants of death, hell, and the grave, these are the horror-mongers-in-chief.' The new Southern fiction, full of murder, suicide, rape, incest, lynchings, castration, miscegenation, and insanity, presented a South even more savage than the abolitionists had described in the 1840s or the sociologists turned up in the 1920s…Thus Southern Gothic had its birth…

Taking Fred Hobson's description of the characteristics of Southern writing — as defined by its Renaissance in the 1920s and '30s (and which Flannery O'Connor referred to as "The School of Southern Degeneracy") — one could argue that *The Black Mass of Brother Springer* was Willeford's first "Southern" novel, especially if we delineate the spectre of slavery and racial segregation as an essential component of Southern writing (although Willeford had already attempted to write about race — rather obliquely — in *Pick-Up* (1955), but to say *how* would be a major spoiler, so I'll refrain). Likewise, *Cockfighter* is intricately bound up with its regional setting. But when approaching *Cockfighter* as a novel positioned firmly within the tradition of Southern writing, it's important to consider a writer whose presence is directly discernable in *Cockfighter*: Flannery O'Connor.

The final championship of *Cockfighter* — the Southern Conference Tournament, or SCT, where Frank wins his Cockfighter of the Year medal — takes place in Milledgeville, Georgia: the hometown of American author Flannery O'Connor, one of the foremost pioneers of the Southern Gothic tradition. In his 2003 review of *Cockfighter* for the

6 The notion of Poe as Southern Gothic not only disrupts the periodisation of the genre as a creation of the Reconstruction Era, but only one of his stories (*The Gold-Bug*) is definitively set in the South. And yet, as Gothic scholar Tom F. Wright has asserted (with convincing supporting evidence and reasoning) in his essay "Edgar Allan Poe and the Southern Gothic," "The Fall of the House of Usher" is "widely seen as one of the founding texts of the Southern Gothic."

Chicago Reader, critic Jonathan Rosenbaum suggested that this setting was perhaps a deliberate nod to O'Connor (on the part of Willeford — the location is named in the book and carried over into the film). Fittingly, this icon of Southern Gothic first tasted fame as the subject of a Pathé newsreel in which she showed off her pet chicken, whom she had trained to walk backwards.[7]

The critic goes on to say that "the mean, caustic bite of the humour in Cockfighter" especially reminded him of Flannery O'Connor. "The evangelist hero of *Wise Blood* observes at one point that any man that's got a good car don't need to be justified, and the obstinate pride and conceit of the Oates character about his own stature seems to belong to much the same world."

Rosenbaum's comparison between the protagonists of *Cockfighter* and *Wise Blood* is apt — even though Willeford was not channeling the latter novel in any deliberate way. An admirer of O'Connor's short stories — he taught them as part of his university curriculum — Willeford is on record stating that "*Wise Blood*, it's not very good. It was too much for her. The novel was not her forté."[8] Nevertheless, there are points of comparison to be made between the two books.

As Michael Stultz points out in a 2006 essay on existentialism in the work of Flannery O'Connor, "O'Connor wishes for a retreat to the fundamental Christianity of 'other ages' whose believers 'felt less' and 'saw more' with a 'blind, prophetical, unsentimental eye of acceptance, which is to say, of faith.' This previous age was not governed by tenderness, in fact it wasn't governed by

mass theory or doctrine at all because it was an age of the solitary believer who was not ashamed of his faith." The hero of *Cockfighter* is not a religious man, not in any discernable, traditional sense. But religious fervor is baked into his bones through his commitment to cockfighting, even as the world changes and modernises around him and his passion becomes more marginalised. Much like the fiery Hazel Motes in *Wise Blood*, Frank Mansfield is noble in spite of himself.

Hazel's landscape may be more apocalyptic — its anxieties clearly calling back to post-Civil War poverty, crime, carpetbagging, hucksterism — but Frank is equally without place; there may be a town bearing his family's name, but he has no hesitation in contesting his father's will (which left the 400-acre family farm to his younger brother Randall) and selling the Mansfield home out from under his brother, who is subsequently left homeless without so much as a second's thought or explanation. Like Hazel, Frank's "got no people," and he knows, as Thomas Wolfe famously wrote, that "you can't go home again." He needs to be free to move to follow the calling of his profession; for Frank and Hazel both, mobility is nobility. Some of *Wise Blood*'s most famous passages

7 "Do You Reverse?" Pathe Newsreel 1932. Accessed online March 20, 2017 at: https://www.youtube.com/watch?v=dtnV-iD2QlI.

8 Qtd. Herron, Don. *Willeford*. Dennis McMillan Publications, 1997. Pg. 354.

Above, Flannery O'Connor, photographed in Milledgeville in 1963 next to a self-portrait.

Wise Blood

— made so for my generation via their sampling in the 1990s Ministry song "Jesus Built My Hotrod" — extol the virtues of the automobile: "Where you come from is gone. Where you thought you were going to weren't never there. And where you are ain't no good unless you can get away from it."

The word "justify" comes up frequently in *Wise Blood*: not only in Hazel's mantra that "Nobody with a good car needs to be justified," but by other characters who are less critical of their own need to justify their actions — to others, to their congregations, to God. The repetition of this word is a direct reference to the many instances in the bible where it is used to mean "counted righteous by God." One such instance — the parable of the tax collector and the Pharisee in Luke 18:14 ("I tell you that this man, rather than the other, went home justified before God") also gave us the oft-quoted line spoken by Joel McCrea in Sam Peckinpah's *Ride the High Country*: "All I want is to enter my own house justified." As with Hazel, whose nihilism demands that nothing he do be "justified," Frank Mansfield likewise doesn't feel the need to justify himself to anyone but himself. As he says in *Cockfighter*, it's a man's broken promises to himself that yield the harshest moral and spiritual despair.

Other similarities with *Cockfighter* involve the transference of an irritating teenage girl between two men in the same profession, and most importantly, the protagonist assuming a pronounced asceticism following a tragic event — after an act of self-sabotaging humiliation, Frank refuses to speak for two years, but Hazel takes a more permanent form of penitence by blinding himself with lime, wrapping himself in barbed wire and walking with glass and rocks in his shoes until one day he is found nearly dead in a ditch by policemen, who deal Hazel the final blow that kills him. Blinding himself is an action that his doppelganger Asa Hawks (played in the film version by Harry Dean Stanton, as is Frank Mansfield's nemesis Jack Burke in *Cockfighter*) cannot bring himself to do and only fakes — but despite Hazel's professed disdain for Christ, in blinding himself he demonstrates the kind of fundamentalist zeal typical of historical Christian martyrs.

In his review of *Cockfighter*, Rosenbaum summons another shared touchstone of both Willeford and O'Connor: Nathaniel West, who was not a Southern writer but penned a classic of American Gothic in 1939 with *The Day of the Locust*. As Rosenbaum writes: "The cockfights themselves inevitably suggest the depiction of one in Nathaniel West's *The Day of the Locust*, and O'Connor is one of the few serious disciples of West, most of all in her treatments of violence." Willeford himself once wrote a thesis on West, in which he cited him as the first novelist to criticise the 'American Dream,' in regarding "the absurdities and horrors of American life as a comic experience."

Though West's book is a staple of California Gothic specifically — a genre in which "California is the place where Midwesterners go to die"[9] — it remains important to the Southern discussion not only through Willeford and O'Connor's direct nods to his work, but through its linkage of cockfighting with contests of masculinity that ultimately reveal how fragile and desperate that masculinity really is. John Schlesinger's 1975 adaptation of Nathaniel West's grotesque indictment of Hollywood's

9 **Murphy, Bernice. *The California Gothic in Fiction and Film*. Edinburgh University Press, 2022. Pg 10.**

den
kobylek
DRAMATICKÝ
OBRAZ
HOLLYWOODU
TŘICÁTÝCH LET
AMERICKÝ FILM
S KAREN BLACKOVOU
V HLAVNÍ ROLI
REŽIE / JOHN
SCHLESINGER

spiritual corruption hit decidedly more screens than *Cockfighter* and featured an even more repulsive cockfighting scene, fueled by a trio of men drunkenly fighting for the attention of desperate wannabe starlet Faye, played by Karen Black. William Atherton plays Tod, the romantic young Hollywood art director who has irresponsibly fallen for the neighbourhood floozy, while his rival for Faye's affections, Earle Shoop (Bo Hopkins), is a habitually out-of-work cowboy actor who is paired throughout the film with equally homeless Mexican cockfighter Miguel (Pepe Serna, of the Corman-produced *Student Nurses*). As Miguel's roosters cluck and pace restlessly in the background, the four of them get drunk on tequila around a fire and the sexual tension builds to overt, violent aggression against the woman. In West's book, Tod describes her "swordlike legs" as holding an invitation "closer to murder than to love." This Hollywood loser's club culminates in an amateur cockpit set up in the garage of the sexually repressed Homer Simpson (Donald Sutherland in a truly frightening performance), where a disorganised and low-rent chicken fight is intercut with shots of Faye trying on different outfits in front of the mirror. This depiction of a lone woman wielding a destructive power in the immediate milieu of a cockpit possesses an undoubted resonance with the centuries of folklore that excludes women from the sport, in fiction and in real life (as we'll see in a later chapter). But, as writer Alex Vernon notes, the cockfight here is also part of the larger context in which these characters are struggling to assert their individual identities in "a society suffering a general loss of distinction."

While California Gothic is largely informed by migration in pursuit of utopian dreams that fail to materialise, and where decaying glamour leads to destitution, addiction, and other forms of self-destruction, Southern Gothic is a poison from within, defined/ characterised by poverty and crime in the aftermath of the Reconstruction era. But the crumbling white mansions of the Antebellum South have no place in the dusty, workaday milieu of *Cockfighter*, where only Senator Foxhall's mansion — filmed at a historical plantation home with surviving slave quarters — stands as a remnant of this desperate Southern pageantry. Instead, Frank's world is one of itinerant workers, travellers, hustlers; likewise in *Wise Blood,* Hazel Motes recalls a carnival coming through town when he was a child, the travelling carnival and revival shows and medicine shows being a common facet of life in the South and a staple of Southern gothic fiction. *The Bastard* (1929), the first novel of celebrated yet controversial Southern Gothic writer Erskine Caldwell — with whom Willeford corresponded — begins with the birth of its antihero Gene Morgan, whose mother gives birth to him "during the heat of a Southern August on the little six by four platform in her hoochie-coochie tent."

It's this brand of Southern Gothic that ties Willeford to Harry Crews, who in his later years came to be considered the father of "Grit Lit" — Southern literature suffused with squalor and petty crime that grew out of the Southern Gothic tradition — though he was never fond of this particular label. Crews' Southern pedigree includes having been a student of Andrew Nelson Lytle, an early champion of both Flannery O'Connor and James Dickey, the author of *Deliverance*, and he is more synonymous with the 'Rough South' than

Left: Czech poster for *Day of the Locust* by artist Clara Istlerova.

Willeford; Willeford's characters have more financial and social mobility than Crews', who perhaps share a much more direct lineage with the morally depraved protagonists of Erskine Caldwell. Crews was a proponent of writing from one's own experiences, and his essay on cockfighting in *Esquire* reads more like Willeford's *Cockfighter Journal* than it does *Cockfighter* itself.

Throughout the 1970s Crews shared stories of cockfighting, dog-fighting and gator-poaching in the pages of *Esquire* and *Playboy*, drawing on that decade's obsession with what was dubbed "The New Journalism' that prioritised first-person experiential storytelling (think Hunter S. Thompson, Joan Didion, Gay Talese and Tom Wolfe). Crews walked the walk; so determined was he to survive dangerous assignments that *Grit Lit: A Rough South Reader* co-editor Brian Carpenter refers to him as a "performance artist."

But it was his 1978 autobiography *A Childhood: The Biography of a Place* that cemented his place atop the pantheon of Rough South writing that took hold in the 1980s, described by NPR librarian Nancy Pearl as "filled with angry, deranged and generally desperate characters who are fueled by alcohol and sex."[10] It's like all the anxieties of Southern Gothic come to pass: fears that the genteel ways of the old South would degenerate, decay, and be lost.

10 **Pearl, Nancy, Qtd in Carpenter, Brian and Tom Franklin. *Grit Lit: A Rough South Reader*. Columbia: University of South Carolina Press, 2012. Pg vii.**

The writing lays bare the outcome of these fears without pretension. As the title of Crews' autobiography suggests, these writers tend to come from the very same milieu they write about, often doing working class jobs and encountering so-called 'high culture' through alternative means, not from institutionalised education but from secret compulsions to find poetry in their harsh surroundings. As *Grit Lit* anthology co-editor Tom Franklin notes, "they're the generation between bigotry and progress, still reeling from their own enlightenment."

Like Willeford, Crews had a varied resume preceding (and concurrent with) his writing career — boxer, falconer, carny — but more firmly stuck in the rough-and-tumble. He was a hard drinker for much of his life, and had a face that one reviewer described as that of "a madman who eats roofing nails for breakfast."[11] In a 1984 essay for *Playboy* called "The Violence That Finds Us," Crews refers to "blood moments" — those instances when the imminent threat or experience of violence finds us — and insists that being face to face with violence is more effective than any psychiatrist in curbing existential anxieties. And while acknowledging the propensity for that violence that historically permeates the South, Crews also felt that bloodlust was just a magnified view of the National character: "stubborn, wrong-headed and self-destructive."[12]

Being active in the same region, and the same literary milieu, it's probably no surprise that Willeford and Crews' paths would cross professionally. "In the mid '70s Charles attended a writing conclave in Orlando," Betsy Willeford told me, adding that literary editor David McDowell — who had been behind the Crown Publishers re-issue of *Cockfighter* in 1972 — "was there drinking Scotch with milk because he had an ulcer. Harry Crews, in one of his darker moods, attacked McDowell for what he considered insufficient respect for the liquor, and Charles had to pull Crews off McDowell. I think McDowell was twice Crews' age and half his weight."

That said, Betsy maintains that Charles liked Harry Crews' books, with his earliest novels *The Gospel Singer* (1968) and *Naked in Garden Hills* (1969) among his favourites. But where Crews bared all (sometimes to his own detriment), Willeford played his cards closer to his chest. He knew who he was and had nothing to prove. Still, I would maintain that Willeford's "Southern-ness" is comparatively studied, and that despite his extensive field research on projects such as *Cockfighter*, he writes about Southern issues with a deliberate observational distance, and — importantly — as an educated reader with an awareness of previous Southern writings. However, this does not erase the fact that the themes that preoccupy *Cockfighter* are deeply informed by Southern mythologies about its own past.

11 Carpenter, Brian and Tom Franklin. *Grit Lit: A Rough South Reader*. Columbia: University of South Carolina Press, 2012. Pg xiv.
12 Crews, Harry. "A Day at the Dogfights" in *Florida Frenzy*. Gainesville: University of Florida Press, 1992.

Chapter Three.

Cockfighter The Film:

Origins

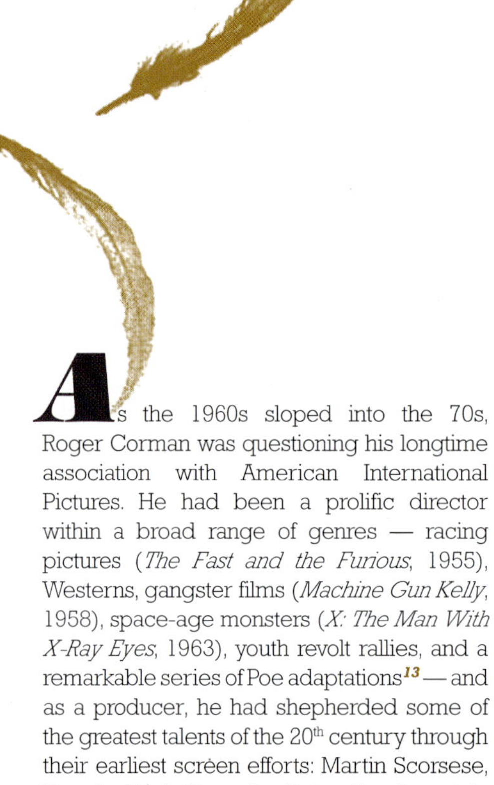

As the 1960s sloped into the 70s, Roger Corman was questioning his longtime association with American International Pictures. He had been a prolific director within a broad range of genres — racing pictures (*The Fast and the Furious*, 1955), Westerns, gangster films (*Machine Gun Kelly*, 1958), space-age monsters (*X: The Man With X-Ray Eyes*, 1963), youth revolt rallies, and a remarkable series of Poe adaptations[13] — and as a producer, he had shepherded some of the greatest talents of the 20th century through their earliest screen efforts: Martin Scorsese, Francis Ford Coppola, Peter Bogdanovich, Jack Nicholson, Dennis Hopper and Monte Hellman among them.

But by the late 60s AIP's co-head James H. Nicholson (who was more uptight than his partner Sam Arkoff) was growing increasingly uncomfortable with Corman's pivot to bold countercultural visons like *The Wild Angels* (1966) and *The Trip* (1967). For his part, Corman felt that as he was getting more experimental, AIP was getting more conservative. Corman had even brought them *Easy Rider*, which they turned down due to Dennis Hopper's inexperience as a director. AIP's fear of change would soon cost them their most reliable collaborator. When they meddled with the editing on Corman's post-apocalyptic environmental satire *Gas-s-s-s* (1969) without his authorisation, he left — and took his handle on the progressive youth market with him.

Corman had a good head for business, that was already apparent. But he was also an artist who had guiding principles and a vision. He was stubbornly independent; not incapable of collaboration, as his many partnerships and co-productions can attest, but in some ways, he was nevertheless a defiant loner.

Corman was also, by this time, burning out as a director. When he set out to establish his own company New World Pictures in 1970 — initially in partnership with Southern drive-in king Larry Woolner, who bailed for his own operation after a year — its mandate was to back pictures by other up-and-coming writers, directors and producers using his tried-and-true formula of low budgets, speedy production schedules and sensational subject matter.[14]

There was only one movie Corman had ever lost money on: the largely self-financed 1962 picture *The Intruder*, starring William Shatner as a white supremacist demagogue who infiltrates a rural community and fuels the racist anxieties of civil rights-era small

13 See Chris Alexander's *Corman/Poe* (Headpress 2023) for a full history of this cycle.

14 1970s graduates of the "Corman School" would include the likes Jonathan Demme, Jonathan Kaplan, Stephanie Rothman, Ron Howard, Joe Dante, James Cameron, Gale Ann Hurd, John Sayles and many more.

town America. The production was plagued by difficulties, ranging from threats of violence in the real town where they were filming, to denial of a certificate by the MPAA, and the film's distributor threatening to back out. In his autobiography, Corman describes therapy sessions he underwent following the failure of *The Intruder*, wherein he mused that, "Maybe I steered clear of the mainstream because of a fear of getting lost as an artist... Perhaps I needed to prove my ability to make it outside the system... worse, it may have exposed me to failure, critical or commercial... but after *The Intruder* I was obviously not particularly eager to take risks and set myself up for another beating." His comments are especially interesting in light of the hubris at the centre of the story we're here to talk about — *Cockfighter* — because the trifecta of Frank Mansfield, Roger Corman and Monte Hellman are connected by that defining moment when they think they have it all figured out, only to be smacked down unexpectedly. Corman has frequently cited *The Intruder* as the picture he's most proud of directing — "the first film I directed from a deep political and social conviction,"[15] he recalled — but swore he would never take such a commercial and financial risk again. Fast forward a decade. Corman was about to eat his words.

It was actually Julie Corman, Roger's wife and producing partner, who discovered the Willeford book and proposed it for an adaptation. "One day in 1972 or so I was reading a review of Willeford's *Cockfighter* in bed," she said. "It featured a man with a mission — to become Cockfighter of the Year in Georgia and it gave a whiff of Willeford's wry sense of humour and his humourous maxims and musings: 'When a woman starts to scream unreasonably it's time to leave'. I showed the review to Roger." By coincidence, Corman's barber was a cockfighter. At the time he'd been ousted from LA, which had the country's strictest anti-cockfighting laws, and set up a game farm in the country where he bred and conditioned roosters. He was constantly regaling Corman with stories of the pit, and insisted that if everyone fought cocks, there'd be no war. "I didn't agree with him," Corman told me, "but he was holding the shears, so I didn't argue!"

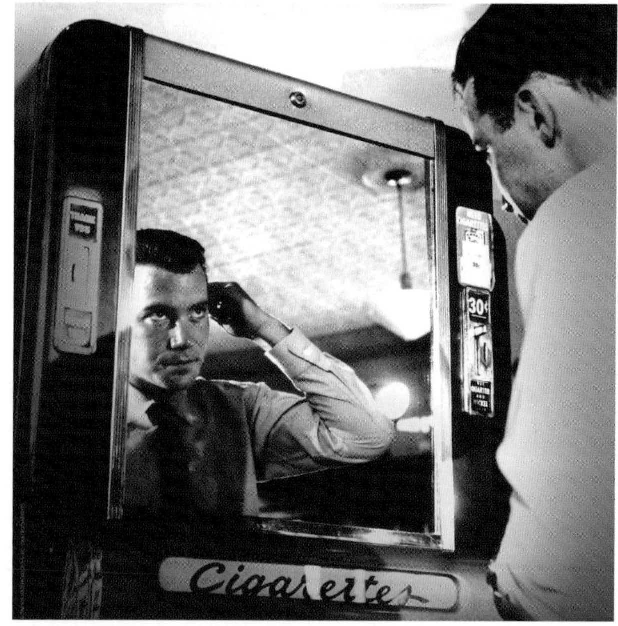

15 **Corman, Roger with Jim Jerome. *How I Made a Hundred Movies in Hollywood and Never Lost a Dime*. London: Muller, 1990. Pg 97.**

According to Corman's longtime script editor Frances Doel[16], Roger never actually read the book, "but he understood that it was structured loosely based on *The Odyssey*. And that was good enough for Roger, because he said the title alone *is* the movie."

Roger's impetuousness was nothing new to Frances. She came into the Corman orbit in a similar fashion to many of his hires — he often looked outside of the industry, for people with various arts and academic skills that could be used to elevate low-budget filmmaking. Frances had a degree in English from Oxford University, and it was when Corman was shooting the last of his Poe films in England that they crossed paths. "He had just made a deal at Columbia, which he was very excited about," recalls Frances,

> and he thought it would be good to try having an English secretary/assistant. So he put an ad in the appointments board. And I answered, mainly because I wanted to work outside of England. I didn't want to be a teacher or work for the Civil Service. I wanted adventure, quite honestly. I knew nothing about movies. So he did interview me but quickly discovered I couldn't drive, and couldn't type — 'cause I've never needed to — and that I've never passed a math exam in my life. So he told me that he thought American girls had more initiative, so he was probably going to hire an American girl. And that was it. Then I was just about to take a job for Penguin books, when I got a telegram from Los Angeles from a temporary secretary working for Roger saying that the assistant he hired had a nervous breakdown and the job was now available and open, and I should leave immediately![17]

"We bought the rights for our company New World Pictures," Julie Corman continues. "Roger hired Willeford to write the screenplay, Monte Hellman to direct and Warren Oates for the lead." When the acquisition was first announced in the trades, Willeford himself wrote in to the *Hollywood Reporter* to correct the spellings of both his name and the film.

Production assistant Steven Gaydos — who went on to be a VP at trade bible *Variety*, and appears on the Anchor Bay commentary alongside Monte Hellman — recalled Corman saying that his acquisition of the book rights was due to research implying that cockfighting was the biggest sport on the planet, which he thought would translate into the film being a hit. Not to mention it was an untapped market. "I like to be, whenever possible, the first one," said Corman. "You can't be the first one very often, but I had never heard of anybody making a picture about cockfighting. And I thought, I can really be the first one here, I can blaze a new trail, so I was very optimistic." Corman-produced films had touched on the sport before, largely as a shorthand for deviancy — there is a pivotal cockfighting scene in the Philippines-shot *Women in Cages* (1971) — but as former New World PR man Jon Davison has pointed out, *Cockfighter* was essentially meant to be Corman's "redneck version of *The Hustler*." However, lone wolf cocker Frank Mansfield never captured the public imagination like Newman's Fast Eddie Felson, nor did the film approach the acclaim of Robert Rossen's Academy Award-

16 In her many correspondences with Charles Willeford referenced throughout this book (and in her credit on *Cockfighter*), she is credited as Frances Kimbrough; she was married to actor Clint Kimbrough and used his name for a time. But she started and ended her association with Corman under the name Frances Doel and that's the name I will consistently use throughout this text.

17 It's worth mentioning that the assistant Corman hired first was Stephanie Rothman, who would soon graduate within the Corman ranks to producer and director. The other person who applied for the position was Julie Halloran, who didn't get the job, but she "got the guy": she's now Julie Corman.

winning picture. "When the picture came out and didn't do any business," Corman told me, "I realized why nobody had ever made a picture about cockfighting."

It wasn't entirely true that no one had made a picture about cockfighting, but not one on US soil. Two overseas films beat Corman by a year: the first a great character study from Iran by director Shapur Gharib called *Khurus* (aka *Rooster*, 1973) in which a decades-old love triangle is played out against a backdrop of cockfighting in a small village. The central cockfighter (Saeed Rad, who became a marquee star with an award-winning turn in *The Morning of the Fourth Day* the previous year) is repeatedly urged to give up cockfighting and marry, because "fighting cocks is like a spring sky — you can't trust it." The film was part of an emerging "tough guy" genre in Iran that explored deviant forms of masculinity, and the western symbolic connotations of the fighting cock are certainly present.[18] That same year, the Filipino-made *Logro Diyes* by director Romy Villaflor examines the world of cockfighting from the perspective of the country where the sport remains the most popular. "For the first time on any screen — the never-before seen — no holds barred, no-punches-pulled inside story of the country's most popular sport — COCKFIGHTING!" proclaimed the posters, adding that it was "filmed in Cock-a-Doodle Colour!"

Though she thought Willeford's book was "terrific", Frances Doel could see that adapting the book would be a challenge, not just due to the disreputable sport at its heart, but because the protagonist doesn't speak.

18 **See the chapter "Males, Masculinity and Power: The Tough-Guy Movie Genre and its Evolution" in Hamid Naficy's *A Social History of Iranian Cinema Vol 2: The Industrializing Years, 1941-1978*. Duke University Press, 2011.**

"I did wonder privately — I didn't say that to Roger directly — but I wondered if he had actually read it whether he would have so blindly bought it."

Willeford's agent had previously tried to pitch the book for a film adaptation to no avail; a letter in Willeford's papers from Carolyn Lefcourt at Warner Brothers contained a rejection of the proposal on the basis of the cockfighting. "People here were so put off by the sport itself," she wrote, "that no one was able to see it in the proper perspective." She recommended that they get a big star to endorse it, "like Robert Redford or Dustin Hoffman." But in July 1972, the deal with New World was inked. Frances Doel wrote a letter to Willeford informing him that contracts for the book rights had been sent to his agent; the option was inked that same month. She gave him two months to write a first draft, and passed on Corman's suggestion that he read Siegfried Kracauer's *Theory of Film*.

In a *Film Quarterly* article Willeford wrote in 1975 — much of which is repeated verbatim in *Cockfighter Journal* and in an earlier 1974 article he wrote for the *Miami Herald* — Willeford says that once charged with writing the script, he retreated to his beach house on the east coast of Florida, and walked up and down the beach for three days, trying to envision how he would structure his first screenplay.

In the Willeford archives are two carbon-copy remnants of letters from Willeford to Corman, advising the latter on the status of the script. In one, dated November 1972, Willeford refers to an enclosed tape of the songs his stepson Stephen Hooker wrote for Frank — the author says he likes the songs and wonders if one might be right for the "hotel room scene." In another letter a month later, Willeford explains that he kept the voiceover in the script though it "bothers me" — saying that *Deliverance, Last Year at Marienbad* and *Summer of '42* would all have been better without it. Nevertheless, the penultimate draft shows no voiceover, although it was apparently re-incorporated for the final version. "Dad talked about how he, Corman and Hellman grappled with how best to pull off the vow of silence without losing the audience," recalls Stephen Hooker. "It was a big concern. Today, I feel that fulfilling the vow and all the difficulties it creates could have produced any number of funny or defining moments of communication struggles."

After the first draft, Willeford met with Corman in Hollywood and stayed locally while he worked on the script revisions, so that he could show Roger pages in progress. By Willeford's estimation, he wrote at a pace of nine pages per day in his room at the Hollywood Roosevelt Hotel. Here he shares his oft-quoted writing ritual: "It is also my practice to write the first page in the morning when I get up, before I urinate. This vicious practice gives a certain urgency to the first page of the day" (Later versions of the quote — he recycled his own wisdom frequently — go on to state that even if one doesn't get past this first page each day, at the end of the year you have a novel). "I do remember Dad being so excited to be directly involved," says Hooker. "He returned home happy and nearly broke having spent most of his contract money on living expenses during the six weeks he was in LA making re-writes. We didn't care, we were just happy for him and looking forward to the next phase, shooting."

At this point, Willeford was under the impression Corman would be helming the movie — he was an avowed fan of the director and frequently showed Corman pictures in his film appreciation class at Miami-Dade Community College — and wrote certain shots into the script that he felt specifically suited Corman's style.[19]

Many accounts of *Cockfighter* — from my personal conversations with Monte Hellman to Willeford's *Cockfighter Journal* and other writings, Susan Compo's biography *Warren Oates: A Wild Life* and Christopher Koetting's *Mind Warp! The Fantastic True Story of Roger Corman's New World Pictures*, among others — insist that Corman originally intended to direct it, something which Corman himself denied vehemently. "I never planned to direct it," he told me. "When I started New World in 1970, I stopped directing. I never, at any time, had any intention of directing *Cockfighter*." Willeford claims that on his second meeting with Corman — at which point Hellman wasn't attached to the project yet — that Corman planned to direct it himself. Trade newspapers *The Hollywood Reporter* and *Variety* likewise reported in 1972 announcements that Corman was to direct.

In May of 1973, Frances Doel wrote to Willeford that they had been turned down by all the major studios for financing — "they are unanimous on two points of criticism — that there is too much cockfighting in the script, and that Frank emerges as an unsympathetic character" — and reports that as a result, Corman had committed to financing *Cockfighter* himself, but with a more modest budget than they had initially hoped.

Cockfighter was announced in the trades as the first in an eight-picture deal between Corman's New World and Artists Entertainment Complex (AEC) — which had originally started as an artist management company but moved into producing with *Serpico* (1973) — whose vice president Samuel Gelfman would serve as on-set producer on *Cockfighter*. Financing would come from the Richmond, Virginia-based Hawkins Land Development company, who in 1972 finalised a $10 million partnership with New World for these eight pictures. At least according to the trades. Corman told me: "There was never actually a contract. It was anticipated that we might do more films together. Actually we did a couple of other films with Sam, but there was no actual eight-picture deal."

It took a year between Willeford handing in his approved draft and Corman getting the funds together to begin shooting. In December of 1973, Doel wrote to Willeford with the good news that the shoot was slated for March of the following year, and that Monte Hellman and Warren Oates had enthusiastically signed on.

19 Willeford, Charles. *Cockfighter Journal: The Story of a Shooting*. Santa Barbara: Neville Press, 1989. Pg 14.

Right and over: A series of letters from New World to Charles Willeford concerning the option and adaptation of his novel.

July 5th 1972

Mr. Charles Willeford
333 University Drive, Apt. 235
Coral Gables, Florida 33134.

Dear Mr. Willeford:

I am writing to you on Roger Corman's behalf as he is currently away in Europe. The contracts have been received by your agent, who will be in touch with you.

Roger is delighted to be working with you as COCKFIGHTER is the first novel he or I have read in several years which struck us immediately as a first class, original narration. Roger's enthusiasm for this project derives in part from the authenticity and concreteness of detail through which you achieve such a vivid evocation of place and a way of life, and in part from the compelling strength of the central character. An extroardinary feat is accomplished in drawing us into an obssessive way of life by giving us insights into the basic (but rarely found in a "pure" form) human drives of aggression, competitiveness and individual aspiration. There is finally an amazing eloquence in the 'silent' narrator. Frank Mansfield's quest for supremacy grips us because it is told with dry humour, suspense and in authentic detail. It is a kind of American Odyssey, and in the end we have the peculiar satisfaction of seeing that "the wheel has come full circle", that the hero got what he deserved in more senses than one and is thereby brought into perspective as a whole man, in his professional life, his interior life, and in his idiosyncratic relationship to others.

Roger would like to draw your attention to two factors that he feels to be problematical in adapting your work to the motion picture form. Firstly, the question of the hero's vow of silence and his silence. How will the audience know the reason? Possibly you would have to use a stream of consciousness, "voice over" technique. Secondly, Roger does not believe in Frank inviting both his fiancee and Bernice to the tournament at the end.

He feels it might work better dramatically if Frank were to invite Mary Elizabeth and then Bernice showed up unexpectedly. However, if he has missed a motivation that you know to be important here, he would not insist on this change.

Roger would like you to proceed directly with the First Draft screenplay and mail it to him when finished. He will be back from Europe July 22nd, and would hope for a First Draft sometime late in the summer. Then, a week or so after he will have received the First Draft he would like you to come out here for a meeting with him.

Finally, Roger highly recommends that you read Siegfried Kracauer's "Theory of Film" (which is now published in paperback), a critical study which Roger feels is the soundest guide to the understanding of the nature of film as an art form, and ~~indicates~~ will give you an indication of the requirements of the screenplay as opposed to the novel or short story.

As far as the screenplay form is concerned, I enclose a First Draft screenplay by John William Corrington, a novelist you may know of. In general, don't worry about giving specific and various camera angles, unless you need to for a dramatic or story point.

Of course, feel free to call us should you want to discuss anything about the First Draft, but otherwise Roger prefers that you have the freedom of working independently on the Forst Draft screenplay.

Sincerely,

Frances Kimbrough

Frances Kimbrough
(for Roger Corman)

ENCL.

8831 Sunset Blvd. Penthouse "A"   Los Angeles, California 90069

657-2201

January 16th 1973

Mr. Charles Willeford
333 University Drive
Coral Gables, Florida 33134.

Dear Charles,

Thank you for your letter of January 9th and the accompanying revisions. I think the new ending and the addition of the dream sequence successfully resolve and clarify the structural and thematic problems that remained. These and your other modifications have now been incorporated into the Final Draft script, which I am extremely pleased with. I would like to congratulate you on the fine work you have done throughout to achieve the consistently high quality of the finished screenplay.

I am now submitting the script to various major companies to see what kind of deal I can get. Incidentally, regarding your reference to the habits of many actors in assessing the worth of a role, I am of course aware of the potential difficulty in attracting a major star with what might be thoughtlessly described as the most major non-speaking role ever submitted! However, I do think that the script is so good that I still have high hopes for the casting of Frank and for a good production deal. We will of course keep you informed of developments in this area.

Sincerely,

Roger

Roger Corman.

8831 Sunset Blvd. Penthouse "A" Los Angeles, California 90069

213- 657-2201

May 16th 1973

Mr. Charles Willeford
Leonardo Arms - Apt. 129
7400 Estero Blvd.
Fort Meyers Beach, Florida 33931

Dear Charles,

I am writing on behalf of Roger to let you know how things stand with "COCKFIGHTER". Unfortunately, we have been turned down by all the major studios now, and they are unanimous on two points of criticism - that there is too much cockfighting in the script and that Frank emerges as an unsympathetic character. United Artists (for whom Roger has just produced a picture) have offered to look at the script again if we can take out one cockfight and do something to make Frank more sympathetic. In any case, if United Artists turn down the project a second time, Roger will back "COCKFIGHTER" himself and make the picture on a medium budget. Roger and I both believe that this is a good script, but in the light of the same specific criticism being made of it on all sides, we feel that some revisions should be made to ensure a proper balance of sympathy for the leading character, and to take out one cockfight.

The most cogent criticisms of Frank as the leading character are that his actions and behavior suggest he is one of the worst guys on the cockfighting circuit and it is hard to see why Middleton, Sanders etc like and respect him, (it is suggested that one of the reasons he seems "one of the worst guys" is that he seems always to be taking and never giving e.g. food and money); and that because his singlemindedness appears so totally cold and selfish in pursuit of his goal the audience is likely to identify with Mary Elizabeth's point of view of Frank expressed at the end.

Of course, we do not wholeheartedly endorse these criticisms because to meet them at their face value would entail telling a completely different story of a more conventional character. However, we do have one suggestion which we think might help to counteract the basic criticism without destroying the integrity of the theme and story - which is, that Jack Burke could be made more of a "heavy" (possibly in regard to Dody as well)from the beginning so that we would have an opening somewhat more akin to "Shane", in which the audience would really root for Frank to make his comeback and beat Jack Burke into the bargain.

It might also be a good idea to have anpther look at the details of Frank's progression to Milledgeville in that, for example, the accumulation of detail does suggest that Frank gets a lot of minor help (starting with the $50 from Middleton when he is really down and out) which perhaps obscures the fact that the story starts out with Frank at rock bottom and that he has to wage a single-minded struggle back.

Roger and Julie will be out of the country for a month, but if you would like to discuss any of this, please do call. We would very much like your thoughts on what cockfight could be dropped, and any ideas you might have on looking at the script again on what modifications or slants of emphasis might help to make Frank more sympathetic as the leading character.

How is your new novel going?

Very best wishes,

Frances

Frances Kimbrough

8831 Sunset Blvd. Penthouse "A"   Los Angeles, California 90069

657-2201

December 14, 1973

Mr. Charles Willeford
333 University Drive, Apt. 235
Coral Gables, Florida 33134

Dear Charles,

This is just a quick note to let you know the good news - that Roger is going ahead with arrangements to shoot COCKFIGHTER, starting in March, in Georgia and north Florida, with headquarters in Atlanta, Georgia.

Warren Oates (who most recently starred in "Dillinger" and is currently shooting in Sam Peckinpah's latest film) has been signed to star as Frank, and Monte Hellman has been signed to direct. You may have seen, or remember, the film Monte Hellman and Warren Oates did together - "Two Lane Blacktop".

I hear that Monte Hellman and Warren Oates are both extremely enthusiastic about the project, and like the script.

Meanwhile, we wish you a good Christmas and a happy New Year,

Kindest personal regards,

Frances

Frances Kimbrough.

P.S. As Roger is anxious to let you know the news right away, I'm sending copy of the letter to the other address we have for you, as I'm not sure which one you're at currently!

8831 Sunset Blvd. Penthouse "A" Los Angeles, California 90069

657-2201

Jan. 10th 1974

Mr. Charles Willeford
Miami-Dade Community College
South Campus
11011 S.W. 104 Street
Miami, Florida 33156

Dear Charles,

It was good to hear from you. Glad you're pleased about Monte Hellman and Warren Oates. Roger suggested I write you now about production plans. We expect to start shooting in Georgia (based in Atlanta, but moving around somewhat, of course) in April. The projected start date is April 1st, and it it will be a 4 week shooting schedule. If you could possibly make arrangements to get away then, we'd very much like you to be there as technical advisor and also play a small part. For which of course we would pay you.

Also, although I know you're pretty well into another normally hectic semester, we will be asking you for a little additional dialogue polish/minor revisions here and there, in conjunction with Monte Hellman's reactions. There is one scene which, after discussions with Monte and the backer, we would like you to rewrite now, if you possibly can. This is the Biloxi motel flashback/dream sequence (PP. 25-28) We are all now agreed that the scene should be a (relatively) straightforward flashback/dream. In other words, we want to drop the surrealistic dream technique and dramatize the scene in naturalistic style, so that we see and hear Burke and Frank's argument, Frank's brag about his chicken, the subsequent motel room challenge match in which Frank loses his chicken and his chance at the medal, and ending scene pretty much as you have it now, except perhaps having Burke tell Frank he should have kept his mouth shut, rather than shouldn't have bragged about his chicken so much. If you could rewrite this one scene now, it would give us a jump on things as other revisions will be minor, not changing a whole scene.

Do let us know whether you think you would be interested in coming up and working on the production, and I will of course keep in touch re start date, etc.

Very best wishes,

Frances

Frances Kimbrough

Chapter Four.

The Space Between: Monte Hellman

Small and wiry with a shock of frizzy hair set far back on his head, Monte Hellman's quiet energy doesn't communicate that he was once considered the most promising director in Hollywood. Like most people, he looks quite severe until he smiles, revealing dimples and a slight diastema. He has the careful movements of a tinkerer. Small details, minutiae carried out in the hidden crevices of vast empty spaces would become a hallmark of his work.

Hellman's relationship with Roger Corman went back to the mid-1950s, when Hellman directed the first LA stage production of *Waiting for Godot* with Corman as an investor.

Monte always found the theatre more artistically pure than the movies. "From the time I was small, my soul was lost to the theatre," he told the *New York Times* in 1971. And though he has famously said that the austerity of his films was the result of austerity in the budgets, there is much in mid-century theatre that one can see reflected in Hellman's films, which operate almost as chamber pieces, but resituated into expansive geographies that fuel their protagonists' pronounced solitude.

Corman then invited Hellman to direct a movie for him, which turned out to be *The Beast from Haunted Cave* (1959). In selecting first-time directors to mentor, Corman would often employ them as assistants, editors and in various other capacities before finally awarding them the director's chair; this had been the case with the likes of Peter Bogdanovich, Jack Hill and Francis Ford Coppola, as well as Hellman, who had initially served as an editor for Corman (and would continue in that capacity off and on for several more years).

Hellman and Jack Nicholson met through the local theatre scene, but it was on the set of *The Wild Ride* (1960), upon which Hellman was employed as editor and associate producer, that they became close friends. The two started working on projects together (including the Fred Roos-produced *Flight to Fury* and *Back Door to Hell*, both shot in the Philippines in 1964) as well as those intended to be financed by Corman — beginning with an aborted production called *Epitaph* (about a struggling actor trying to raise funds for his girlfriend's abortion), which Nicholson described as "a very down, dry, Antonioni, British-naturalist-influenced look at the malaise of Hollywood."[20] Instead, this transitioned into the duo of existentialist Westerns *The Shooting* and *Ride in the Whirlwind*. Critic Damien Love calls *The*

20 Qtd. Crane, Robert and Christopher Fryer. *Jack Nicholson: The Early Years.* (Originally published in 1975 as *Jack Nicholson: Face to Face*) University Press of Kentucky, Lexington 2012. Pg 11

Shooting — written by Carole Eastman under the pseudonym Adrien Joyce — "a cowboy comic book by Kafka, set on a bleak windswept prairie that perpetually folded back on itself."

"Carole Eastman was using a more poetic technique," recalled Nicholson in an early 1970s interview, "where you were using one image, the falling effect at the end was really an attempt to, like a tuning fork, re-attune those impulses that you got from watching the Jack Ruby piece of footage, which, at the time this was written, was a very strong piece of footage."[21] Nicholson is referring here to the assassination of Lee Harvey Oswald by gangster Jack Ruby in November 1963 — an assassination that occurred on live television. This spectacle, and that of the Zapruder footage of Kennedy's assassination itself (though it would not be seen by the public in full until later, *LIFE Magazine* published a frame-by-frame pictorial in November 1963), would have an indelible impact on all forms of media for the following decade, as independent filmmakers repeatedly grappled with its grim implications. Hellman and Eastman also shared an interest in the kind of existential Americana that was emerging as a response to the European art films infiltrating the US market at the time. They would later work together on an aborted project called *Interval* for Universal, described by Hellman biographer Brad Stevens as "a music mystery in the vein of Antonioni's popular *Blow-Up*," which is fascinating when one considers that *The Shooting* and *Blow-Up* (which went in production a year later) certainly share a lineage in terms of their respective references to the capturing of real death on film. In the chapter on Carole Eastman in his book *Always Crashing in the Same Car*, Matthew Spektor confirms that "echoes of the JFK assassination" can be found in the ending of *Interval*.

The Shooting is also the genesis of a direct pathway which continues through *Two-Lane Blacktop* and *Cockfighter*. It is bleak and cruel, full of doubling and substitution, its gloomy vistas impregnated with silence. And it creates an unforgettable role for Millie Perkins, as a mysterious, sadistic woman who corrals various men into helping her fulfil some strange ambition they aren't clear on, but all are pretty sure it ends with a hole in someone.

"Monte was in an acting class when I first came to California, after I shot *The Diary of Anne Frank*," explains Perkins. "I joined an acting class where I met a lot of my new friends: Sandra Knight and Monte Hellman and Jack Nicholson and Warren." She would play a key role in future Hellman/Nicholson collaborations and be forever associated with the AIP roster through her successive marriages to Dean Stockwell and Robert Thom. But it was her relationship with Warren Oates, solidified on the set of *The Shooting*, that would have the greatest impact. "Warren and I became very close and kept in touch for awhile," Perkins told me in a phone call as I was finishing this book. But she didn't remember meeting me 20 years earlier — when I brought her to a film festival in Vancouver for a screening of the Robert Thom-scripted *The Witch Who Came From the Sea* — and what she told me then: that Warren Oates had been the love of her life. As she explained it, their lives just never seemed to match up; they were never single at the same time. But the intimacy and immediacy of the shoot made for impulsive behavior, and the onscreen electricity between Warren

21 Qtd. Crane, Robert and Christopher Fryer. *Jack Nicholson: The Early Years.* University Press of Kentucky, Lexington 2012. Pg 13.

Oates, Millie Perkins and Jack Nicholson was reflective of a behind-the-scenes love triangle that surely benefited the film.

"I loved it, says Millie Perkins of *The Shooting* and *Ride in the Whirlwind*,

> We shot them in Utah, practically in two weeks' time, and we didn't have a good budget. Jack and I went to Western Costume and picked out our own clothes, and they put us up in a motel and we shot those movies really fast. It was really a great experience… Monte was an oddball, and we used to make jokes about Monte because he was, let's say he thinks he's the next Francois Truffaut or Fellini or something. He loved all of those European avant-garde movies. And we respected him for it. And Monte let us be who we were basically. He chose us for who we were and he didn't direct much. He would say, 'You know, Mill, you ought to ride that horse a little faster, don't you think she would?'

The films would form the basis of professional relationships that would carry over into *Cockfighter*, where Perkins would be reunited not only with Hellman and Oates, but with Harry Dean Stanton, who appeared in *Ride in the Whirlwind* as a one-eyed stagecoach robber. But like *Cockfighter*, both films revealed a director whose instincts were disruptive to genre conventions.

The wide shots of the Western would remain a staple in Hellman's films; in his 1986 documentary on Hellman, *Plunging on Alone: Monte Hellman's Life in a Day*, director Paul Joyce notes that they serve to align the actors with the landscape. "That's true," Hellman responds. "Also it enables me to put distance between the actors. And frequently put an actor on one end of the screen and another on the other, and the space in between — it's an expression. It's a way of emphasising a point." Incidentally, the setup of a cockfight utilises this framing by necessity; the birds are on opposite sides of the pit like gunslingers in a duel, the eight feet between them crackling with a tension that will break when their handlers let them go and they rush towards each other.

As Nicholas Pasquariello pointed out in a 1976 interview with Hellman in *Jump Cut*, both *The Shooting* and *Ride in the Whirlwind* succeeded in elevating the source material to a level of mythic and existential import not often seen on US screens, and were the first to define what makes an essentially *Hellman-esque* picture: "The characters here are in search of mysterious, unconquerable forces (perhaps their very souls) which are always

Above: Millie Perkins.

just beyond their reach," he writes. "Yet they are driven on to the very edge of life itself in their search. *In search*. Perhaps more than any other two words, these sum up the theme of Monte Hellman's work. The search for what mysterious forces motivate men to greed (*Flight to Fury*), to compete (*Two-Lane Blacktop*, *Cockfighter*), to understand the nature of life and death (*Ride in the Whirlwind*, *The Shooting*)." Even as recently as *Road to Nowhere* (2010), Hellman was still exploring the theme of the chase, wrapped up in existentialism; the unattainability of that intangible goal at the end of it all, a goal that may well not even exist. Willeford may have fashioned a bristly nod to *The Odyssey*, but Hellman admits that every film he's made has been an unconscious ode to the myth of Sisyphus.

"The two Westerns had a problematic release," Corman told me, "and took a few years to find their footing in the market. I think both pictures were very good, incidentally, but if I had any quibbles, it was that I thought they should, as Westerns, have a little bit more action. I did not have a distribution company at that time. Since I didn't have a distribution company, what I would do is I would finance a number of pictures — often of new directors, like Francis Coppola, Martin Scorsese and so forth — and then I would look for distribution. I had a little difficulty getting the distribution because of the fact that they did not have the action that the distributors were looking for. So it took me a while to make a deal. But I finally made a deal in which I sold the pictures outright for a reasonable profit. So I was essentially happy with the whole thing."

When he produced *The Shooting* and *Ride in the Whirlwind*, Corman was under contract to Columbia, but continued to back films independently. After so many successes at AIP, Corman had been courted by the majors, but his experiences there were a frustrating series of stops and starts; projects developed and then dumped as the studios waffled on their decisions. Corman left Columbia for 20th Century Fox and managed to make one picture there — *The St. Valentine's Day Massacre* (1967) — before realising that the environment the major studios offered was far too stifling for a tornado like Corman. "My recent attempts to work with the majors has led to disillusionment, some bitterness, and anger," wrote Corman in his autobiography, "It was apparent that I was not about to emerge as a 'star' director in the Hollywood establishment." Corman went back to AIP only to face more meddling there. And that's important because in this story, our protagonists all get to the top of their game, but are stopped in their tracks and made to take several steps backwards — with all the accompanying disappointment and self-doubt that entails. Corman was tough but even he admits he was not impervious to hard self-reflection in the face of failure.

After the two Westerns, Hellman spent the years leading up to *Two-Lane Blacktop* (1971) employed in a variety of film roles that had little to do with his own status as an auteur: namely jobs for hire. These included several editing gigs — he was renowned as an editor and this would keep him afloat during fallow periods — including *The Wild Angels* (he disputes Peter Bogdanovich's claim in Andrew Yule's biography that Bogdanovich was enlisted to help with editing[22]), and the musical sequences for Bob Rafelson's *Head*

22 Qtd Stevens, Brad. *Monte Hellman: His Life and Films*. McFarland & Company, 2003. Pg 70.

(1968), the Monkees' phantasmagorical big screen debut penned by his pal Jack Nicholson (Monte's credit is mysteriously absent from extant copies of the film). Corman also hired Hellman as editor for one of his projects at Columbia — *The Long Ride Home*, scripted by Robert Towne, but Roger was ousted from the director's seat in favour of Phil Karlson (*The Phenix City Story*) and Monte resigned in solidarity.

In all of Hellman's less visibly productive periods, he always had projects in various stages of development, which underwent stops and starts as the winds (and the staff) changed at the studios.[23] When Corman was still at AIP, Hellman was slated to direct a Southern racial picture called *Explosion*, but Sam Arkoff cancelled the project and gave it to Sam Fuller instead; only to drag his heels so long that in the meantime MGM came out with a picture with an identical plot called *Tick...Tick...Tick...* (1969). After his ouster from *Explosion*, Hellman turned his attention to a parody of the Kennedy dynasty which was quickly scrapped after Bobby Kennedy was shot on June 5th 1968. Then came an aborted Patricia Highsmith adaptation. He also had a short-lived director's company with Vernon Zimmerman (later the director of *Unholy Rollers* and *Fade to Black*), Bill Norton (*Cisco Pike*) and Stephen Spielberg (by contemporary accounts the least promising of the bunch!), but they disbanded before producing a single picture. Not to mention, he came close to directing such films as *Fat City, The Last Picture Show, Duck, You Sucker, Logan's Run, Kid Blue* and *Pat Garrett and Billy the Kid* — the latter one of many intersections with the career of Sam Peckinpah (who later called Hellman "the best director working in America today").[24]

Maybe it's like this for everyone, but it seems Monte had especially rotten luck.

But in early 1970, things looked like they were about to turn around: Hellman was offered a five-picture deal with Cinema Center, and given his pick between a cautionary tale of Hollywood excess called *The Christian Licorice Store* or a zany cross-country racing picture called *Two-Lane Blacktop*. James Frawley — who also picked up *Kid Blue* (1973) — would take *The Christian Licorice Store* (whose title was derived from a Tim Buckley song) in which Monte would have a brief role onscreen playing himself (incidentally, so would Tim Buckley — and Jean Renoir!). The other picture, written by Will Corry, was — in Hellman's estimation — not good. But it had potential... if the script were thrown out.[25]

Now something to know about Monte Hellman — he frequently took on scripts he didn't like, and completely refashioned them to fit his vision, with the help of a collaborator of his choosing. This was essential to his artistic process and his authorial control over the work (and as we shall see, it's going to be a problem later). Corry's script may have been an ensemble comedy in the vein of *It's a Mad Mad Mad Mad World* (1963), Saturday morning cartoon *The Wacky Races* (1968), or the soon-to-be smash hits *The Cumball Rally* (1976) and *The Cannonball Run* (1981) — a staple format of America's gearhead culture, really — but what appealed to Monte were the gambling stakes at the narrative's core. As he told biographer Brad Stevens, his father was a gambler, and this was

23 I'm leaning heavily on the research of Hellman biographer Brad Stevens in this section about Monte's "in-between" years.

24 Peckinpah said this on *The Tonight Show* in 1973.

25 In Sylvia Townsend's exhaustive book about *Two-Lane Blacktop*, Floyd Mutrux, who wrote *The Christian Licorice Store* and had originally been tapped to rewrite Will Corry's script before Wurlitzer came on, says history gave Corry a bum rap: "Nobody gives Corry credit," he says, asserting that many of the film's notable elements were already present in Corry's script despite the fact that Hellman and Wurlitzer claim to have started from scratch. Plus, says Mutrux of Hellman: "He did not understand anything about cars."

something he could work with. It was also something that would clearly continue through *Cockfighter*; in his contemporary review of the latter film, critic Jonathan Rosenbaum noted that "the fascination with games and competitions that persists through *The Shooting* and *Two-Lane Blacktop* is always tempered by the dryly comic notion that all of them are pretty silly." Hellman biographer Brad Stevens also points out the ubiquity of games in Hellman's oeuvre — from solitaire to chess and checkers up to drag racing, cockfighting and more — but says it was Jack Nicholson's character in *Flight to Fury*, "obsessed with both games and death, who most clearly suggested something clarified in *Two-Lane Blacktop*: that it is the inescapable fact of our ultimate demise which reveals how random contests of chance or skill function as substitutes for more meaningful action."

Hellman's choice in co-writers was not always the obvious one. When he hit up Rudy Wurlitzer to rewrite *Two-Lane Blacktop*, the decision was based on the latter's experimental novel *Nog* (1968) and his script for Jim McBride's post-apocalypse film *Glen and Randa* (1969). While *Nog* is a questing bohemian drama from the POV of a shell-shocked, unreliable narrator, it too has been likened to post-apocalypse SF of that period. There was something in the science fiction of the time that Hellman clearly saw as transmutable to the road movie, and I would argue he was early in that acknowledgement. Science-fiction in the late '60s was going through the same changes as the Western; it was the ideal outlet for stories of existential crisis, youth alienation and misdirected belief. Both genres had taken a dark, dystopic turn, and with the emergence of writers like JG Ballard, Michael Moorcock and Samuel R. Delany, science-fiction had positioned itself as a key platform for radical political thought and sexually transgressive experimentation.[26] SF of this period was

Above: *Two-Lane Blacktop*.

26 **For more on this topic, see Andrew Nette and Iain McIntyre's *Dangerous Visions and New Worlds: Radical Science Fiction, 1950-1985*. PM Press, 2021.**

also adept at channelling the themes of isolation so important to Hellman's life and work. Thus the quote from a group sex scene in Wurlitzer's *Nog* that Hellman taps in his introduction to the published version of the *Two-Lane Blacktop* script that accompanied the 2007 Criterion Collection DVD release ("Meredith finally came with a long shuddering spasm followed closely by Lockett, whose arms and legs wrap over Meredith in his final embrace. I plunge on alone"), which also provided the title for Paul Joyce's aforementioned documentary about Hellman.

Likewise this rebellion against social norms, an emphasis on masculinity in crisis, and an atmosphere of existential malaise would soon come to characterize the road movie. Despite proto-road movies like *Stagecoach* (1939) or *The Grapes of Wrath* (1940), the fusion of man and vehicle that was a dominating motif of the road movie really arrived with the post-war car culture boom accompanying the expansion of the nation's highway system and the introduction of the Rocket V8 engine in 1949, which became a staple of muscle cars in the 1960s. *Two-Lane Blacktop* was a natural successor to *Easy Rider* (1969) and was accompanied the same year by Richard Sarafian's *Vanishing Point*. With gearhead culture at its peak in America, expectations were high.[27]

So high, in fact, that in April of 1971, *Esquire* made *Two-Lane Blacktop* their cover story, with a preemptive vote for "movie of the year," and printed Rudy Wurlitzer's entire screenplay over nine pages in the magazine. It was an endorsement they would publicly retract.

Once Hellman's edit was finished — in keeping with the New Hollywood's experimental tactic of giving directors final cut — the studio execs realized what they had on their hands was *not* the next *Easy Rider*, as they had hoped. Where Hopper's film was full of anthemic rock n' roll propulsion, *Two-Lane* was comparatively "sedate and unembellished."[28] Other than a few early champions — Vincent Canby in the *New York Times*, Jay Cocks in *Time* — critical responses were not good. As the film's biographer Sylvia Townsend notes, it would take decades for the film to reach the canonised status it enjoys now. But at the time, reviews were more likely to echo *Newsweek*'s comment that "Hellman turns the voltage so low that one is tempted to take the film's pulse to see whether the projector is still rolling."[29]

The lack of sustained acceleration in Monte's career certainly put pressure on his marriage; he told me himself that his wife Jackie was always disappointed that they didn't have the same success, recognition — and *money* — that "Jack and Sandra had." During *Two Lane*'s development and casting, Monte and Jackie separated — though she continued to work with him on the film. She was there when a very young, rail-thin New Yorker named Laurie Bird came in to screen test.

It's a very special kind of disappointment when you aren't where you think you ought to be in life. When your peers seem to skate past you with their opportunities and successes, even though everyone is so quick to tell you how special you are, how unique, how what you're doing just can't be compared with anything else because it's just *on another level*.

Two-Lane Blacktop, in the context of the New Hollywood and its priorities — for supporting visionary, rogue young iconoclasts — should have had a very different outcome for Hellman.

---

27 The very first car magazine was an 1895 American periodical called *The Horseless Age*.
28 Townsend, Sylvia. *Bumpy Roads: The Making, Flop, and Revival of Two-Lane Blacktop*. University of Mississippi Press, 2019. Kindle edition, Pg 109.
29 Qtd in Townsend, Sylvia. *Bumpy Roads: The Making, Flop, and Revival of Two-Lane Blacktop*. University of Mississippi Press, 2019. Kindle edition, Pg 116.

APRIL 1971
PRICE $1
Esquire
THE MAGAZINE FOR MEN
Read it first!
Our nomination for
the movie of the year:
Two Lane Blacktop
See Page 104

While in post on *Two-Lane*, the buzz around the film gave the director his choice of opportunities; he had been offered *Kid Blue*, but turned it down because he already had a Western on his slate: *Pat Garrett and Billy the Kid*, which would again see him teamed with Wurlitzer as screenwriter. It was in development at MGM, who dropped it when *Two-Lane Blacktop* flopped. Wurlitzer kept working on the script without Hellman, and MGM ultimately offered the project to Sam Peckinpah. It was one of many times Hellman's career would intersect with Peckinpah's, not only in terms of specific projects — Hellman had also been offered *Junior Bonner (1972)* — but through their shared relationship with Warren Oates as well. Additionally, Hellman had worked on developing *The Mechanic* (1972) before it was finally given to Michael Winner instead. *Two-Lane Blacktop* had clearly landed Monte Hellman squarely in movie jail.

Instead he found himself cobbling together another project — an Alain Robbe-Grillet adaptation that never materialised — for Corman, ever the underappreciated benefactor. Because while all the Corman graduates are quick to praise Roger for the career kickstart he gave them, he's also considered something to *get past*, a stepping stone on the way to making "real" movies. And no one likes to take a step backwards. But it's really not fair to Corman. He was always there with a paycheck, welcoming of idiosyncratic — even difficult — personalities. Not everyone is deemed "employable," trust me, I know. When doors close it's important to acknowledge those who hold another door open.

Still, for Hellman, having touched the periphery of substantial critical and financial success, there was no question that going back to B-pictures was a defeat. It was a moment of hubris that would be crucial in establishing Monte's receptiveness to the character of Frank Mansfield.

165. Interior. Car. Close on Driver.

His face is completely concentrated, completely involved in the moment. His lips are tense, his eyes slightly squinted. Inside the Car it is absolutely QUIET. All SOUND ceases until the end of the movie.

The Driver's right hand: the hand grips the stick shift and pushes it into first.

The Driver's hands on the steering wheel. The airstrip is visible and the '32 Coupe lined up on the right. The sun is sinking fast. On the left, the starter chops down his hands.

The race starts. We're instantly propelled forward within the Car. The Car seems suspended outside of time. It is as if the projector is running down as the Car floats slower and slower towards the finish line. The film stops. The heat of the projector lamp burns a hole in the frame and the entire frame DISSOLVES.

Chapter Five.

When A Man's Soul Gets Into His Head

100
FEDERAL
100
Secretary of the Treasury
Treasurer of the United States
100
FEDERAL R
LK8465
K11
UNITED STATES
FEDERAL RESERVE SYSTEM

"What matters is not the idea a man holds but the depth at which he holds it."

Ezra Pound, quoted at the opening of Willeford's *Cockfighter*

Let's talk about obsession

If you are a fan of *Cockfighter* — the film or the book — what you likely admire is the singularity of Frank Mansfield's obsession. Even the most superficial observation of *Cockfighter* will reveal that obsession is a core theme; on the cover of the book's very first edition, the logline touts its subject as "the dedicated obsession of a fanatical sport."

The roots of the word "obsession" lie in the Latin *obsidere*: "to sit before, besiege, or occupy." From a purely clinical perspective, obsession is acknowledged in the DSM in terms of Obsessive-Compulsive Disorder and Obsessive-Compulsive Personality, which have separate diagnostic numbers and are very different things, but the long and short of it is, obsession is categorised as a *mental disorder*. And yet, that isn't how most of us use the word. In his broad study of the changing diagnosis and perception of obsession over time, *Obsession: A History*, Lennard J. Davis says that at the beginning of the 21st century, "obsession is seen both as a dreaded disease and as a noble and necessary endeavour." He then goes back centuries to explore how it got this way — how "obsession" was interpreted as a type of demonic possession up until the Enlightenment, when it was recast as a medical phenomenon. But its perception changed most dramatically as a result of industrialisation, which relied on "a greater sense of precision, repetition, standardisation and mechanisation." As Davis relates, the 18th and 19th centuries saw the rise of specialisation: "The older idea of the Renaissance man or woman whose fame comes from the variety of his or her knowledge gives way to the expert with a single focus." As a result, there came to be an accepted cultural distinction between *good* obsession (where one's focus and productivity serves the community economically or creatively) and *bad* obsession (that which detracts from one's ability to serve the greater goals of the society). So it comes down to: how *useful* is your obsession?

This is not only what determines whether or not Frank's obsession is pathological but it also calls attention to the fact that there are different societies at work within *Cockfighter*, and each see his obsession differently. To those within the cockfighting milieu that Frank's activities are largely confined to, his single-minded, forensic attention to the details of his trade is an admirable quality. And given that this specialisation is in service to an endangered tradition, it is also perceived, in this context, as noble.

Of the story's many characters, it is primarily Frank's hometown sweetheart Mary Elizabeth who pathologises the sport (but even this is colored by her own agenda to be married before a certain age) — and his father, long-dead at the start of the story, who left everything to Frank's younger brother Randall on account of his eldest son's 'disreputable' profession. Randall, who went to law school and did everything 'by the book,' has turned out to be an alcoholic loafer, selling off parcels of the family's once-extensive property. Having gotten himself in debt to Frank, the latter uses the opportunity to legally exercise his birthright and seize control of the family's remaining assets — which he promptly sells to restock his game farm.[30] Thus both sons squander the Mansfield legacy to support questionable habits.

Of the various modes of obsession, it's apparent that Frank's obsession sits under the banner of "perfectionism."[31] Perfectionism can be self-sabotaging, but it rarely hurts anyone other than the perfectionist; the worst it can do is lead to inaction when one fears being unable to live up to one's own standards of excellence. But Frank never succumbs to inaction. When he fails, he takes time to re-strategise, and tries again. This was certainly a quality that Monte Hellman could appreciate. "I think there's something very human and very understandable about obsession with perfecting one's craft," he said.

But in those moments when the story moves outside of the protective bubble of the cockfighting circuit (which are more numerous in the source text), Frank's perfectionism in his chosen field has no witness. The sport's ugly reputation among the uninitiated is extended to Frank, who is perceived solely as a gambler. He is even perceived by some as a tragic character, connecting more to the 19th century notion of the *idee fixée* — a singular fixation in an otherwise rational person that "overvalues" the object of their obsession. English philosopher Jeremy Bentham (1748-1832) — fittingly, also a key figure in the driving philosophy of animal rights activism (he is the source of the oft-repeated quote, *"The question is not, Can they reason?, nor Can they talk? but, Can they suffer?"*) — referred to it as "Deep Play," where the price of the obsession is much greater than what can possibly be gained from it. He described it as "play in which the stakes are so high that it is irrational for men to engage in it at all."[32] Bentham believed that deep play was morally destructive and should thus be outlawed (and indeed early prohibitions of cockfighting were focused largely on the gambling aspect of it), but the appeal of deep play and its promise of reputation, dignity, honour and status remains steadfast.

Among what Frank risks and loses because of his obsession: all his money (save ten bucks contingency), his car and trailer (which he needs to travel on the circuit), and eventually, what remains of his family's ancestral property. He has no emotional attachment to any of these things. He even puts himself on the hook for the $500 fighting cock Icarus, knowing he'll be disgraced if he doesn't follow through on the purchase. This one is more of a sticking point for Frank, because it involves his reputation, which is all a cocker has. But it's intended to get him back on track in time for the Southern Conference Tournament, where he will have a shot at the Cockfighter of the Year Award.

30 In the film this convoluted process is simplified: Frank inherits the farm and his brother Randall is his tenant. In both cases Frank leaves his brother homeless.
31 According to a basic Wikipedia search these are considered to be "perfectionism (related to symmetry, organization or rules), relational (doubts or worries about relationship, typically a significant other), contamination, causing harm, and unwanted intrusive thoughts (often with sexual or violent themes)"
32 Geertz, Clifford. "Deep Play: Notes on the Balinese Cockfight" in *The Cockfight: A Casebook*. Madison: University of Wisconsin Press, 1994. Kindle. Loc 2494.

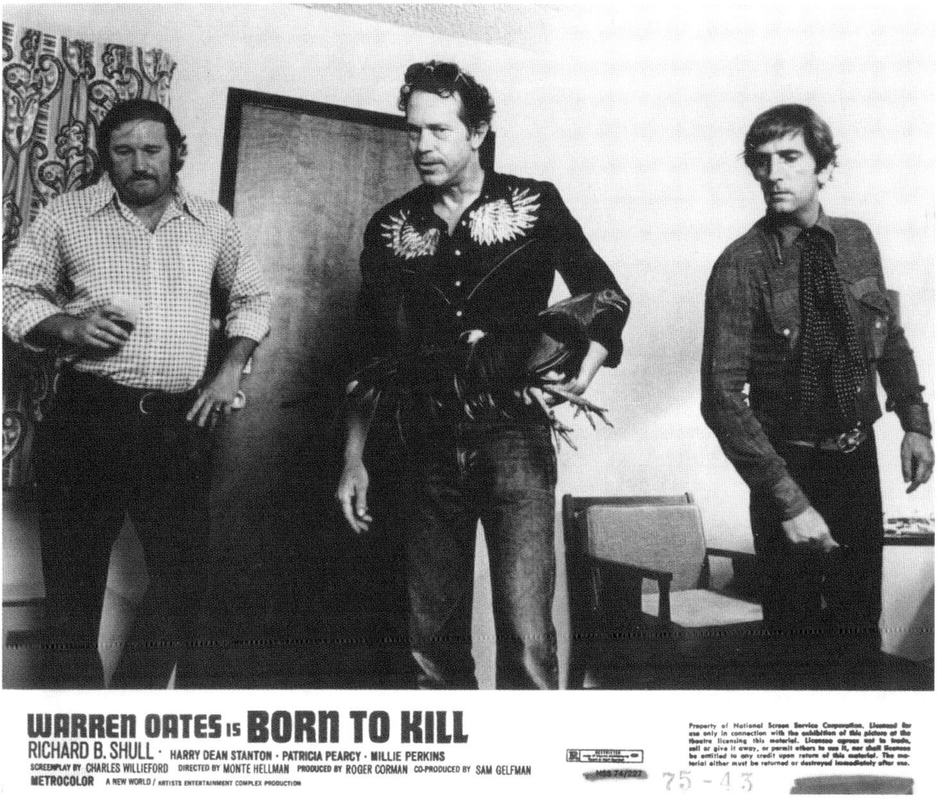

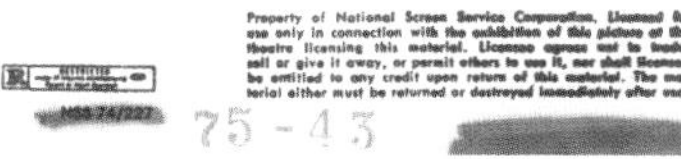

In the book and film, the Cockfighter of the Year Award is a holy grail of sorts to the cockers; it is not given out annually, but at the discretion of Senator Foxhall at the Southern Conference Tournament, or SCT — which is an invite-only tournament. Not only does it confer upon its beholder a coveted title, but it also guarantees him a paid job as a referee for life. For Frank, who wants to make his living solely in the cockfighting arena, this award is the culmination of his greatest ambitions.

"To a cocker this medal means as much as the Nobel Prize does to a scientist," Frank narrates in the book. "If that doesn't convey an exact meaning of the award, I can state it simpler. The recipient is the best damned cockfighter in the South, and he has the medal to prove it."

While Bentham's concept of deep play was prompted by the corruptive and addictive qualities of gambling, Frank's obsession is not an obsession with gambling — it is an obsession with *winning*, and what author Francesco Duina called "the hidden qualities of victory"; namely, that it acts as a gateway to something else that is of singular importance to the winner. And there is a deep American-ness to Frank's ambition.

Being a sport that was transplanted to North America with the first waves of European (and specifically British) settlement, cockfighting assumes a unique social significance in the context of the so-called New World. This transatlantic move promised a new social mobility, unfettered by the hierarchical constraints of the Old World, the freedom to aspire to individual greatness. America embraced competition, and has never let go of this goal of "indefinite perfectability."[33]

At the very beginning of Monte Hellman's film of *Cockfighter*, Frank's voiceover conveys his movement through different hobbies before arriving at cockfighting, stating that he lost interest in all the others, "but this is one thing you don't conquer." This dialogue does not appear in the book or any version of the script — it was taken verbatim from informal interviews Hellman did with real-life cockers on location. While Frank goes on to say that "the drive in it is to be the best," there is nevertheless an unspoken awareness that being the best is elusive and that the barometer for "best" is constantly changing, which puts the competitor in a constant state of chase. Monte Hellman told me that he thought every film he did was just a version of the myth of Sisyphus, and here it is, right in that very statement.

Key to the thrill of chasing victory is close competition — ergo the birds having to fight within the same weight class — because it provides the most accurate test of one's differentiation. Erik Erickson's mid-century studies into the nature of identity found that most people could only understand their own identity when compared to someone else. Differentiation from one's peers is a key goal of competition, and it's where competition has its most significance from an existential perspective. Frank could make more money on other circuits, but the Southern Conference Tournament with its strict standardised rules ensures the competition is a close one. The tradition of this circuit appeals to Frank more than the newer, bigger contests that are less selective.

Close competition also increases one's risk of loss (which is where deep play comes into effect), but the threat of loss also requires more labour, which is important to Frank. While a strong element of luck is at play in cockfighting ("I can't look into his heart and tell you how game he is"), that bird is there because of the work they have done together, and Frank's knowledge of breeding, his skill in selection, and his conditioning methods — which are frequently mentioned throughout the book as a source of repute. Winning reinforces the effort he has put in.

As Duina points out in his book on the subject, most Americans are obsessed with winning, but few can articulate exactly why they want to win. The trophy or title is the object at the most superficial level of winning; from there is a ladder representing ancillary prizes that have social, cultural or even spiritual significance.

But critic Jonathan Rosenbum, reviewing *Cockfighter* in a 1974 issue of *Film Comment*, sees Oates' character as less honourable than merely deluded. "For all the arcane bits of inside information that Oates imparts about his trade," he says, "he mainly comes

33 **De Toqueville, Alexis. Qtd in Francesco Duina, *Winning: Reflections on an American Obsession*. Princeton: Princeton University Press, 2010. Pg 3.**

MAMMOT

across as a likable, brainless twerp who nurtures a mythical sense of purpose, like some variant of Hemingway's Old Man of the Sea recast as Don Quixote in a hillbilly context." But any attempt to cast Frank as a quixotic character is superficial: if we deem the quixotic as a romantic idealism that lacks practicality or common sense — Cervantes' 17th century protagonist is an obsessive reader who escapes into chivalric romances and reinvents himself as the knight-errant 'Don Quixote,' refusing to see the world for what it is — then Frank is far from that. He has clarity in his goal, which, while uncommon, is not impossible, and he has a practical timetable to reach it. It's the "why" that people struggle with; Frank is not considered a fool because he is incapable of reaching his goal, but because the goal *itself* is considered foolish. As Captain Ahab says in Herman Melville's *Moby Dick*, "my means are sane, my motive and my object mad."

Even Willeford's own *oeuvre* contains more pathological examples of perfectionist-obsessives; it was a theme he would return to throughout his career, from early novels like *The Woman Chaser* (1960), through *The Burnt Orange Heresy* (1972) to his Hoke Moseley detective novels. In *The Woman Chaser* — one of the few Willeford novels to be adapted into a film (structurally, it even has segments written to mimic the style of a script) — his used car salesman-turned-movie director Richard Hudson hustles his way into making a studio-financed feature with no experience, thanks to the connections of his has-been movie producer stepfather, and makes a perfect 63-minute film, an artistic statement on American savagery, an indictment of greed and inequality — but it's 20 minutes too short. Rather than making him pad it out to feature length, the studio heads offer to salvage the film by using it to launch a weekly television playhouse-type series, but the commercials would require further cuts and Hudson refuses to bend either way — he thinks the film is perfect as it is. His response: to set the studio on fire, destroying his film and destroying any chance he has of conventional success. I regret never asking Monte Hellman if he had read this book.

In his essay "The Fable of Failure in Modern Art" examining various quixotic characters, Paul Barolsky talks about Balzac's short story "The Unknown Masterpiece" (1831) — in which an aged and obsessed painter spends 10 years on portrait of a courtesan, only for the painting to finally be revealed as a jumbled mess, which the artist sets aflame when he realizes that after all that effort, what he created was merely "nothing." This story was adapted more tragically by Emile Zola in his book *The Masterpiece* (1886) and also prefigures what is likely Willeford's own masterpiece, *The Burnt Orange Heresy*, in which an art critic tracks down a reclusive artist (considered one of the world's greatest) to see what he has been holed away working on — only to find that all his new paintings are essentially blank canvasses; the artist has been unable to create for years. Unwilling to report back to the art world that his idol is a has-been, the critic sets fire to all the aborted works and himself forges a painting that he claims is the artist's final masterpiece (setting off a chain of intrigue and murder).

Still, the tendency to make Frank Mansfield a tragic character is a persistent one. *Cockfighter's* cinematographer Nestor Almendros, who wrote of Frank in his autobiography in just those terms, said that he was "dominated by an *idee fixée* — like other characters in Hellman's universe — which has its genesis in Greek tragedy." The central characters of Greek tragedy are often brought to ruin through their own actions, and this is certainly the case for Frank at the point where we enter the story. His trajectory is much more that of the classical hero's journey: he is on a quest and must pass through a series of tests before emerging with his final reward. In his study of the American obsession with winning, author Franco Duina specifically summons *The Odyssey* as an example of how "our mythologies are heavily preoccupied with the close relationship between effort and rewards."

Frances Doel likewise brought up its "Odyssean" qualities in a letter to Willeford confirming that Corman was proceeding with buying the rights. "An extraordinary feat is accomplished in drawing us into an obsessive way of life," she writes,

> by giving us insights into the basic (but rarely found in a "pure" form) human drives of aggression and competitiveness and individual aspiration... It is a kind of American Odyssey, and in the end we have the peculiar satisfaction of seeing "the wheel has come full circle," that the hero got what he deserved in more senses than one and is thereby brought into perspective as a whole man in his professional life, his interior life, and in his idiosyncratic relationship to others.

What's interesting about references to *The Odyssey* in particular is that unlike its predecessor *The Iliad*, *The Odyssey* uses song and story to recount what would have been recent events, stories of travelling and hardship endured by those still living. Furthermore, *The Odyssey* features autobiographical storytelling: Odysseus and other characters frequently recount tales of their own travels to others. The storytelling itself — as with Frank's first-person narration in *Cockfighter* — frees Odysseus from the constraints of his own narrative and allows him the agency to change his ending. Even though Frank remains outwardly silent, his storytelling is similarly cathartic.

It's also important because it overturns the deterministic tendency of tragedy; the classic Greek tragedy is a play about man and his fate; the tragic hero is revealed to be a small part in a much bigger machine. "The tragic is the space in which a protagonist acknowledges, willingly or not, his or her limitations before it," says scholar Richard Rader. But Frank doesn't accept these limitations, and telling his story, even though he doesn't speak it aloud, becomes his reminder to himself of why he does what he does and what waits for him at the end if he can push himself to do it. Though it is less explicit in the film, part of Frank's goal is also to have Icarus defeat Little David in particular — Jack Burke's champion bird whose win in that ill-fated hotel room hack set our story in motion.

In a really simple but poignant comparison of *Don Quixote* and *The Odyssey*, scholar Colin Cavendish-Jones says that, "Both protagonists are questing heroes, but Odysseus has been on his quest and, by the time The Odyssey begins, is only trying to get home." Indeed, *Cockfighter* — even moreso in the film than in the book — takes place after a two-year journey, in that final season before Frank at last gets where he's going. It is not destiny that makes Frank the Cockfighter of the Year, it is his own obsession and refusal to settle for anything less than the ideal, which guarantees his differentiation, and his immortality.

But the question of whether Frank Mansfield's alignment (in terms of classical literature) is "epic" or "tragic" perhaps highlights the differences in how the character was perceived and portrayed by Willeford and Hellman, respectively. Hellman was reaching for something with that character that isn't quite in the book; an almost monastic self-reflectiveness that was certainly to be found in Monte himself.

In the documentary *Plunging on Alone*, Hellman reads aloud from Ernest Becker's 1973 landmark *The Denial of Death*:

> The work of art is then the ideal answer of the creative type to the problem of existence as he takes it in. Not only the existence of the external world, but especially his own. Who he is as a painfully separate person with nothing shared to lean on. He has to answer to the burden of his extreme individuation. His so painful isolation He wants to know how to earn immortality as a result of his own unique gifts. His creative work is at the same time the expression of his heroism and the justification of it. It is his private religion. His uniqueness gives him personal immortality. It is his own beyond, and not that of others.

"There's a very solitary quality to a lot of [Hellman's] heroes," says film historian and programmer Dennis Bartok.[34] And that solitariness emanated from Hellman, who strove for philosophical insights that were perhaps beyond the remit of the B-picture milieu he frequently worked in, insights that remained frustratingly enigmatic to those charged with carrying out such a vision. So while Hellman and Frank Mansfield share a pronounced tendency towards obsession, there are fundamental differences that would keep the director from being able to tell Frank's story in a way that felt true to him. In many ways Hellman would remain an outsider on his own film, never quite able to crack its code. But if there was one person who could translate the director's unarticulated vision to the screen, and be a mediator of sorts between the brutal compulsiveness of Willeford's Frank Mansfield and the concave existentialism of Hellman's Frank Mansfield, it was Warren Oates.

34 Qtd in Hickenlooper, George. *Monte Hellman: American Auteur*. 1997.

Chapter Six.

"Nobody Loses All The Time": Warren Oates

I've seen fans lament the fact that an actor as respected as Warren Oates ended his career predominantly back in the realm of television — often in small screen retreads of classic big screen films like *True Grit*, *The African Queen*, *Black Beauty* and *East of Eden*. But it was one of those remakes that served as my introduction to Oates: *My Old Man* (1979), based on the Hemingway story of the same name and previously adapted to the screen in 1950 as *Under My Skin*. However, Warren Oates wasn't the reason I watched it — that honour belongs to Kristy McNichol, arguably the most important person in my life in 1979. Oates stars as Kristy's deadbeat dad, an "unlucky" horse trainer trying to win back his daughter's affection. I noted in my previous book *House of Psychotic Women* that this redemptive story offered catharsis-by-proxy, considering that my own emotionally-withholding father was nicknamed "Oates" due to his resemblance to the great character actor. Thus my receptiveness to *Cockfighter* probably began percolating decades before I first saw it.

There are a few major differences between book and film, and Oates would have to reconcile these differences in his performance as Frank Mansfield. Not many actors would have been able to play this complex character with the right degree of toughness, grace and goofiness (in the book, this goofiness comes out only in the insincere letters he writes to the women in his life) — almost silently, to boot. Corman wanted Oates in the lead, and Oates was in fact first in the configuration, even before

Above: Kristy McNichol and Warren Oates in *My Old Man* (1979).

13225

STAR WARREN OATES AND DIRECTOR MONTE HELLMAN RELAX BETWEEN TAKES DURING THE FILMING OF "BORN TO KILL," THEIR THIRD PICTURE TOGETHER.

Monte Hellman. "I thought that Warren Oates would be an excellent actor for the lead," Corman told me, "and Monte was a good friend of Warren. So I told Monte you can direct the film if you can bring in Warren, because you're a good friend of his, and I think you can do well working with him in this particular role."

Having done two films with Warren Oates, including Hellman's favourite of all his films, *Two-Lane Blacktop*, the director knew Oates was the man to take on the challenge — even though Mansfield is 32 in the book and Oates was over a decade his senior. "I think the key to any film is casting," said Hellman in a 1986 interview. "Warren became the alter-ego and the focus of literally every film that I did after [*The Shooting*]. I don't think it was accidental. I think he had a quality that harked back to the great Western actor heroes... the silent man whose very honesty and integrity is apparent from his face."[35]

The two had met while Oates was starring in an L.A. theatre production of *One Flew Over the Cuckoo's Nest*, after which Hellman cast him in *The Shooting* and they got along famously. "We really had a close kinship," said Hellman in the Anchor Bay *Cockfighter* commentary. "I really felt like he was my brother."

Oates was born a few hours after the Fourth of July in Muhlenberg County, Kentucky, made famous in the song "Paradise" by John Prine. Like his character in *Cockfighter*, Oates' family had been one of the original pioneers of his hometown and he worked the family farm until high school in Louisville, after which he left to join the Marines. Returning to the University of Louisville, Oates caught the acting bug when he made his debut in a campus play, then hit the bright lights of the Big Apple hoping to pursue an acting career. But New York didn't suit him and he bolted for the West Coast when he heard cowboys were in high demand for what was then a TV renaissance of Western shows. It was here he first met long-time collaborator Sam Peckinpah, who directed him in *The Rifleman*. Moreover, it was a way for Oates to draw upon his rural experience, to let his regional accent play freely, and unlike in NYC, he soon found that he didn't have to be a pretty boy to get a lot of work.

A transition occurs in Oates' roles — and his delivery of those roles — as the 1970s come into view. He outgrew the under-educated, impulsive country-boy type seen in films like *Private Property* (1960), *Ride the High Country* (1962) and *In the Heat of the Night* (1967), and emerged as a decisive, charismatic leading man. He even found himself playing fast-talking, fame-hungry Depression-era bank robber John Dillinger, whose exploits Oates followed on the local radio as a child. By the time *Cockfighter* came around Oates was one of the most in-demand actors of his generation.

35 Qtd in Joyce, Paul. *Plunging on Alone: Monte Hellman's Life in a Day* (1986).

In Bud Yorkin's *The Thief Who Came For Dinner* (1973), Oates steals every scene as a frustrated insurance investigator locked in a game of cat-and-mouse with the cocky title character, played by Ryan O'Neal. At one point, Oates enlists a newspaper chess columnist (Austin Pendleton) to engage in a public match with the thief, who leaves a chess piece and move at the site of every burglary. These chess pieces provide the primary visual motif of the film, standing in as symbols of composure and wit. I mention this because several photographs survive that show Warren Oates himself hunched over a chess board, sometimes resting on a rickety surface devised haphazardly on a set between takes. A behind-the-scenes still from *The Wild Bunch* captures him mid-game, lost deep in thought. In interviews, Monte Hellman would frequently reference his silent chess matches with Oates as a staple activity of their unusual friendship. "We almost didn't have to talk," Hellman said in an interview with filmmaker Allison Anders. "We talked a lot on *The Shooting*, but on the other three movies, you know, we just kind of like, *knew*. We would play chess and talk about other things, and we just knew that we were on the same wavelength."

What's most relevant here is that to succeed in chess, you always have to anticipate the opponent's next move — or more accurately, their next six or seven moves. When Hellman refers to a "silent understanding" between himself and Oates, what that actually means — since we already know Hellman to not be the best communicator — is that Oates was anticipating what his director would want (or at the very least, what he would be receptive to). This is a skill continually honed through playing chess, which is routinely used to develop focus, and pre-visualize potential outcomes and thus act quickly when they happen. It's also a skill that likely came in handy when navigating the unpredictability of the mercurial Sam Peckinpah.

Peckinpah's media-baiting reputation — as a confrontational, belligerent director — was already firmly established as early as 1965, in the wake of such troubled productions as *Major Dundee* and *The Cincinnati Kid* (the latter of which he was fired from after only four days). However, the dominant narrative that everything he touched was bloodily, operatically violent ignores that the fact that Peckinpah also made quiet, introspective films like *The Ballad of Cable Hogue* (1970) and *Junior Bonner* (1972). But it was *Bring Me the Head of Alfredo Garcia* (1973) that future *Austin Chronicle* founder Louis Black — then writing the October 1980 programme notes for film society Cinematexas — said got the worst shake: "Released at a time when coy, self-serving liberal sweetmeats such as *The Long Goodbye*, *California Split*,

Coca

Save the Tiger, *Carnal Knowledge* and *One Flew Over the Cuckoo's Nest* were the critical rave, its atmosphere of paranoia and desperation prefigured (and less glibly so) *Taxi Driver* and its ilk."

His role as the doomed Benny in *Bring Me the Head of Alfredo Garcia* may be an even more iconic turn for Oates than that of Frank Mansfield in *Cockfighter*; indeed, the two are often discussed side by side, as much for the mutual intensity of the characters as the presumed intensity of the experience of switching from one role directly to the other. Oates transitioned to *Cockfighter* straight off a promotional tour for Alfredo Garcia — which was, at the time, getting largely negative reviews. Even *Cockfighter* scribe Charles Willeford had little good to say about it, feeling it was largely nonsensical. But Willeford had some funny things to say about Peckinpah, based entirely on information relayed by Oates during their time together on the *Cockfighter* shoot:

> He's down in Durango. He lives down there, you see, all the year round. He's got his house down there. He shoots all those Westerns, so that he doesn't have to leave his house. The crews hate it. The people hate them down there… Warren Oates told me one night he had to see Peckinpah, down there in Mexico, that miserable goddam town. He said he went there, you know, knocked on the door. Nobody answered, so he went on in. He went down the hallway, came into the bedroom, and Peckinpah pulled a forty-five from under the pillow and had it on him, you know. "Jesus Christ, don't shoot!" He was all set to blow him away. He was an alcoholic. He was drunk half the time, you know. He had cancer, I think, toward the end. He was on his way to perdition when he made *Alfredo Garcia*…[36]

While Oates was one of Peckinpah's repertory players, sometimes (as in *Bring Me the Head of Alfredo Garcia*) enlisted to play a version of Peckinpah himself, on Hellman's films the vision seemed very much dependent on, and shaped by, Oates. As though Hellman didn't know what he wanted until Oates was there doing it. In that way Oates was a muse to Hellman in a way he wasn't to Peckinpah, despite the symbiotic relationship Oates had with the latter.

Hellman also says the appeal of Oates for him, as an actor, is the latter's ability to play roles in either a theatrical style, or a documentary style. There is so much versatility in his face, and in his voice; in *Two-Lane Blacktop*, the character of GTO is the one character in the film who is "bigger than life,"[37] whereas his role in *Cockfighter* is muted to the point of actually being silent. When Hellman tried to prep Oates for how difficult the almost

36 Herron, Don. *Willeford*. Tucson: Dennis McMillan Publications, 1997. Pg 365.
37 Pasquariello, Nicholas. "Monte Hellman on Corman and Cockfighter" in *Jump Cut: A Review of Contemporary Media* No 10-11 (1976): 17-18.

wordless role would be to execute, Oates scoffed: "Are you kidding? This is the easiest part I ever played — I don't have to learn any dialogue!" Oates literally had two lines, apart from the voiceover which would be recorded later. But it bears reiterating that not any actor would have been able to pull it off, communicating so much with just a subtle twinge of his face or a shift in his eyes. "His forte lay in observation," said writer Damien Love of Oates' acting, "watching other people, letting us see his characters thinking: the toughest, least showy stuff that actors can do."

It's clear from the differences between the ending of the book and film of *Cockfighter* that Hellman didn't want to end on Frank's triumph; in typical fashion, he instead sought to imbue the ending with an ambiguity — which he did through the closing line "She loves me, Omar" (a line that will be discussed in more detail in various further chapters). The director needed Frank to remain a mystery — even to himself — because what appeals most to Hellman is the unknowable. Importantly, both Hellman and Willeford felt that Oates was playing Frank in a way that remained true to their respective versions of the character, which is a sign of a superlative interpreter. Willeford's Frank is defiant; Hellman's Frank is sentimental. Oates manifests these entirely different versions of the same character in the final moments of the film through a sequence of facial gestures that allowed both creators to see what they wanted. It's this ability that has seen critics using seemingly conflicting adjectives — like "tender" and "brutal" — to describe Oates' face at the same time.

Like the character he would play in *Cockfighter*, Oates maintained a complex air of mystery about himself. He liked to pretend he was simpler than he was. "He had the kind of persona that attracted you to him, and yet kept you at a distance," said Hellman. "I believe one of the great appeals of movies themselves is this kind of sense of mystery, of many layers that you have to peel away in order to get to the core — and I think that this was his personality, he was just like that. He seemed to be so open, and to reveal everything and yet he revealed very little."[38]

"There's something in his face, the way he looks at things, that suggests a readiness for failure, or darkness," said writer David Thomson in the documentary *Warren Oates: Across the Border*. In the same film, Thomas McGuane, who directed Oates in the 1975 adaptation of his own book *92 in the Shade* said "his face in repose was sombre. It comes from the solitude that was kind of his interior environment. I don't know where it comes from… but it may be part of what happens to everybody who leaves home and never goes back."

38 Love, Damien. *Supporting Features: Writing and Interviews on Movies and Moviemakers*. CreateSpace, 2016. Kindle. Loc 7112.

Chapter Seven.

The Semiotics of Silence

C

"The mouth of an impetuous man brings danger near."

Clement of Alexandria

In his book *Absence in Cinema*, Justin Remes talks about the disruptive function of a moment of silence in Godard's *Band of Outsiders* (1964) wherein the characters challenge each other to pass a minute in silence, and after a countdown — one, two, three — all sound in the film halts. But it doesn't even last a minute; neither Godard nor his characters have the necessary patience.

At the start of Willeford's book *Cockfighter*, it's been two and a half years since Frank Mansfield has spoken. The book exists in interior monologue; Frank is an outwardly silent character whose inner world is filled with constant chatter, recitation of facts, statistics and sage-like wisdoms, all of which conceal what is really going on for him emotionally. His transient lifestyle facilitates this refusal to investigate; the constant movement leaves no time to dwell on what lies beneath his motivation to abandon the possibilities of "normal" life in favor of a relentless, silent pursuit of the Cockfighter of the Year Award. But while Frank remains silent to everyone around him, he does not remain silent to us, the readers. We are privy to his thoughts at their most horrid, pompous and contradictory. A real sense of Frank's silence only comes to us through the film — through Monte.

It's interesting to remember that Monte Hellman did not choose this material. It was a job he was offered and a job he needed to take. But I'm positive the material chose him.

When I first saw *Cockfighter*, it was the silence — not the beloved character faces, not the violence or singular obsession of the cockfighting — that first fascinated me. As a relentless over-sharer, I was envious of Frank's ability to just turn off his voice like a faucet. Just *no more talking*.

But the silence was something I always assumed appealed to Monte too.

I first met Monte Hellman in 2015. I was in Los Angeles to promote my anthology

collection *Kid Power!* with a series of related screenings at LA's once-beloved Cinefamily theatre, and I'd heard he ran an AirBnb out of his house, so I was determined to stay there during my trip. For someone who doesn't drive, being way up in the hills of Laurel Canyon was a decided inconvenience — it would take me well over an hour to walk down the windy roads out to Sunset — but the idea of staying in a classic Laurel Canyon bohemian pad, being served breakfast by one of my favourite directors, was too much of a surreal thrill to pass up. Furthermore he claimed in his AirBnb writeup that he loved talking to the guests about movies. I knew I would be too shy to bug him much otherwise — this was before I'd decided to write a book about *Cockfighter* — so this declared proclivity for conversation was a hopeful sign.

But a talkative person was not what I encountered when I went to stay at that storied house at 8588 Appian Way. Let me clarify — there was another woman staying at the house, and he seemed to enjoy talking to her. But I would get vague and terse answers to everything — which admittedly began as soon as I uttered the words, "my favourite film of yours is *Cockfighter*." He scowled and said, "That's the worst picture I ever made."

Monte Hellman's artistic interest in silence was already evident in his earlier films, most notably *Two-Lane Blacktop*, where it hangs over the proceedings like a sheet of suffocating numbness. The two protagonists (The Driver and The Mechanic) are so embedded in silence that the intrusion of the talkative Girl played by Laurie Bird seems exceptionally disruptive. But they don't even attempt to voice protest against her presence. They just remain elusive to her. She adapts to the silence, while GTO, the Warren Oates character, grows increasingly frustrated by the impenetrable wall this silence presents. At the end of the film, The Driver's been dumped by The Girl — after breaking character by breaking the silence with a pathetic appeal for companionship — and he locks himself into the chamber of the car with a thud that sounds like a prison door locking behind someone. The film burns. The ensuing silence lasts throughout the end credits.

I asked Monte's longtime friend Deanne Mencher whether she felt Monte valued

Above: Monte Hellman's longtime home at 8588 Appian Way, where he lived and hosted guests through Air BnB.

silence. "Yes, YES. Oh my god," she said emphatically. "Monte's like a mute, he just doesn't say anything," she says. "I mean, if you really think about it, it's really *hostile*. It's really dismissive. Monte was notorious for that. He was basically a very anti-social guy. Monte is not a talker. I mean, he can talk about film, but on a personal level he was quite remote."

A *New York Times* piece preceding the release of *Two-Lane Blacktop* echoes these sentiments: "Although he has a certain kind of nervous openness, people close to him insist that at the core he is totally inaccessible. "Like an iceberg," says an acquaintance. "You can't get through to him. The weirdest thing is that when he gets angry, there is no heat. Anger only seems to make him more self-contained." His actors have corroborated this:

Warren Oates: "Inaccessible."
James Taylor: "Distant...Untouchable. Shy. It really bothered me."
Jack Nicholson: "Secretive. He's very private, very covert. He's not intentionally secretive. It's just the nature of the beast. That makes him a difficult director to work with."

I couldn't help but think of Monte's many similarities with *Cockfighter*'s antihero Frank Mansfield. But it's not just *Cockfighter*. Silent characters dominate his films. "His films mirror their director," continues the New York Times article. "The thing that makes them unique — and unnerving — is his inability to present more than the ice cold surface of his characters, his absolute refusal to burrow inside them. While editing *Two Lane Blacktop* he was 'shocked' and 'amazed' to discover how wordless the film is. 'In some 10-minute reels, there are only two minutes of dialogue.'"

There are many types of silences, at least two of which I believe are applicable to Frank Mansfield, and likewise to Monte Hellman. As philosophical historian David Kleinberg-Levin proposed, these include:

> the heavy silence of one going deep into her grief; the silence of one whom unspeakable horror has rendered speechless; the awkward silence of shame or embarrassment; the aggressive silence of one who is hiding his guilt; the benumbed silence of a deep depression; the silence of an anger which accuses and causes hurt by using silence as a weapon; withholding the kindness of speech; the heroic silence of the political prisoner, who refuses to surrender the names of his comrades even under extremes of torture; the guarded silence of citizens who must endure constant surveillance under the rule of a police state; the silence of timidity; the silence of shyness; the silence of rapt attention; the silence of prayer; the silence of spellbound anticipation; the silence of a joy that needs to be deeply felt.

The two types of silence most apparent in *Cockfighter* — the silence of prayer and the silence of withholding — are in opposition with each other; scholar Thomas Gould refers to these as Apophasis (transcendence and unknowability) and Reticence (withholding and self-possession). "Apophasis," he says, "proceeds through a logic of linguistic impotency, whereas reticence implies a logic of linguistic potentiality." Phrased simply: the power of words (to manifest or to harm) versus the powerlessness of words (that they are merely 'noise' obfuscating the truth). In *Cockfighter* this creates an interesting tension between punishment and healing; Frank's withholding silence affects his external social world in a way that is deliberately manipulative, but there is an element of magical thinking to his vow, a type of abstention and an exercise in self-discipline that takes a dramatic presentation in line with ascetic spiritual traditions.

To investigate what Monte Hellman brings to Frank Mansfield's silence — and to *Cockfighter* in general — it is necessary to situate the film in the context of mid-century modern art and the silence that became a hallmark of that era, beautifully addressed by Susan Sontag in her 1967 essay "The Aesthetics of Silence."

Sontag begins her essay with an examination of the ways that art itself in that era was seen as something to be "terminated" or "gotten past" — citing several artists (Wittgenstein, Duchamp, Rimbaud) who disavowed their vocations. "Art is more than ever a deliverance," she writes, "an exercise in asceticism. Through it, the artist becomes purified — of himself, and eventually of his art." She points out that in this period the most respected modern artists tended not so much toward *literal* silence (though Samuel Beckett certainly did) but began a process of obfuscation — obscuring things to deliberately break down pathways of communication with the audience. Consequently, audiences were frequently frustrated by modern art and saw it "as an aggression against them."

Filmmakers such as Oskar Fischinger and Maya Deren willfully insisted on silence (before receiving a musical score courtesy of her husband Teiji Ito in 1959, Deren's 1943 film *Meshes of the Afternoon* had always been screened silent), becoming hugely influential on the American experimental films of the 1950s and '60s, in particular the films of Stan Brakhage. "Brakhage had a deep distrust of language," says Justin Remes, "Brakhage is interested in precisely that which cannot be reduced to language, the purely sensuous experience that effortlessly slips out of any linguistic straightjacket. He claims one of his goals as an artist is to 'drive the mind beyond words.'"

In the published version of his 1965 Masters' Thesis, "The Immobilized Hero in Modern Fiction," Charles Willeford coins the term for what he sees as a critically dominant sub-literary genre that had become firmly entrenched by mid-century, and as Sontag does, uses the word "hostile" to describe their effect on the audience — particularly taking aim at Beckett. "Samuel Beckett's solipsism is directed toward the innermost self in ever-narrowing circles," Willeford writes, describing the theme that all immobilized heroes share as "the frenetic, endless and impossible attempt to escape from the restriction of the self, the personality, into a freedom that simply does not exist."

But this stagnant domain of "paradoxes and ambiguities" was clearly a place that Monte

Hellman comfortably inhabited. It should come as no surprise then, that Hellman mounted the first stage production of Samuel Beckett's *Waiting for Godot* in Los Angeles — a play that was famously described by critic Vivian Mercer as one in which "nothing happens, twice."[39]

It's no coincidence that silence is a leitmotif in Beckett's work — his prose, his plays, even his criticism. Scholar Thomas Gould has pointed out that there are two types of silences in Beckett: "an extra-textual theoretical silence, which is exposed or intimated by Beckett's aesthetic, and a textual, narrative silence, which torments Beckett's speakers." Especially relevant here is his claim that "the former silence relates to a position of impotency and failure," which is so important to Hellman films such as *The Shooting*, *Two Lane Blacktop* and *Cockfighter* where sparsity is representative of impotency — explicitly so in *Cockfighter* with its stacked innuendo. But as Sontag notes, "the space of the missing or ruptured dialogue, can also constitute the grounds for an ascetic affirmation."

Historically, the purpose of a vow of silence is spiritual contemplation. Most spiritual practices involve the use of silence for clarity, meditation, and place value on its spiritual properties — Judeo-Christianity, Buddhism, various folk practices — all recognise that there is a transcendence or magic inherent in silent practice, even if all don't have a formal system of asceticism. And it would be easy to ascribe a certain monastic quality to Frank's silence, seeing as it is an isolating sacrifice in service of a higher goal. In monastic communities, silence keeps the focus on work; idle chatter and superfluous preoccupations are discarded in favour of tireless devotion to one's vocation. But in the book, Frank's internal monologue is busy, rife with petty remarks — his appearance of silence is not reflective of a quieted mind. We get a clearer picture of a transcendent silence in the film, and this demonstrates just where Monte Hellman and Willeford diverge artistically. As a writer, Willeford's talent is for shaping words to dramatic effect, whereas Hellman's *modus operandi* as a filmmaker is to strip them away entirely, giving Frank an infinitely more pensive quality.

In his essay on the theme of silence in the writings of the mystic Clement of Alexandria, scholar Raoul Mortley addresses how, for Clement, silence was a religious and ethical attitude signifying "a capacity which lies beyond speech. Silence is a quality which is becoming to all men; it is the victory of mind over speech... the word is the symbol of the physical world: on the other hand, silence is

39 Qtd. Remes, Justin. *Absence in Cinema*, Pg 13 Epub edition.

Above: Joey Faye and Jack Albertson in Hellman's stage production of *Waiting for Godot*.

the symbol of pure thought." In *Cockfighter*, as in the mystical beliefs of many cultures, silence is a sign of strength of character, whereas language is an obstacle to clarity.

Mortley continues on to say that for Clement, "speech, which is too animated, expresses the unstable, wavering part of the human being." There are moments in the film where such animation is apparent physically — Frank slapping his knee in response to a joke, the emphatic hand signals, the caricature of Frank monkeying around his prospective mother-in-law's car — but overall Frank's composure is maintained, and his voiceover kept to a minimum of elaboration, leaving the audience to interpret or decode him as they might any silent mystic. I appreciate that Frank's silence removes the banal — he can't engage in small talk, so every communication is significant. If there is an evil Frank is trying to negate or deny by his silence, it is the evil of gluttony — in this case a gluttony of words. This particular vice needed to be excised because it caused him to sin against himself.

Sontag writes that the artist's traditional use of silence is as "a zone of meditation, preparation, for spiritual ripening, an ordeal that ends in gaining the right to speak." The parameters of Frank's vow — namely that it concludes when he wins the Cockfighter of the Year award — convincingly illustrates Sontag's assertion that he is *earning* the right to use his own voice, when he emerges from the silence as a perfected version of himself. Even Frank's spirit animal — the fighting cock, known for its heraldic voice, relates to Frank's quest for regeneration through silence: in Ancient Greece the chicken was a powerful symbol of healing and resurrection, and the totem of Persephone, the goddess of renewal.[40] If Frank is successful, the 'resurrection' of his voice will also accompany a changed man, detached from the ostentation that was his undoing.

In the meantime, Frank's muteness makes confessors of everyone around him — something he shares with the silent protagonist of fellow Southerner Carson McCullers' 1940 book *The Heart is a Lonely Hunter*, but also Ingmar Bergman's *Persona* (1966), both widely digested examples of silent characters who become ciphers for their chattier counterparts. In "The Aesthetics of Silence" Susan Sontag addresses "the spiritual vertigo" of *Persona*, pointing out that the actress Elisabeth Vogler (played by Liv Ullman)'s decision to not speak is — like Frank's — voluntary. *Persona*, like *Cockfighter*, explores that tension between what Gould referred to as 'Apophasic' and 'Reticent' forms of silence: while Elisabeth's silence can be seen as "a wish for ethical purity" it is also, as Sontag notes, "a means of power, a species of sadism, a virtually inviolable position of strength from which she manipulates and confounds her nurse-companion." The nurse (Bibi Andersson) projects integrity and nobility onto Elisabeth's silence, and is compelled to fill the space between them with talking — specifically using that space to confess a troubling past indiscretion, only to realize the actress has been silently mocking her.

Willeford's earlier novel *The Black Mass of Brother Springer* also featured a protagonist who, like Frank Mansfield, makes a personal vow, the purpose of which is only known to him, and finds himself a reluctant receptacle

40 Lawler, Andrew. *Why Did the Chicken Cross the World?: The Epic Saga of the Bird that Powers Civilization*. Atria Books, 2014. Kindle edition. Pg 51.

for the town's secrets. In *Cockfighter*, this is what Frank has the hardest time swallowing: he is repeatedly tortured with one-sided conversations that he has no interest in but tolerates "as an unwelcome part of the deal I had made with myself."

There is a strong emphasis on the spoken word in Southern culture — tall tales, songs, oral folk wisdom — that marks Frank's rejection of the spoken word as yet another way he is distinguishing himself from the traditional milieu he operates in. Elaborate boasts shared between Southerners had the effect of "spurring each other to new heights of self-magnification" and engendered "a sense of theatricality and display."[41] Frank's braggadocio in the motel room flashback therefore recalls a Southern oral tradition — in these boasts, men would liken themselves to wild animals, exaggerate their skills or the extent of their property — in time, the boast itself became an art form. When we see this earlier incarnation of Frank, it is obvious he was a big personality. But ultimately, his own tongue-wagging betrayed him.

Still, Frank is very conceptual-minded and stubborn, and even though no one knows why he no longer speaks (Mary Elizabeth for instance, believes he simply lost his voice), he knows, and he's too obstinate to crack, even though the secretive nature of his bargain means he wouldn't lose face were he to do so. But Frank's silence is a protest against himself; it is a pact aimed at restoring his internal sense of value. To break it would reveal a weakness he could never live with.

"It's a funny thing," Frank says,

> A man can make a promise to God, break it five minutes later and never think anything about it. With an idle shrug of his shoulders, a man can also break solemn promises to his mother, wife or sweetheart, and except for a slight, momentary twinge of consciousness, he still won't be bothered very much. But if a man ever breaks a promise to himself, he disintegrates. His entire personality and character crumble into tiny pieces, and he is never the same man again.[42]

But importantly, Frank's silence — while he'll maintain it's "a bargain he made with himself" — it is also a trauma response. Losing his ace cock in a meaningless hotel room hack, and by extension not only the financial promise of its probable triumph in the pit, but the months of work, the expertise he has spent years accumulating to get him to *this* point where *this* bird was going to win him that damn medal, creates a momentary fracture in Frank's sense of identity. Sure, his need to control his own narrative will insist it's a personal choice, but Frank is struck dumb by his loss, not unlike those who experience selective mutism following a traumatic event. While silence has disruptive potential, it is also such a powerful method of healing that sometimes it will become a physiological imperative. The body will insist on it. Even *Sideswipe* (1987), the third book in Willeford's Hoke Moseley series, begins with his burnt-out Miami homicide detective protagonist having a dissociative episode and retreating into silence. "There was no need to think about anything, to worry about anything," Hoke narrates, "because as long as he kept his mouth closed and refused to react to anybody, he

41 Gorns, Elliot. "Gouge and Bite, Pull Hair and Scratch" in *The American Historical Review*, Vol. 90, (February to December 1985): Pg 8.

42 Note this same quote opens Willeford's earlier exercise in developing the character of Frank Mansfield, "Guitar Interlude" (date Unknown).

would be let alone. When a man didn't talk back or answer questions, people couldn't stand it for very long." Hoke apparently can't stand it for very long either, and by the fourth day he is talking again, having emerged with a new resolve to quit the force and adopt a quieter, simpler life; to abandon his children and his partner without sendoff or ceremony.[43]

And so we can add another category of silence to the roster: silence as escape hatch.

"I learned later in life never to say goodbye to anyone," Charles Willeford wrote in his memoir *I Was Looking for a Street*. "As an adult, I have never said goodbye. I have left wives and lovers, naturally, but I have always disappeared without a word."

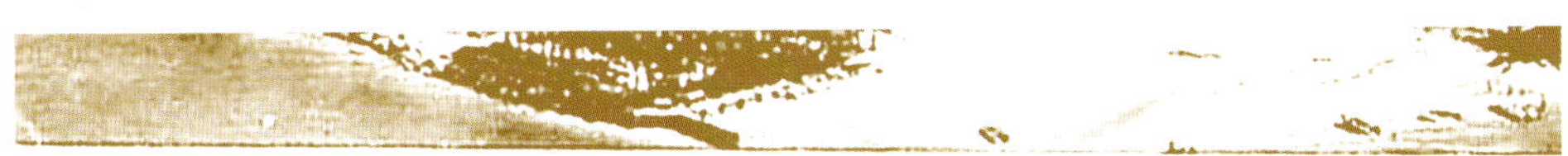

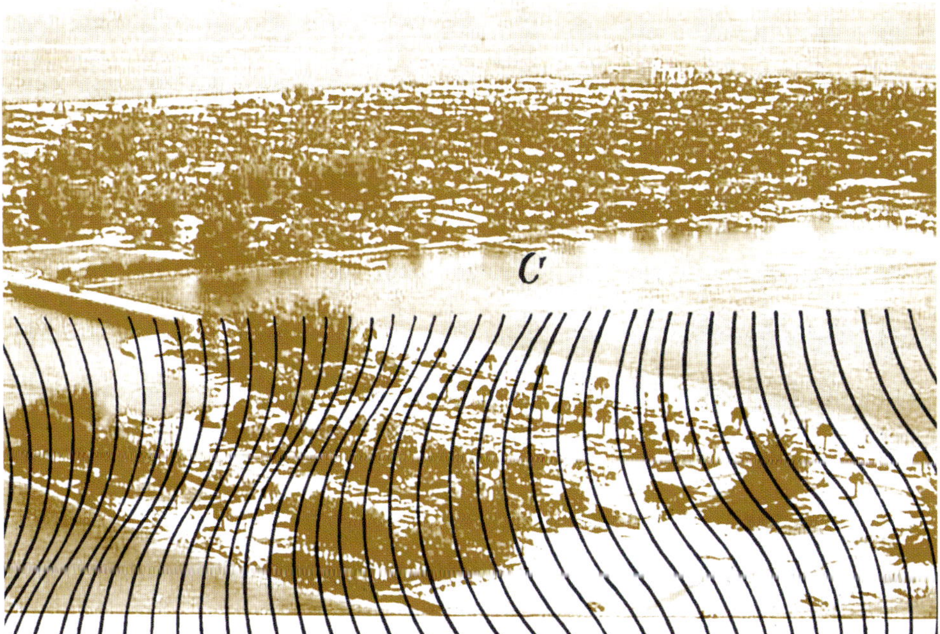

43 ***Sideswipe*'s first act is transplanted from that of the proposed second book in the Moseley series, *Grimhaven*, only in the latter, Hoke's breakdown results in a distressing cross-country crime spree. *Grimhaven* was ultimately deemed too dark (or at least, prohibitive as far as franchise potential) and never published; parts of it also ended up in the second (published) Moseley novel, *New Hope for the Dead* (1985).**

Chapter Eight.

Independent People

One of the many things that resonates about *Cockfighter* is Frank's relationship to work, which is generated by a deeply-engrained ethos that was already decades old by the time of *Cockfighter*'s publication.

During my brief stint at University, compensating for the lack of medieval courses I needed to finish my degree I gobbled up whatever non-film departments offered film courses and managed to register for a course in Scandinavian literature and film that ended up being the most rewarding of any electives I took. But I still remember my reaction the day the teacher told us we were going to read a 600-page novel about Icelandic sheep-farming called *Independent People*. I really did not want to read this book, which sounded like the antithesis of the kind of high-minded literature I was hoping to be challenged by while attending university. But with the teacher ignoring my not-very-well-disguised disapproval, we began.

Independent People (1934/5) is indeed an epic about sheep farming. Its central character, Bjartur, is a stubborn, single-minded and sometimes cruel man with a lazy-eyed daughter (actually the product of his dead wife's affair with another man) who lives on an isolated farm situated in the midst of a bleakly inhospitable landscape. He eschews materialism, luxury, progress and personal relationships in favor of work — work that almost kills him on numerous occasions and from which he reaps very little reward other than his own self-satisfaction. He takes pride in his heartiness, his adaptability to misfortune, and although people around him drop dead as he soldiers on, Bjartur never sways from his beliefs. Because even though this attitude eventually leaves him completely alone, it more importantly reinforces his independence.

I have never stopped thinking about this novel, and in fact, I even mentioned it twice in my previous book *House of Psychotic Women* (including using a line from it as one of my chapter titles: "You Carry a Coffin Today"). But it was only in recent years that I started to think about it in relationship to the character of Frank Mansfield in *Cockfighter*. An association that was vindicated by going through Willeford's personal papers and coming across the line in his introductory notes to the original screenplay of *Cockfighter* that the cockers he's interviewed "remind you of the Icelanders in Laxness' *Independent People*."

That cockers are a hearty people who take great pride in their work is evident not just in the extensive rule books and conditioning guides that have remained in print over several centuries, but even in the letters and ads that can be found in the major gamefowl magazines. In a 1958 copy of *Grit & Steel* from Willeford's personal collection, there is an ad for an apprentice gaff-maker in Oklahoma that states: "This is not a get rich quick trade and cannot be learned overnight... There are two things I will not tolerate, drunkenness and a filthy mouth."

As writer Nick Pinkerton points out in his review of the 2011 reissue of the novel, "Frank silently evaluates all of the men around him against their relationship to their jobs." This refers to his partner Omar Baradinsky who gave up a successful advertising career to fight cocks; Doc Riordan "who waits in his sepulchral office for a windfall that's never coming"; his lazy, alcoholic brother Randy (the most personal affront to Frank's dignity given Randy's undeserving usurpation of his birthright); the fruit tramps that come and go in the background of the story; veteran cocker Ed Middleton, persuaded into retirement by his wife and thus doomed to an early grave. "Even gamecocks are evaluated in terms of their work ethic," Pinkerton writes, "as Frank ponders the superiority of fighters raised free-range: 'Like members of a welfare state, chickens who don't have to get the hell out and scratch for their living will soon learn to stand around waiting for a free handout, getting fat and useless.'"

Money is a means to an end, but the work is the thing. The work leads to a different calibre of reward. "All of us in America want money because we need it and cannot live without it," says Frank, "but we don't need as much money as we think we do. Money isn't enough. We must have something more, and my *something more* was the Cockfighter of the Year Award."

In the book we are given rather more to work with regarding Frank's background; by his own admission he's rarely had a regular job in his entire life — and yet he has developed an unwavering work ethic. He is selective about what employment he takes on, favouring work that requires specialised knowledge. Even in the most temporary employment intended only to serve immediate needs, he is compelled to distinguish himself. In her examination of portrayals of American labour in 1930s and '40s art, Erika Doss notes that, "it is a commonplace assumption that what we 'do' as Americans is often the most outstanding indicator of who we 'are'" and this is a belief that Frank Mansfield subscribes to in both practical and existential terms. But Doss also makes an important point that I had pondered myself regarding exactly where it is that Frank's relentless work ethic

WORK
PROMOTES
CONFIDENCE
WORKS PROGRESS ADMINISTRATION

WORK WITH CARE.
W P A FEDERAL ART PROJECT PENNSYLVANIA

Work Pays America!
PROSPERITY
WORKS PROGRESS ADMINISTRATION

A YOUNG MAN'S OPPORTUNITY
CCC
FOR WORK PLAY STUDY & HEALTH
APPLICATIONS TAKEN BY
ILLINOIS EMERGENCY RELIEF COMMISSION
ILLINOIS SELECTING AGENCY
MADE BY ILLINOIS WPA ART PROJECT CHICAGO

comes from. She points out that despite the crucial moral importance the notion of work plays in the American psyche, it is only in Depression-era art that we see the image of the worker celebrated prolifically. This would be the very same era of Willeford's youthful recollections of migrant workers and transient camps as recounted in *I Was Looking For a Street*. This brand of artwork was specifically promulgated by the New Deal initiative the Works Progress Administration, or WPA, which was established in 1935 to provide employment to millions of unemployed and displaced workers through public works projects — which included infrastructure projects like building roads, bridges, parks and schools, but also cultural projects such as visuals arts, theatre, music, as well as significant historical/archival projects.

As to why image-makers sought to lionise the worker at a time when work was scarce, Doss cites the writings of Barbara Melosh and Karal Ann Marling in their assertion that such imagery "helped to deflect Depression-era anxieties about unemployment, and undercut worries about the roles and responsibilities of masculine breadwinners." Frank emerges from this era of workers needing to be adaptable, independent and mobile, and anxieties around work of this era are more closely aligned with Frank's perspective than the 1940s idea of work as a more collective, unifying enterprise full of opportunity and prosperity. The vulnerability of workers in the 1930s is something that drives Frank's need for a self-sufficient path, but it's one that allows no room for laziness or distraction.

An interesting aspect of this labour-infused 1930s artwork is how in the midst of this crisis in masculine identity, it sought to prop up ideals of the physical male body, with frequent semi-nude portraits in multiple media — sculpture, painting, photography — attempting to "sustain a sense of the masculine self through depictions of the manly body."[44] It's also been noted that men's beefcake and bodybuilding magazines experienced a simultaneous boost in sales during the Depression[45], and I mention this aside only because it seems to have had an ironic effect on Frank's obsession with health and muscle — but not his own. Throughout *Cockfighter* there is evidence of Frank's identification with the birds, and his projection onto them of his own ideals of focus and fitness; it seems only fitting that his attempt to master masculine anxieties would manifest in this way.

It's also important to acknowledge the influence of American Tramping literature on *Cockfighter* — the novel, at least — with its combination of mobility, individual freedom and shifting perceptions about the tramp's relationship to work. In the late 19th century, railroad expansion gave rise to a new type of worker referred to 'tramps' or later, as 'hobos'; Willeford's memoir reinforces this changing perception via his deliberate distinction between the two terms, describing a hobo as "a man who uses freight trains as a free means to get from one job to another" and a tramp as "on the road by choice... uninterested in employment of any kind." As scholar Christine Photinos points out in her study of the tramp in American literature, such people were originally viewed in terms of

44 Doss, Erika. "Toward an Iconography of American Labor: Work, Workers, and the Work Ethic in American Art, 1930-1945" in *Design Issues*, Vol 13, No. 1, Spring 1997. MIT Press. Pg 62.
45 Hooven, F. Vallentine. *Beefcake: The Muscle Magazines of America*, 1950-1970. Pgs 20-22.

deviancy and criminality, but by the onset of WWII they had been reconfigured through a nostalgic lens.

A large-scale depression in 1873 called "the Great Panic" originally gave rise to the tramp figure, after millions of workers were displaced from their jobs. However, most tramping literature of this era does not describe tramps as job-seekers, but as people with an aversion to work — shifty, parasitic, and very often drunk. At their best, they were sometimes depicted as political agitators who riled up the unemployed against the establishment.[46] Josiah Flynt's 1899 study "Tramping with Tramps" — in which he went undercover as a tramp himself — asserted damningly that tramps were not victims of circumstance, but *chose* to live how they did. Flynt's study was widely read and contributed to notions of the tramp as a voluntary outcast worthy of disdain, rather than one desperately roaming the country looking for work.

By the 20th century the transient worker was now seen as a strong survivor and adventurer rather than a suspect social deviant. The popularity of Jack London's writings had a bearing on the social elevation of the tramp — London himself had been a tramp for many years and his adventure stories drew significantly on this experience. Photinos describes a 1907 *Atlantic Monthly* story about a hobo whose shirt, washed in the river and hung from a tree to dry, takes on the aspect of a flag representing his personal freedom. "The very figure that had been understood as an inscrutable 'other,' dangerously immune to dominant ideologies of success and domesticity, is here described as a quintessential freedom-loving American man."

Floyd Dell's 1926 short story "Hallalujah, I'm a Bum" has its protagonist find true happiness by hitting the road to become a migrant worker, but in a twist we'll see replayed later in *Cockfighter*: "This freedom, though, has to be vigilantly defended against female domesticators." In Dell's story, when its protagonist meets a woman he is drawn to, he thinks, "I saw myself settling down in that little town and buying a house for that girl to live in, and spending the rest of my life paying off the mortgage… I walked up and down thinking about it, and then just before daybreak I lit out and took to the road again."

This idealisation continued throughout the 1920s, with the middle classes becoming weekend hobos and going on camping trips to 'rough it', lacking all context of the tramp's very tangible economic woes. This all changed with the stock market crash in 1929, and Depression-era accounts of tramping like Frank Conroy's 1933 novel *The Disinherited* once again summoned a bleak picture of the tramp's reality. But the idealisation of pre-Depression-era tramps persisted — albeit with a certain irony.

46 Photinos, Christine. "The Tramp in American Literature, 1873-1939" in *AmeriQuests* Vol. 5, No. 1 (2008): Pg 2.

Rolling with the Punches at 14

He rode the rails, warmed himself by the fires in hobo jungles and became a professional boxer while barely in his teens. Here, a noted Miami novelist-screenwriter talks about growing up in the Depression — and his battle with a boxer named Soldier

By Charles Willeford

When I decided to turn pro at 14, it seemed like a good idea at the time. And the fact that I had never been in the ring before made my decision that much easier.

There were four of us road kids ...
around a small ...

Photograph: Battle Vaughan

Author Charles Willeford often rode the rails for free as a youth. Today, he returns to some of his old haunts

... dodged, however, shouting, "Grab him, Tiny!" — and the big guy, moving with incredible speed, tore the root out of my hands and tucked me under his left arm.

CHARLES WILLEFORD is the Miami author of The Burnt Orange Heresy and Cockfighter. He recently adapted the latter novel into a movie version starring Warren Oates.

I struggled some as I was carried across the tracks toward the station where they had parked their pick-up truck, but I calmed down when the man in the suit told me that they weren't going to hurt me. He was merely looking ...

... you look a lot ...

"Not to me," the giant said. "He looks a lot younger."

I had lied because I didn't want to get locked up as a runaway, or lose out on the possibility of the prelim. Actually, I neither looked older nor younger than 22. I was so dirty it would have been impossible to guess my age. I hadn't had a bath in two months, and I hadn't washed my feet since I left the Colorado River jungle in Yuma, about two weeks before.

"How much do you weigh?"

I shrugged, because I had no idea.

"What do you think, Tiny?"

The big man ...

... know what I would have done if he had accepted my challenge. I knew only that my ribs were sore from being held under his arm, and I didn't appreciate his sarcasm. As a sensitive, novice liar, I still resented it when people expressed any doubts about the stories I told. But on the road lying is a means of survival, and I had already developed the ability to say outrageous things with a straight face.

When the man in the suit, the promoter of a monthly card in Bisbee, explained that I would be paid $20 if I won, and $10 if I lost, I climbed eagerly into the back of the

BUNT BROS. CIR
SIDE SHOW

Even though millions of jobless people were forced to leave home and ride the rails looking for work across the country, in mainstream publications like *Readers Digest* and *New York Times Magazine*, tramps were given pictorials and nostalgically referred to as "Vanishing Americans." Mid-century writers like Willeford and Jack Kerouac — with his highly influential *On the Road* — played a part in propagating this nostalgia. As Willeford relates in *I Was Looking for a Street*, when his family found itself with too many mouths to feed in the early 1930s, "I left home and went on the road. I wasn't alone. For the next few years there were thousands of boys my age riding freight trains to nowhere. But no one can ever tell me I didn't have a happy childhood."

While he was still a child during the Depression, one could sense that Oates could relate to his *Cockfighter* character's transitory lifestyle; like Frank Mansfield, Oates was a man in perpetual motion. As his biographer Susan Compo noted,

> Although he would live in the arty atmosphere of New York's Greenwich Village, the cowboy flats of Southern California's San Fernando Valley, the faux wilderness of the Hollywood Hills, the faded glamour of Los Angeles' Los Feliz district, and the dramatic Montana landscape, Warren Oates never really found a home. 'I always feel in motion,' he would insist. 'You start moving a man around and he doesn't have time to adjust. It's *The Grapes of Wrath* all over again.'"

In what comprises a large section of the book *Cockfighter* that is excised from the film adaptation, the penniless Frank — who has lost everything in the fight with Jack Burke's Little David — gets a job playing music nightly in a small cabaret. He refuses to take more than he feels he deserves, and won't take the money at all if he suspects people are being patronising to him. He wants to earn a living, and adamantly refuses charity. According to notes by New World script reader Katharine Seyster, who was charged with giving feedback on Willeford's first draft of the screenplay, this detour outside of the cockfighting milieu was originally intended to be part of the film. But Seyster bluntly comments that the section doesn't work, because any attempts to depict Frank doing whatever he can to scratch by are undone the minute he arrives in the hometown bearing his name.[47] In the film, we see the town's name emblazoned on the nearby water tower when Frank steps off the bus: Mansfield, Georgia. Through it is never explicitly stated, in the film or the book, it is more than likely the town is named after Frank's family. In the novel, when Frank sells the house and a large parcel of land in his quest to secure financial resources for the Southern Conference Tournament, this exchange of real estate is given a substantial wordcount. Because it illustrates the true weight Frank is operating under: this down-on-his-luck grifter who knows only how to navigate a world that is considered sleazy and embarrassing by most, comes from *money*. He has turned his back on his family name and legacy in order to be a cockfighter. In the book, it is made clear that Frank could choose to settle down with Mary Elizabeth, run the farm and be relatively comfortable financially. Her family has even offered financial incentives if he will just stay still long enough to marry the poor girl.

47 **Seyster, Katharine. Notes on Willeford's first draft of *Cockfighter*, in his personal papers at the Dianne and Michael Bienes Special Collections and rare book Library, Bienes Museum of the Modern Book, Broward County Library. As early drafts contain more surreal setpieces and flashbacks It was also Sesyter's recommendation that Willeford stick to a straightforward story structure : "It seems to me that this film, centering as it does around one earthy, single-minded man, calls for simplicity of style."**

And so Katherine Seyster found a conflict in something that I see as a central point of the story, namely that Frank finds no satisfaction in doing anything the easy way, nor does he find security and stability in the same things that other people do. Frank's sense of security comes from knowing that he is reliant on no one, and responsible to no one.

Frank's relationship to the guitar as a secondary form of labour underpins this determination to remain independent and mobile. I've often joked that if I only knew how to play the guitar better, I'd have some currency in the post-Apocalypse. But it's true — there's a reason wandering troubadours are often depicted playing the guitar and not the piano. Because they can follow the work. And so Frank's cockfighting and guitar-playing are all part of a very specific lifestyle that is transient by design. And that design is to avoid being a victim to the country's larger economic fluctuations, a design specifically informed, I would argue, by his author's experience of the Depression.

It is important that even though Frank's repertoire consists of only three songs — "Empty Pockets," "Grandma's Quilt" and "Georgia Gal" — he is revered as a transcendent guitar player by both the audience and the house band whose act he is supporting. Furthermore, all three songs are self-composed, as he describes it, as an aural interpretation of specific visual and olfactory memories. Faced with additional time to fill, he launches into an improvisational piece recalling "the dry rasping of locusts," "bright, silvery moths circling the lamp on the corner," the creaking chains on a metal porch swing, the laughter of children, the swishing of a lawn sprinkler. His mother rewarding his naughtiness with kisses and cuddles. The crowd erupts with applause. If he only knew more than three songs it is implied that he could be a master guitar player. But instead, it is left there as evidence of Frank's limitless potential. Here is a guy, it is suggested, that could do anything he set his mind to. But you can't serve two masters, and his heart belongs to cockfighting.

The scene of *Cockfighter*'s silent protagonist onstage performing the three named songs onstage has a precedent in Willeford's short story "Guitar Interlude,"[48] Interpretations of these songs were composed by Willeford's stepson Stephen Hooker and recorded on cassette in 1972 (these very sweet lo-fi recordings — which include both vocal and instrumental versions — can be heard at the Bienes Museum of the Modern Book in Florida which houses Willeford's personal papers). "I remember recording them in my bedsitter using a consumer two-track Sony tape recorder," he explained. "The only instrument was my 1967 Gretsch Chet Atkins Nashville electric guitar with a double cutaway. For the two songs, I had both the guitar and the amp set up for a very clean, almost acoustic sound. I first recorded a rhythm track while singing using a single mic and then I added a second track with some improvising here and there. The track balance is poor, probably intentional since I was a shy singer and let the guitar drown me out somewhat."

Hooker clarified that Willeford actually wrote the lyrics for the songs "Empty Pockets" and "Georgia Gal" himself, and asked Stephen — whose interests had turned to music as a teenager — to put music to them. Hooker's musical endeavors were put on hold by the

48 **The date of this story is unknown, but notes in Willeford's papers suggest it predates *Cockfighter*.**

Vietnam War, and it wasn't until afterwards, as talk of a film version of *Cockfighter* intensified, that he sat down and began composing. As he recalls:

> At university, I wasn't doing well and was about to be drafted into the army and sent to Vietnam. My parents encouraged me to escape to Canada, primarily my mother, but I said no and would knuckle down on my studies. I think Dad was quietly proud of my choice. As insurance however, Dad said I should join the university's army ROTC program. That would put a hold on me being drafted. The logic went that by the time I would graduate, 1968, I would be commissioned in the army but the war would be over by then and I'd be safe. Most of all that came to pass except the part about the war being over. So off I went and served a year in Vietnam, mostly as an infantry combat commander. When I returned home the war experience had focused my future… I had a new interest and it pushed music into a secondary interest. I wanted to make films.
>
> Dad knew I needed a complete break and suggested a total change of scenery, The London Film School. Perfect. In the first year of school, *Cockfighter* was picked up and script writing began. Dad kept me informed and many times I weighed whether to cut and join the effort in California. Then Dad sent me the lyrics of the two songs he had written and asked me if I'd put music to them. To my disappointment, my musical skill had slipped since the distractions of university and the army. There wasn't that old eureka excitement. I tried very hard but to me my efforts seemed to miss something. Perhaps Dad knew I'd be rusty and wanted that level of quality.

Nevertheless, in one of his letters to Corman, Willeford suggested using one of the songs during the hotel room hack that precipitates Frank's vow. There's no indication that this was ever considered; instead Michael Franks' simple country guitar-picking is laid against warped strings, like the sound of something circling a drain. But the Willeford/Hooker compositions stand as compelling curiosities, further evidence of the author's understated world-building.

Aside from being a means of income, the guitar is also linked symbolically to the fighting cock in a way that reinforces Frank's view of the cock as extension of himself. "My guitar was an old friend," Frank muses. "The guitar served as a substitute for my lost voice, and I don't know what I would have done without it." Nevertheless, when the widow Berenice Hungerford overpays Frank for a private concert at a house party, presumably as a means of buying sex from him, he takes the money and the sex — but snaps the neck of the guitar and leaves it broken on her front porch. It is a scene that foreshadows the ending of the story, when he steps on Icarus' neck and pulls the gamecock's head off, handing the bloody mass to Mary Elizabeth. Both guitar and gamecock are tools of Frank's trade, and their offering in mutilated form is an act of defiance — and a warning: attempt to domesticate me, it says, and you'll get half a man.

Right: Lyrics for 'Georgia Gal' in an early draft of the *Cockfighter* script.

into the mirror.

LOSE SHOT. MIRROR. Frank's mottled face.

OSE. SENATOR FOXHALL, ED MIDDLETON, + PEACH OWEN,
medal, all of them smiling, at Milledgeville pit.
eton suddenly disappears from the three-shot.
rns away, opens his guitar case on the bed.

CLOSE SHOT. Frank, with one foot on the chair, tun
tar. He begins to play "Georgia Girl."

FRANK's VOICE (O.S.)

Good girls don't wait too long,
(voice over) But a good girl will hear my song. . .

CLOSE SHOT, over Frank's shoulder, of mirror. Mar
eth is SUPERIMPOSED on the mirror. Her hair, long
, is pinned on top of her head in a bun. Her mout
m, and she looks disapprovingly at Frank. She wears

So, wait, wait, Georgia girl,
You've got to wait for me.

I know that--

oks into the mirror.

M CLOSE SHOT. MIRROR. Frank's mottled face.

IMPOSE. SENATOR FOXHALL, ED MIDDLETON, + PEACH OWEN,
ng medal, all of them smiling, at Milledgeville pi
ddleton suddenly disappears from the three-shot.
turns away, opens his guitar case on the bed.

UM CLOSE SHOT. Frank, with one foot on the chair,
guitar. He begins to play "Georgia Girl."

FRANK's VOICE (O.S.)

Frank's gamecocks reflect his ideal of workmanship and discipline, and he puts them through brutal tests of gameness that are not depicted in the film adaptation (although the various drafts of the script make it clear that much of this violence was excised by Willeford himself.) In the book there is one particularly shocking sequence where Frank must prove a new strain by selecting one young Mellhorn Black from the brood and putting it through a regimen of torture to see if the cock will still fight through the pain. In this instance he cuts off its legs, and, satisfied that it still projects the same determination even when balancing on painful stumps, he sets it on fire — disgusting even his partner Omar, who can't bear to watch. The bird prevails; it fights until it is completely consumed by the flames and killed, filling Frank with adulation for the charred, legless creature that will never enjoy the fruits of its own valour.

Of course, Frank's identification with the cock is a projection of his own ideals; the truth of it is that the birds work at the behest of those who keep them. In an *Atlanta Journal-Constitution* set visit from the time, cocker Jimmy Williams corroborates the 5-fight rule I've been told by the cockfighters I've met personally: namely that a cock who wins five fights gets to retire "with a harem of hens and all the feed he can eat." The retired cock gets to live in a virtual barnyard paradise, enjoying legendary status as the patriarch of his own brood of baby fighters. "You walk by him there and you remember how he fought for what he's got," says Williams, "and it makes you a little proud."

Chapter Nine.

Jimmy Carter Says Yes

The $400,000 film[49], like the book, is largely set in Georgia, where cockfighting was already illegal at the time, and had been since 1933.

As of this writing, the film industry in Georgia is America's most prolific — more films are now shot in the state than anywhere else in the US, including Hollywood, a position it has held since 2016 due to a diversity of tax incentives. But back when Cockfighter was shot in spring of 1974, the fledgling Georgia Film Commission was only a year old.

Despite its negatively stereotypical depictions of Georgia mountain people — which was vociferously protested by locals — John Boorman's *Deliverance* (1972) put the state on the map as a viable film location. Political leaders in the Sun Belt felt the benefits of inviting future movie productions outweighed the risks of such negative characterisations; the film generated significant financial returns for the state, which prompted then-governor Jimmy Carter to greenlight a state film commission in 1973 to market Georgia as a cooperative and desirable location for outside productions.

The first film commissioner was Ed Spivia, who, according to *Cockfighter*'s production

49 **Though this is the film's official budget, Monte Hellman has stated in interviews that he brought it in for considerably less.**

Above: Jimmy Carter in triplicate, from his controversial 1976 interview in *Playboy*.

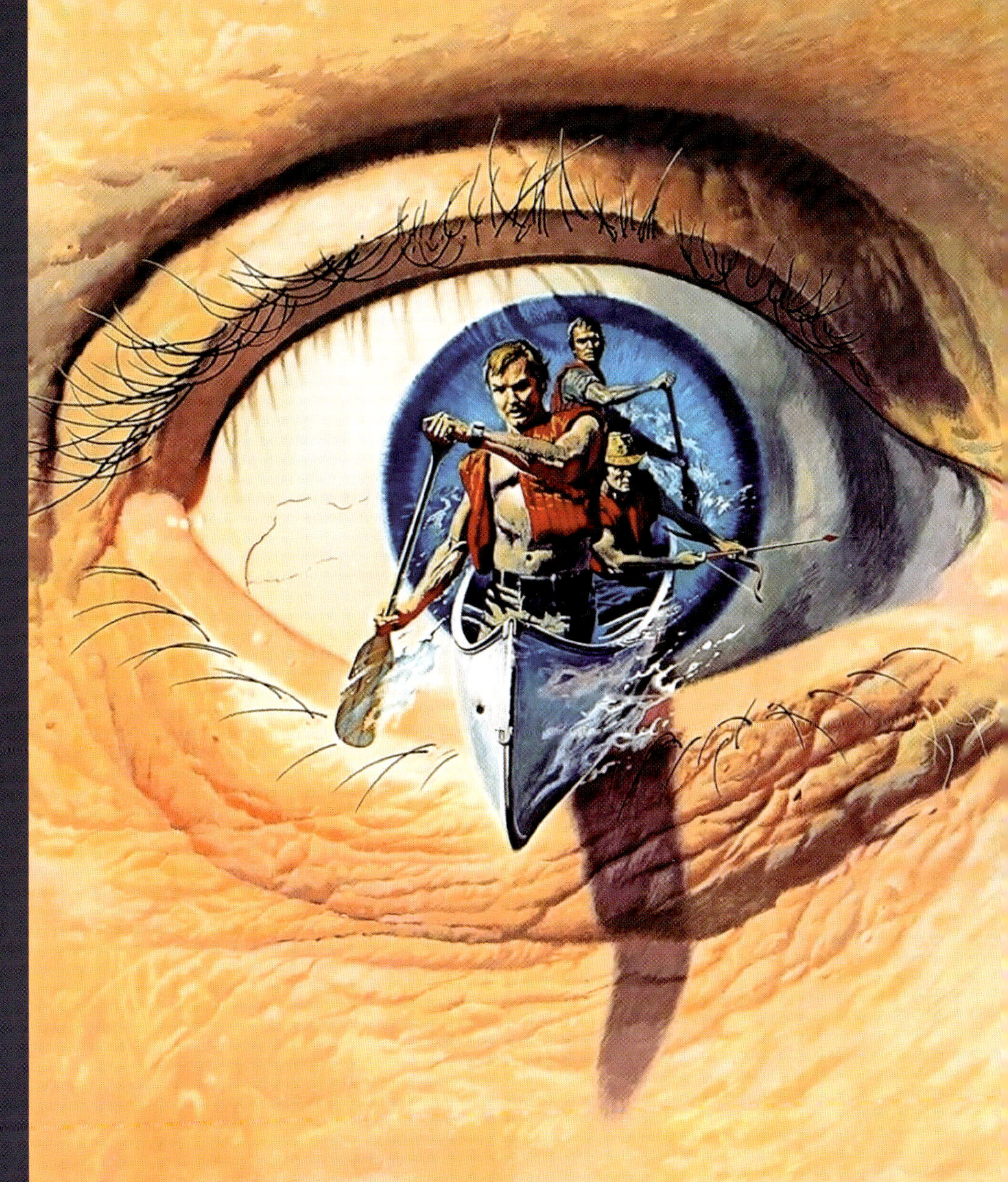

Deliverance

manager Peter Cornberg, helped pave the way for the film. Spivia had been a radio announcer in Atlanta in the 1960s, and when *Deliverance* set up shop in the state in 1972, he wrote a set visit piece for Georgia Trend *magazine. There he met Burt* Reynolds and the two went on to forge a lifelong friendship that would see Reynolds-fronted blockbusters like *Smokey and the Bandit*, *Gator* and *The Longest Yard* shot in the state. It was after this set visit that Spivia came back to Atlanta and pitched Jimmy Carter on the idea of establishing a formal film commission to encourage filming in the state. Jimmy Carter said yes.

Though Spivia would be instrumental in introducing complex tax incentives to shoot in Georgia in the 1980s, at the time of its establishment these incentives were more about welcoming productions by opening doors with locations assistance, and ensuring simplicity and expedition in permitting. From the mid-1960s, location shooting outside of Hollywood eventually resulted in the establishment of formal film commissions or bureaus in several states, beginning with the Mayor's Office of Motion Pictures and Television, launched by New York mayor John Lindsay in 1966: "Working against the notion of New York as unwelcoming to film crews, the film office offered a streamlined 'one stop shop' for shooting permits, a full time film commissioner with direct access to the mayor, and even a dedicated police unit to work with film crews."[50] It also allowed for less controlled depictions of the city itself, which was important because it didn't require a rosy view of the location and its people in order for a production to get municipal or state support. Lindsay's program would become a model for other film bureaus that proliferated in its wake; by the mid-1970s there were 30 municipal or state film departments vying for Hollywood dollars.

Above: *Deliverance* author James Dickey on the set of the film with Burt Reynolds.

In Georgia, Jimmy Carter founded the Motion Picture and Television Advisory Committee in response to Deliverance, which had spent half of its production budget in the state. Even aside from the boost to the economy from such revenues, tourists flocked to the Chattanooga River locations, creating subsidiary revenues through film tourism. Carter recognized both the hard and soft benefits of encouraging filming in the state.

Ironically what the Carter-backed film commission strategised was a move away from the unregulated rural lifestyle depicted in *Cockfighter*, that would "enable the South to break free from the tradition-bound, agrarian-oriented values of its past and spur an ever more rapid rate of regional-industrial development."[51] This was already happening in a major way with the help of an unlikely — and rather symbolic — ally: air conditioning. "It changed the landscape of America, opening up whole new frontiers to migration and development," says author Jeff Goodell

50 Bleich, Joshua and Lawrence Webb. *Hollywood on Location: An Industry History*. New Brunswick: Rutgers University Press, 2019.
51 Nystrom, Derek. *Hard Hats, Rednecks and Macho Men: Class in 1970s American Cinema*. New York: Oxford University Press, 2009.

in *The Heat Will Kill You First*, describing how the technology of personal comfort made previously "sluggish" environments more amenable to a consumerist vision of prosperity. "Corporations moved their headquarters south," he writes. "Factories and manufacturing plants, fertilised by cheap real estate and non-union labor, blossomed in abandoned cotton fields. The political ramifications of this demographic shift to the Sun Belt was enormous. The flood of conservative retirees to the South, once a Democratic stronghold, shifted the balance of power in American politics."

It simultaneously revitalized the economy in the South, but also served to deepen a rift between the different kinds of people who lived there — highlighting class distinctions but also challenging long-entrenched racial hierarchies. "In the past, Georgia has had a provincial Southern image," said Ed Spivea in a 1976 interview in the *Atlanta Journal-Constitution*. "I know of no better way to change it than to get the image-makers on your side. People like Bob Aldrich, Burt Reynolds, Bill Cosby — who could ask for a better group of salespeople?"[52]

Even though cockfighting was still legal in neighbouring Louisiana (it remained so until 2008), Corman opted to shoot in Georgia, knowing that, illegal or not, the sport was still widely practiced there, and politicians tended to look the other way. "It was being done, but not in the big cities," Corman told me. "We knew some people in Georgia and I just asked them, where can I go to find this, and they gave me several places to look. And so we went to one place I remember, it was sort of a big, tin-roofed arena with light was streaming through the roof, and I thought, this is really great, and I started getting into it, and I bought some moonshine whiskey and I started betting on the fighting cocks — I lost every bet! I thought, how do these guys know which one looks good? They all look the same to me! I didn't know the hand signals, so I was just betting against guys at random."

But the Georgia Film Commission was not directly involved in the production, nor did they offer specific incentives at that time. "It was more sort of cooperation," explained Corman. "They would help you find locations, find local people who were trained in motion pictures and so forth. But I never really went to any of them, I thought, I just want to go in and shoot quietly, I'm not announcing to anybody that we're shooting this picture here. The *last* thing I want is the Georgia State government involved in the making of this film!" But Unit Production Manager Peter Cornberg said that Georgia's Department of Community Development — via Ed Spivea — was instrumental in clearing the way for the shoot.[53]

One of the biggest incentives for shooting in Georgia at that time was the availability of non-union crews in the "right-to-work" environment of the Sun Belt. Even Frank Mansfield, in the pages of *Cockfighter*, comments disparagingly on unions: "The idea of any free American male paying gangsters money for the right to work struck me as one of the most preposterous customs we have."

As scholar Derek Nystrom points out in his book *Hard Hats, Rednecks and Macho Men*,

52 😐

53 Cornberg, Peter, qtd in *Variety* April 10, 1973.

> By moving production to areas that were both geographically scattered and removed from the histories of trade unionist struggle that produced the film unions in the first place, the studios, like other US corporations, limited the ability of Sun Belt workers to build solidarity with each other and connect with the larger traditions of the film unions. Decentralized production also made it more difficult for the film unions to monitor and enforce union pay scales and work rules.

Unsurprisingly, the Hollywood unions fought this tendency to hire below-the-line non-guild crew on location, and the South duly fought back. When SAG tried to stop members from working for North Carolina producer Earl Owensby — who established a mini-studio of his own in Shelby, North Carolina in 1974 with non-union labour — "the state's attorney general ruled that North Carolina's right to work law forbade the refusal of employment to nonunionized workers... in short, Southern location shooting not only enabled cheaper film productions through the use of nonunion labor but also restricted the ability of the film unions to defend and advocate for the interests of its members both in and out of Hollywood."[54] Owensby convincingly argued his case in *Variety* interview, stating that in an E.O. Studios picture, the lack of union rigidity regarding specific expertise allowed for crew roles to be more fluid, so that "a grip today could be tomorrow's assistant director."[55] Consequently, the frustrated unions looked for any fissure through which they could exert their influence, and Monte Hellman himself would become embroiled in a labour dispute as a result of *Cockfighter* — but more on that later. For now, Georgia looked like a very attractive proposition indeed.

Aside from the on-the-ground assistance provided by Ed Spivea and the Georgia Film Commission, Corman had a couple guys in mind with specific experience shooting in Georgia, namely Peter Cornberg and Don Walters, who would come on as *Cockfighter*'s Production Manager and Assistant Director, respectively. As a bonus, the two had already worked together before.

Don Walters got his first on-set experience working in adult films — and continued to work on adult films after *Cockfighter*. "All the guys that went out [to California], all of them had worked in adult films before they ever went out there. And of course in those days, they weren't all-out; you had restrictions, you couldn't do this, you couldn't do that. And in '69, that all changed. But that was one of

54 Nystrom, Derek. *Hard Hats, Rednecks and Macho Men: Class in 1970s American Cinema*. New York: Oxford University Press, 2009.
55 Owensby, Earl, Qtd in Nystrom, Derek. *Hard Hats, Rednecks and Macho Men: Class in 1970s American Cinema*. New York: Oxford University Press, 2009.

"That which we call freedom,
that which we call liberty,
are not tangible things.
They are principles,
they are questions of the spirit,
and the people must have
a consciousness that they
not only have the term liberty
and freedom, but they must
have the power and the right to
exercise these great attributes of life."
SAMUEL GOMPERS
Founder of the
American Federation of Labor
SAMUEL GOMPERS
National Right To Work Committee
8316 ARLINGTON BOULEVARD • FAIRFAX, VIRGINIA 22038

the ways you could learn filmmaking. You can play with the equipment, you can learn all the things you really need to learn." This theory is borne out through the infamous history of another Georgia-shot film of the early 1970s (thought not released until 1975) that was crewed largely by folks with adult film experience: the wonderfully degenerate *Poor Pretty Eddie* — surely a candidate for a book-length study of its own. "I was working on a couple of things," continues Don Walters, "and then a friend of mine went on a gig in Europe or something and he couldn't do a job on *Moonrunners* as an AD. And his girlfriend said, 'Well, why don't you do it?' And she was on the film as a script girl. So she talked to Peter Cornberg and said, 'Peter, I got a good AD for you.' And so they just gave me a call and I flew out that day."

"I went to Roger Corman university, did a number of films," said Cornberg, "and I really wanted to work as a production manager and I got a job on a film called *Moonrunners*, directed by Gy Waldron — that spun off into *The Dukes of Hazzard* — and that's where I met Don [Walters]. That was shot in Georgia." Like *The Dukes of Hazzard*, *Moonrunners* featured country superstar Waylon Jennings as the balladeer and running commentator for the misadventures of bootlegging cousins who sell moonshine for their Uncle Jesse while being pursued by Sheriff Roscoe P. Coltrane. It's also an instrumental building block in the changing face of the rural South, which sought to transform the 'redneck' into the 'good ol' boy.' Walters recalls it as a great experience, despite having to wrangle the film's hard-partying stars Jim Mitchum and Kiel Martin, who were ignoring set calls and even leaving the state to score weed in North Carolina. "I got to do a lot of second unit shooting of car chases and fights and all manner of fun stuff," Walters says. He continues:

> Filming in Georgia at that time was fairly active because Georgia was a right-to-work state and was not subject to heavy union rules. There were several very active film crews in the state (centered in Atlanta) at the time and there were plenty of TV crew guys who also worked film sets. There was plenty of equipment available including some supplied by crew members who had their own inventory. It was fairly easy working also because the people in the state were still dazzled by the idea of someone filming in their neighborhood and locations and other amenities were readily and cheaply obtainable. The film commission was very helpful to filmmakers and advertised the state

2-A The Atlanta Journal and CONSTITUTION SUNDAY, JAN. 11, 1976

$30 Million Fattens Economy

Georgia Becomes a Shooting Star in Filmmaking

Ed Spivia, Burt Reynolds, Mike Douglas on 'Gator' Set, left; 'False Face' Filming in Oakland Cemetery, right

and helped bring in producers to investigate the wonders of "Filming in Georgia". It was also very helpful that Georgia taxes were and are low for filmmakers and that helped bring in a lot of productions.

Jimmy Carter didn't just give the film a "tacit approval"[56] via the film commission's collegial assistance — he visited the set. "One thing I'll never forget was this mansion that we were using," says Peter Cornberg, referring to Bulloch Hall, where the final SCT Championship takes place. "And Jimmy Carter stopped by on the day we were shooting to say hello to people. And that was a real thrill 'cause he was still a hero to some of us more radical people." "It was wonderful," says Don Walters. "Five or six big limos came, screeching up with a siren and the whole deal, and he jumped out and of course he's kind of small. So we were thinking this big guy was going to get out of the car. Nope." Production assistant Steven Gaydos also recalled being there that day. "Jimmy Carter came down and shook hands with everybody on the set," he says. "We got a little bit of guff about that, because the people in the great state of Georgia who didn't appreciate cockfighting didn't appreciate their governor coming down and endorsing this." And while it could be argued that Carter was fulfilling a diplomatic obligation on behalf of the freshly-minted film commission, he may have had more personal reasons for visiting the set: according to the website *Atlanta Time Machine*, Carter told Hellman that his family had been involved in cockfighting for several generations.

56 **Willeford, Charles. *Cockfighter Journal: The Story of a Shooting.* Santa Barbara: Neville Press, 1989. Pg 61.**

COCKFIGHTER

Screenplay by

arles Willeford

from his novel

Chapter Ten.

Duelling Scripts

ad hard enough to make him grimace.

MARY ELIZABETH
That's the way I feel sometimes...
like shaking you!

e releases his hair and leans back supporting herself wit
layed hands. She stares thoughtfully at nothing and her
ops.

MARY ELIZABETH
What about us, Frank?

ank frowns slightly and moves backward in the water looki
at Mary Elizabeth. She takes off dark glasses and puts
one side. She cups her breasts (which have not as yet p
osed), and smiles ruefully.

MARY ELIZABETH
They aren't as firm as they used to
be are they? In a few months I'll
be thirty years old, Frank, and officially a thirty year old woman who
hasn't married is called a spinster!

ank grins slightly, but she doesn't notice.

MARY ELIZABETH
I want to be married and have children.
And I want to have them <u>here</u> where we
both have roots. I'm not going to marry
you and live on a gamecock farm in Ocala!
I thought that as you got older you'd
see how wrong cockfighting is...morally,
legally, and every other kind of wrong!

ank jerks towel away and pulls her into the water. He pu
s arms around her, tries to kiss her, but she pulls away
grily shaking her head.

MARY ELIZABETH
No! I want to talk to you and for
once I want you to listen!

ank shrugs, gives up, and climbs out of the pool. He dri
h her towel and begins to get dressed. Head and shoulde

I asked then-production assistant Steven Gaydos if over the course of their long friendship he ever found out what it was about *Cockfighter* that Hellman didn't like. "The answer is mysterious," he offered. "Monte says to me over and over again that, you know, he's not looking at writing, he's not looking at stories. He's looking at revealed moments. He's looking for life to unfold."

There are a lot of improvisational and verité moments in *Cockfighter*, largely involving the background characters, and those are the parts Monte always liked best. But something in the script — or more accurately, something that *wasn't* in the script — was proving to be a creative block. Monte needed more time. But the production was ready to go. Things needed to move.

Though some would argue that you can barrel into production without a completed script — the makers of *Lawrence of Arabia* (1962) and *Jaws* (1975), for example — the fact is it's hell for those making the schedule and not economically feasible on on a Corman-level picture. Hellman was still insisting on significant revisions dangerously close to the production date — which was testing Corman's patience.

As far as Corman was concerned, he already had a script he'd commissioned and largely approved, penned by Willeford himself. Hellman, like any director Corman enlisted, was not involved in its development. "My usual plan is to work with the writer and get a first draft script," Corman explained to me, "sometimes even a second draft script I'm pleased with, and then I bring in the director, so the director can have some input on the final script, with thoughts of his own. But I want to make certain that the basic line is what I want as a producer myself."

Frances Doel had been charged with working closely with Charles Willeford to get the script to a realistic state for shooting, initially hashing it out over the phone several times a week, and then daily once they got on location during pre-production. But the latter was limited to excision, not dramatic rewrites that would affect the production schedule.

"Charles Willeford was very cooperative," she recalls,

> I mean, he knew some of Roger Corman's movies, he liked movies, but he recognized that he had never written a script. And he also recognized that the whole novel couldn't be transposed because it would be way too long.

So he knew some things had to be cut, dropped, simplified, and so on. So actually he was very good to work with. It was when we got to Atlanta, and Sam Gelfman, the producer was there, and I was to work with Charles Willeford on the next draft to really cut it down quite heavily because it was still way too long. And often dialogue heavy and all the things that, you know, a beginning screenwriter doesn't necessarily know, and full of very detailed screen directions. Again, I don't know how it is today, things have changed a lot, but at that time writers were discouraged from calling for specific shots. That was the director's job to decide how to shoot it. I mean, a writer could put in an emphasis where something was really crucial, a close up with something that was going to pay off. They could do that. But Charles Willeford initially thought that he really had to lay out the shots. So then it was a little more tricky working with him. Not that he was uncooperative in any way, but I remember sitting on his bed in the motel and me summing up what needed to be done and how much it needed to be cut, trimmed, simplified. And he looked very downcast, because I believe he thought that he'd done pretty well — which he had, really — and that he hadn't expected it to be this much work.

Willeford really *had* come a long way in re shaping the script from earlier versions, which were not only doubled in page count, but also featured surreal flashback sequences with characters talking in chicken squawks — which he was urged to remove in favour of a more realistic treatment quite early on.

But as soon as he'd gotten the gig, Hellman made plans to begin his own rewrites. With the supposed blessing of Corman, Hellman hired a relatively green screenwriter named Earl Mac Rauch (author of *Dirty Pictures from the Prom* (1969) — which he had written while still a high school student — and 1971 rural Americana novel *Arkansas Adios*[57]) to work with him on rewriting the script,[58] because what appealed to Hellman was not the cockfighting — the 'hook' that Corman was banking on to sell the film — but the character and the way that character moved around in his own very particular world. "I had no experience with cockfighting before, other than a tendency to avoid death sports," Hellman told me, adding that "I didn't change during the making."

57 In her book *You'll Never Eat Lunch in This Town Again*, Julia Philips mentions that both she and Tony Bill independently proposed that Sydney Pollack make a film adaptation of *Arkansas Adios*. Which he didn't.

58 This didn't stop *Box Office Magazine* from reporting on March 4, 1974 that Bill Norton (*Cisco Pike*) had written the script. Corman denied there had ever been another writer besides Willeford.

The choice of Earl Mac Rauch as a writing partner is an intriguing one; his earlier novels indicate a writer with a strong penchant for the absurd and irreverent (later veering to the outright fantastical, as his screenplay for *The Adventures of Buckaroo Banzai Across the 8th Dimension* can attest). He could, however, be categorised as a Southern writer, and one that could flesh out dialogue authentically; his novel *Arkansas Adios*, for example, is hilariously degenerate oversexed psychosis with a country twang… from the perspective of an eleven-year-old. I can only speculate as to whether Rauch's "Southern-ness" was a selling point for Hellman, or whether other aspects of Rauch's previous books suggested him as a suitable writing partner. Hellman admitted to me that he had not read Rauch's books and said that he hired him on Terence Malick's recommendation (the latter's *Badlands* — also featuring the involvement of Hellman alumni Warren Oates and James Taylor — had debuted just a few months prior, signaling the arrival of another major talent).

But while it's been remarked in a few places that Rauch was a 'protégé' of Terence Malick, this just wasn't the case. It's possible Malick introduced him to Monte — Rauch thinks it was more likely Bob Rafelson — but Rauch never worked with Malick. Furthermore, Hellman's retellings of this story make it seem more transactional than it was; the two of them had a friendship predating any work on *Cockfighter*. "I had known Monte since '72," Rauch tells me,

'Cockfighter'

Novelist Turns His Book Into Screenplay-- And Learns Some Tricks in the Process

By CHARLES WILLEFORD

CHARLES WILLEFORD is a Miami novelist and English professor. His movie, starring Warren Oates, opens in Atlanta on July 31 and comes to Miami this fall.

> I had just come out to LA and was living in an old, badly ventilated apartment building and Monte would come over on occasion and we would go up on the roof to get some air and shoot the breeze. He was genuinely unassuming and funny, just an easygoing guy with a wide-ranging intellect. We tossed around a few movie ideas that never quite crystallized, and sometime in '73 he mentioned *Cockfighter* and gave me the novel to read, along with a first draft by Willeford. I had very little screenwriting experience, but knew enough to recognize that the draft wasn't quite a screenplay. Willeford had simply taken sections from his novel verbatim and strung them together, cut-and-paste style.

For his own part, it was when he had met emerging director W.D. Richter in the early 1970s that Rauch transitioned from novelist to screenwriter (with a stint at law school student in between). "A seduction took place," Rauch explained in a 1984 *Starlog* interview:

> Novel writing is such a lonely pursuit. Then, the book comes out and there's no support behind it. It disappears in a matter of months and you wonder why you worked so hard. If you can live off the ego trip of having a novel published and getting good reviews, I guess it's a good way to stay alive. It is a pure way; you have integrity. It's wonderful, it's artistic and blah-blah-blah. I couldn't see that life for me, especially with the kind of novels I was writing, ones which didn't have a prayer of ever becoming bestsellers. It simply became an ego thing. The day-to-day process of screenplay work allows you to get by. There are story meetings, you interact with people, and you get well paid for all of it. A movie may never get made, but at least you're adequately compensated.

That said, Rauch knew *Cockfighter* rewrites were not going to be his meal ticket — especially given Corman's notoriously austere budgets. But it was a challenge he and Hellman were eager to take on together. "We both understood that a movie dealing with cockfighting would be a tough sell," Rauch explains,

> but also fertile ground for an array of Willeford's quirky characters — which was what appealed to us both about the project. Monte said he would talk to Roger Corman about getting me some money to do a draft. But since I had no Hollywood track record, he wanted to show Corman a sample, so I did a little work — mostly editing and shifting pieces around, but also writing some dialogue and a couple of new scenes for him to show Corman. Unfortunately, Monte came back and said Corman didn't want to pay for a rewrite, so that was how we left it for the time being. Finally, a few months later, Monte called and said the project seemed to be going forward, and asked if I was still interested in working on it. I'm pretty sure it was late '73. Monte brought me in to doctor the script once production started, even offering to pay me something out of his own pocket if Corman didn't come through. He would direct me to certain scenes, mainly to punch up dialogue, add character stuff and humour wherever possible, but I was always free to send him whatever new idea occurred to me.

As Monte Hellman explained in an interview with fellow director Allison Anders (*Gas, Food, Lodging*, *Grace of My Heart*) for the Director's Guild of America:

> We started to do a page one rewrite; he started at the beginning and just really just rewrote everything. And after about a week, Roger kind of saw it slipping out, you know, from his control, and so he got very, very nervous, and he said, "Okay, you've only got another week." And so then, for the rest of it, Mac, which is his nickname, started just doing key scenes, you know, that he and I would choose together.

"I didn't go to Georgia," Rauch clarifies, "Everything was by express mail in those days, but it was actually pretty fast and dependable, a day or two at most, coast-to-coast. It was mostly me sending pages, and Monte marking them up or checking in with comments and a call." Faced with the time-crunch they zeroed in on the scenes with Frank's fiancée, Mary Elizabeth. "The Mary Elizabeth character deserved better treatment," insists Rauch,

> On the one hand, it was important to show that she cared for Frank because her feelings for him give us permission to find him somewhat sympathetic. At the same time, we wanted to guard against the stereotype of the loyal, ever-patient, good-hearted woman back home waiting for her no-account rambling man to finally settle down. Frank is an enigmatic, seriously challenged individual, and sorting *him* out, much less their relationship, was always going to be complex. Obviously, the through-line of the book and the movie is the journey of a self-destructive man who throws all that he values into cockfighting and rejects the love of a woman who sees something redeemable in him.

Among the changes added by Hellman and Rauch were an expanded porch scene where Frank is reunited with Mary Elizabeth. The scene existed in Willeford's version but was expanded to give Mary Elizabeth a more obvious hesitance in confronting Frank through sly, passive-aggressive jabs that betray her struggle with being left behind and neglected. This scene also features the sole departure from Frank's habitual stoicism that Willeford spoke out against in his *Cockfighter Journal*, wherein Frank jumps around his senile would-be mother-in-law's car like a monkey, which the author saw as a mockery of the old lady that went against Frank's character. The other major expansion was the scene at 'the Place' — the waterfront hideaway where the pair have their dreamy, sun-drenched love scene. Again, this scene is in both the book and Willeford's earlier scripts, but it is much funnier and more poignant in the Hellman/Rauch version, again due to Mary Elizabeth's conflict about how much she can push Frank without the risk of losing him altogether. In an exaggerated Southern drawl, she tells a childhood anecdote that hints at a morbid cheekiness not seen elsewhere in the script:

> Did I ever tell you about Johnny Owen? Boy who peed on the wall in study hall? Teacher wouldn't let him go to the bathroom. So he kept raisin' his hand, sayin' 'teacher, I can't hold it, I ain't kiddin,!' So finally, she wouldn't let him go to the bathroom after 30 minutes, and he just got up, and walked back to the corner, and peed on the wall. She took him down to the principal's office, and Mr. Tomlin says, 'Son, YOU are expelled!' And he said, 'I don't give a shit, I'm gon' join the Marines!' And he jumped in his '52 chevy, started out to San Diego, and then when he got to New Mexico, he ran into a bridge post and killed himself. He never woulda made a Marine anyhow, I maintain. I think it was suicide. You know what it proves? The value of self-control. If he hadn't had to pee, he'd be alive today!

When I ask Rauch if he was responsible for Mary Elizabeth's anecdote, at first he can't quite recollect, but when I send him a transcript of it, he is surprised to recall that not only did he write it, it's actually a true story. "A high school classmate of mine!" he reveals, "It's all true! I've told that true story many a time."

It's especially interesting to me that for people allegedly working toward different goals — the producer and the auteur, with all that implies, respectively — both were mining the same book for guidance: namely, Siegfried Kracauer's *Theory of Film*. Monte himself told me this was his filmmaking 'bible,' and was surprised when I told him that it was also Corman's; Corman typically advised all first-time screenwriters to read it, including Willeford. Published in 1960, Kracauer's book is both contemplative and opinionated, but far from being an 'instructional' book in the sense of a traditional screenwriting guide, it instead digs into the bigger psychological and philosophical questions of how films communicate to us, and the opportunities that film has compared to other mediums. He specifically addresses the concept of adapting novels to film, and even if Willeford didn't read the whole book (it's rather lengthy) he undoubtedly skipped ahead to this section. Kracauer maintains that the novel has "four formal (or structural) properties which resist stubbornly translation into cinematic language," referring to time, space, tempo and point of view. He says that the novel can be experimental with time, whereas the only destabilising device a narrative film can utilise is the 'flashback' (which *Cockfighter* does). As noted previously, *Cockfighter* all takes place according to a specific schedule, with the motel room flashback as its sole departure into a 'time before' which necessarily condenses a lot of information we need to understand Frank's motivation, and the rippling impact of failure on a perfectionist.

The latter formal challenge — that of point of view — is met by a voiceover narration that, according to surviving correspondence, the production wavered on before ultimately deciding it was necessary. As Kracuaer says, there are certain "psychological events which no combination of physical data would be able to connote."

"I think we could have done more to understand Frank in two ways," offers Rauch,

> by exploring the nature of gambling addiction, and engaging him in conversation. The idea of keeping him mute in the movie was a mistake in

> my view. Let Warren Oates speak! My compromise suggestion to Monte was to allow Frank to at least converse with his birds in private. It could have been funny and revealing and a way to inject some humanity and vulnerability into his character.

Kracauer points to the novel-to-film adaptation of *The Grapes of Wrath* as an example of how "collective misery, collective fears and hopes" manifest in group behaviour that is easier to show onscreen. But perhaps this is why the film's depiction of Frank Mansfield's milieu convinces, and why Hellman was happiest with those documentary-like elements that portrayed the collective.

As production manager Peter Cornberg understood it, Frances Doel had been sent down to Atlanta to work with Hellman on the script and to report back to Roger on a daily basis. But that isn't quite how it shook out. Doel continued to work directly with Charles Willeford, while Hellman and Rauch hammered away separately. She remembers there being a complete disconnect between the dueling script revisions. "On location, I talked with [Willeford] every day or every morning, every afternoon," she told me, "And he would start writing and hand in five pages in the morning, five pages in the afternoon. So, I didn't let him race ahead. I just had to make sure that he did what we talked about, which basically he did. I mean, it was not a difficult process, but I worked much more closely with him right before we started shooting when we were actually on location, while everybody else was there doing their own pre-production."

Doel was aware that Hellman and Rauch were working on revisions independently, but assumed it was being done *without* Corman's knowledge or approval. For her part, she ignored it and focused on coaching Willeford. Since it was Willeford's first time writing a script, she could understand if Hellman wished to work with someone else, but said, "I don't think it was ever really on the table" — which seems evident in retrospect. This fractured writing process was making Peter Cornberg quite nervous. "Monte and Roger were continually revising their ideas about what the film was going to be," he recalls, "And Monte, I think, wanted to have it be much more romantic and symbolic than Roger ever would have imagined. The script controversy continued almost till the last minute."

As Hellman described it, Corman halted the rewrites, giving them one more week to finish up. Monte could never get the script where he wanted to, and as such, has always viewed *Cockfighter* as "incomplete."[59] Among other things, the director maintained that the film was crippled by a screenplay that didn't really get going until 40 minutes in, making the film top heavy and seemingly plodding. Still, Hellman told me, "I learned never to argue with a producer who had already made up his mind." They adjusted to the reality of Corman's timeline.

"I greatly enjoyed working with Monte," Rauch reflects. "We shared a sense of dark humour, and I certainly didn't take the job for the money. Now, based on Corman's comments and his famous tight budgets, I am left to wonder whether Monte paid me himself. If so, I'm doubly grateful — grateful for the kind gesture, and grateful he didn't

59 **How long Hellman and Rauch initially had to work on the script changed in different retellings, but he was consistent in asserting that there was a confrontation in which Roger gave them week to finish.**

tell me. He was a good and generous man in many ways."

The final screenplay does not deviate extensively from Willeford's. Neither Hellman nor Rauch would receive a screenwriting credit, which Corman ascribed to the fact that their changes were quite minimal. "They did rewrite a couple of scenes," Corman admitted, "but it was not a major amount of work that would have deserved a credit for screen writing. That's fairly common, incidentally — having directed so many films myself, I would very often make little changes in the script somewhere after a rehearsal and so forth. So what Monte did was just that sort of thing."

"There was a bit of acrimony, nothing terribly serious, because Roger is never anyone's fool," recalls Peter Cornberg, "And Monte is very laid back and graceful. So between the two of them, they didn't allow it to get totally out of control. Though I don't know what personal, intimate kind of crazy conversations they could have had about it."

But according to Hellman, there was a scene. In his recollection, after Corman read the last of the rewrites, he "came into the production office the next morning, did not say a word, he just took the script and threw it with all his might against the far wall, walked out the door, got in is car and drove to the airport and flew back to L.A. He was absolutely furious about what we'd done to the ending particularly."[60]

First AD Don Walters corroborates this story:

> Roger came pumping into headquarters and said to Sam Gelfman, 'You better shoot this fast and really, really cheap because it's not very good.' And he threw the script across the room. I just figured afterwards that this was Roger's deal since he was not going to be there to control everything, which he liked to do. He wanted to scare everybody into thinking they better do their jobs really fast and well. 'Cause he didn't waste any time. Normally on a regular film with a pretty good budget, you're doing 10 setups a day maybe. And he wanted us to do 25. Which means *move, move, move, move, move.*
>
> Frances Doel: That was very characteristic of Roger — on many occasions I've seen him throw scripts at the wall! Including when Dick Miller was writing something for him: "Dialogue, dialogue, dialogue!"
>
> Beverly Gray: Roger was notorious for throwing scripts at walls. So that wouldn't have been the first or the last time.
>
> Frances Doel: He can be very emotional.

Corman nevertheless maintained that this story is apocryphal. "The script that ended up on the screen was essentially Willeford's script," the producer asserted. "Monte did make some minor dialogue changes, which I approved. I think the ending of the film was pretty close to what the script was, I don't remember — of course it was many, many years ago — but I don't recall any major change in the ending of the film." This bears out in reading several drafts of the script: the last line in Willeford's version, as Frank hands Mary Elizabeth the cock's head, is "Here's my heart."

60 **Hellman, Monte. *Cockfighter* commentary, Anchor Bay edition.**

Furthermore, if Roger left the set after a couple days, this would not be unusual. Hellman himself has acknowledged that while Corman would often be more hands-on at script stage, he would usually not reappear until the first edit of the film to make suggestions. "One of the things that made Roger great was that it was just Roger you had to deal with," said Hellman on the Anchor Bay commentary. Corman could make decisions on the spot, there was no time-wasting bureaucracy. And though Corman supposedly hated the ending of *Cockfighter*, Hellman said, "To his credit he never made us change it."

As to whether Willeford had any problems with the rewrites, Hellman said he didn't remember any specific reaction. "Since the script was set by the time I met Charles, I only related to him as an actor," he offered. Likewise, Willeford doesn't mention any such disappointment in the pages of *Cockfighter Journal*. He seemed happy enough getting a front row seat to the whole process, which few authors are afforded. "He was so unobtrusive, but just so ready to be of help on the set," says Frances Doel. "If a line change was needed, he wasn't persnickety at all about an actor adapting or changing a line if it sounded more natural to them. He would encourage it. He was just a really good presence on the set, you know?"

Willeford functioned as an observer, and ultimately, a chronicler of the whole experience. Despite living with the character of Frank Mansfield for well over a decade, he brought no baggage, nor any expectations to the production. If he was secretly hoping that *Cockfighter* would function as a gateway to other film adaptations, he kept such ambitions to himself. Instead he watched as others squabbled and fretted, catastrophes were presented and assailed, and a peerless illustration of obscure Americana materialized before his eyes.

Above: Charles Willeford arrives on the set of *Cockfighter*.

HATTANOOGA
113
121
129
120
124
131
130
122
125
119
123
LLE
128
118
126
127
ATLANTA
M
GEORGIA
MACON
RY

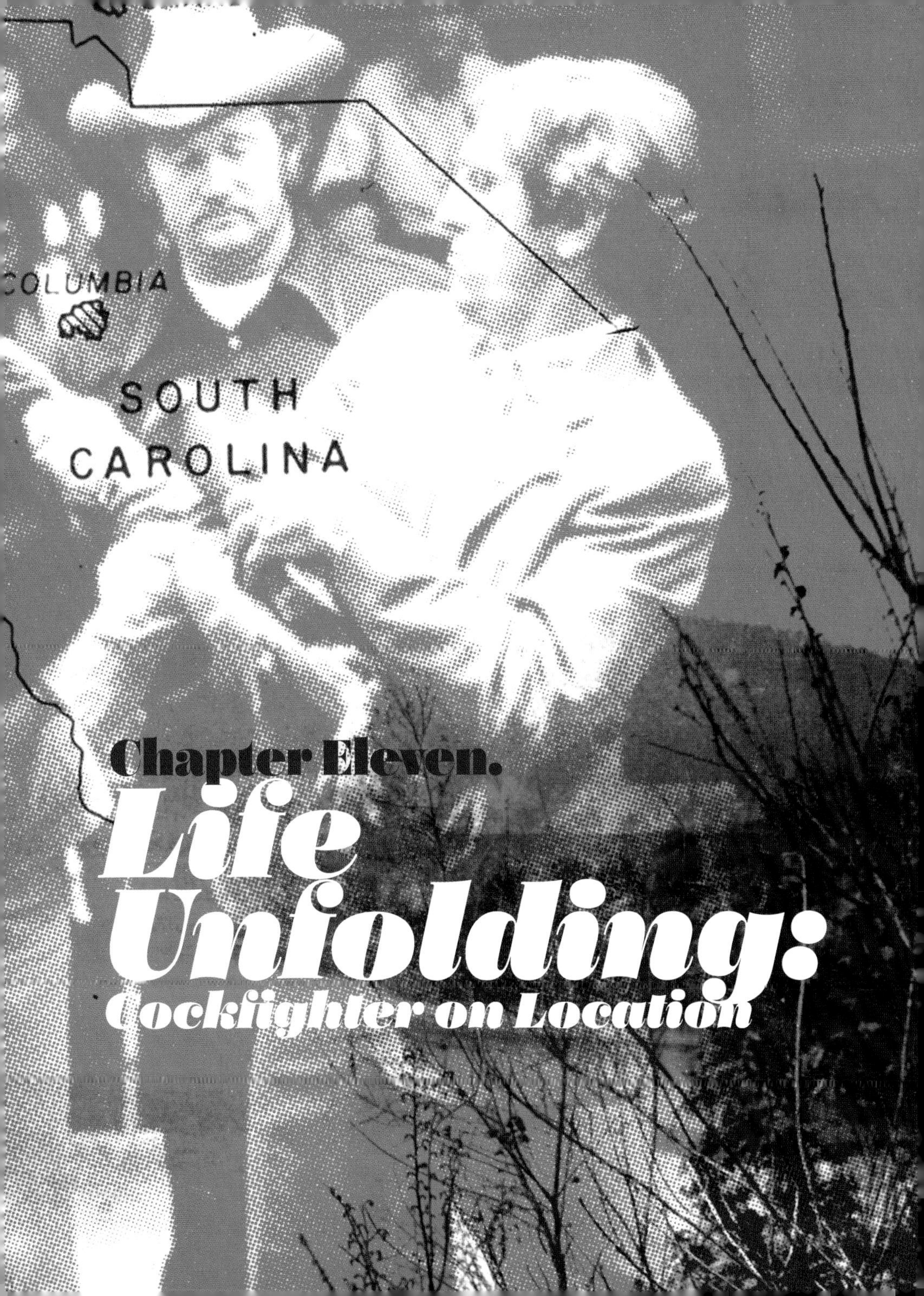

COLUMBIA

SOUTH CAROLINA

Chapter Eleven.

Life Unfolding:

Cockfighter on Location

Hellman did most of the casting in New York in early March 1974, after which he went to Georgia for three weeks of prep. Hellman had a stubborn relationship with casting that was evident on earlier productions; the casting director for *Two-Lane Blacktop*, Fred Roos — who had also cast *Zabriskie Point* — said Hellman was "harder to please than Antonioni."[61]

"The movie was Monte's and he knew what he wanted," casting director Michael Chinich commented cryptically, "Unfortunately haven't seen the movie since then and don't recall the details." Neither he nor his co-casting director Don Phillips cared to participate in an interview for this book, the latter only offering that, "It was my least favorite of all the films I worked on!" The two had first worked together on Otto Preminger's 1971 film *Such Good Friends* and would go on to have a major impact on the teen films of the 1980s; they both cast *Animal House* in 1978, with Philips going on to cast *Fast Times at Ridgemont High* in 1982 (and later *Dazed and Confused*) and Chinich executive-producing four John Hughes films, including *Pretty in Pink* — for which *Cockfighter* alum Harry Dean Stanton found himself playing deadbeat dad to '80s it-girl Molly Ringwald.

Stanton was perfectly cast as Frank Mansfield's rival Jack Burke. Less driven or desperate than Mansfield, Burke's even-tempered business sense nonetheless finds itself upended by the seeming impulsiveness of his enigmatic opponent. Even when Mansfield loses, Burke can't quite escape the suspicion that he's been had; the liminal space of the professional pushover. Stanton excelled at conveying this particular brand of confusion. "He can be wide awake and still seem like he's half asleep," said Hellman of Harry Dean, and indeed there is a part of Stanton's characters that he forever keeps to himself — an interior life that we can only guess at through the exterior pathos he communicates. And he's certainly carved out his own character type, which is apparent even in roles as varied as an impotent junkie (in *Cisco Pike*, 1972) a phony preacher (in *Wise Blood*, 1979) to a veteran repo man in Alex Cox' 1984 film of the same name. And famously, Stanton essayed his own portrait of a man emerging from a solemn vow of silence in Wim Wenders' *Paris Texas* (1984). But as for Cockfighter, Stanton has said in interviews that he can take or leave it.

Stanton had done two films with Oates by the time of *Cockfighter* (*Two-Lane Blacktop* and *Dillinger*) and the two were firm friends;

61 Compo, Susan. *Warren Oates: A Wild Life*. Lexington: University Press of Kentucky, 2009. Kindle.

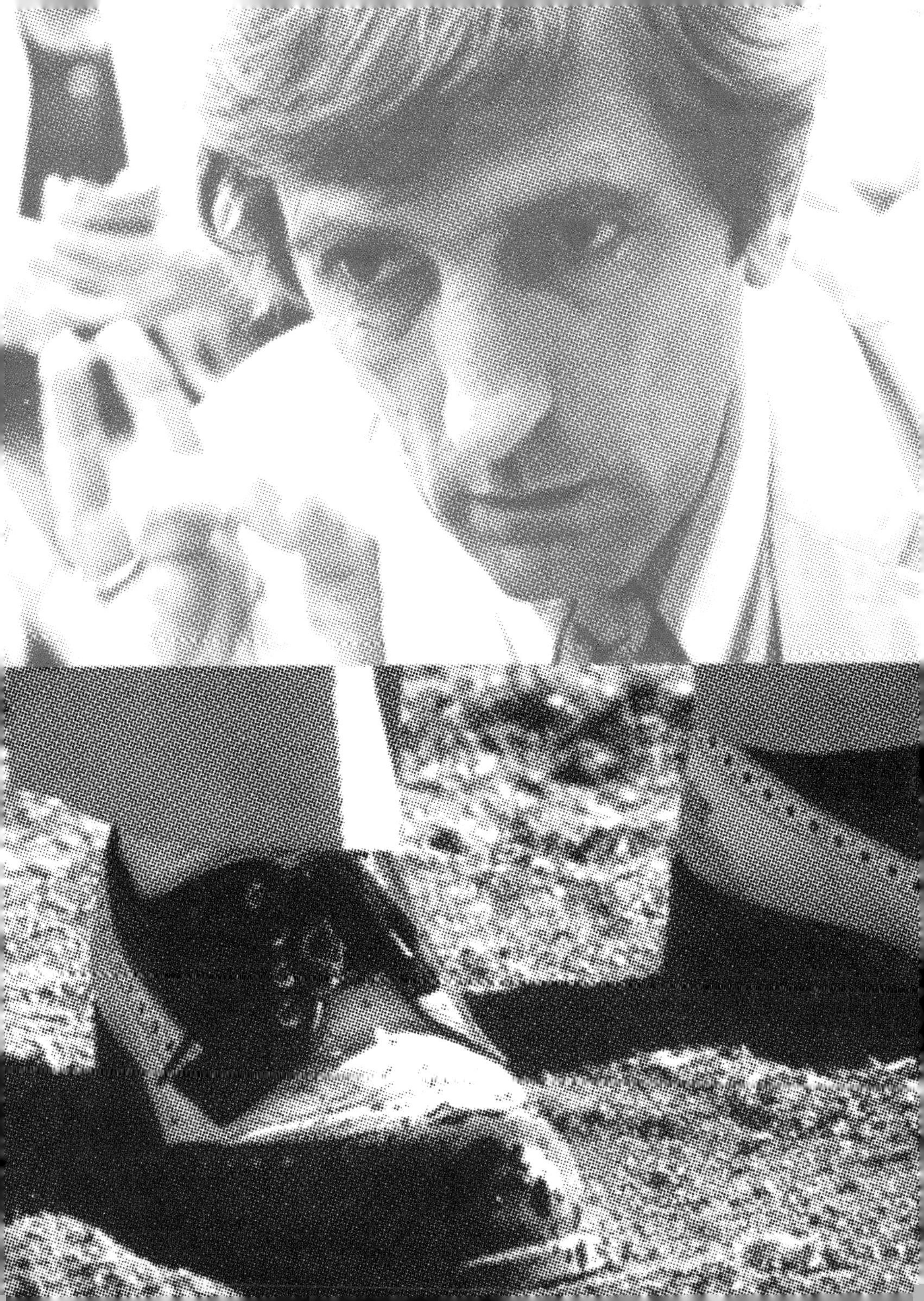

Harry Dean even gave Oates a guitar, which he would play after the day's wrap on set. "We both came from Kentucky," says Stanton, "Sort of the rural, country boys... And we drank together a lot. Had a few jars."[62] Still, the friendly rivalry between their characters in *Cockfighter* was also an element of their real-life relationship. "Harry Dean had an envy of Warren because he was frequently playing second banana to Warren," revealed Hellman. "He really didn't understand why it didn't work the other way around sometimes." And Harry Dean has admitted in interviews that when he appears in a film he plays to the actor opposite him, not the character that person is playing. "So, if it's Warren Oates playing a role," he says, "I play to Warren Oates, not the character... Because to me, it's more believable, more visceral."[63]

Richard B. Shull — who would play Frank Mansfield's cockfighting partner Omar Baradinsky with an exuberance that beautifully counteracts Frank's restraint — has a colourful resume that includes everything from crime capers (*The Fortune*, 1975) to teen sex comedies (*Spring Break*, 1983) to horror anthology shows (*Tales From the Darkside*, *Monsters*) and even music videos (Billy Joel's "Keeping the Faith"). In the '60s he appeared to travel in some exploitation film circles, appearing (uncredited) as a park rapist in 1965 mondo film *It's a Sick, Sick, Sick World* and co-writing the story for Anton Holden's 1966 roughie, *Aroused* — best known for its climactic scene prefiguring that of William Lustig's incendiary *Maniac* (1980). But by 1971 his acting career had taken off; after a role in Sidney Lumet's *The Anderson Tapes* he worked steadily in film and stage for the

next several decades, even heading up his own short-lived television series, *Holmes and Yoyo* in 1976. At the time of filming *Cockfighter* he was just coming off a spate of television appearances on *Good Times*, *Ironside* and *Love, American Style*.

Beverly Gray, a PhD student in American Literature at UCLA who'd been recruited as an assistant in the script department at New World, was given a jill-of-all-trades role on *Cockfighter*, which she remembers being one of her first assignments at the company.[64] Asked by Hellman to bring in Richard Shull for an audition, she recalls that,

> I looked through the classic book that casting people used to have, with the pictures and little bios and things. And I found Richard Schaal. I said, well, that's who he must have meant. So I called in Dick Schaal, Richard Schaal. And I kind of knew who he was because he was the husband of Valerie Harper. And this is at the time when, you know, *Rhoda* was a big deal.[65] I'd always kind of thought that must be interesting and awkward to be married to somebody who's just become a kind of meteoric

62 Qtd in Love, Damien. "The Wanderer: Harry Dean Stanton" in *Supporting Features: Writing and Interviews on Movies an Moviemakers*. 2016 Kindle edition, Loc 4345.
63 Love, Damien. "The Wanderer: Harry Dean Stanton".
64 She also went on to work at Concord New Horizons as the story editor in place of Franci Doel starting in 1986.
65 The TV series *Rhoda* didn't actually start until September 1974, after *Cockfighter*'s release, but the character Rhoda was well known from *The Mary Tyler Moore Show*.

> TV star. So he comes in and he looks really excited that somebody is wanting to interview him. And he got there and Monte was clearly thinking, 'That's not the guy I wanted. I wanted Richard Shull.' And here I could see right in front of me, this guy's heart breaking just a little bit.

Frank's African-American farmhand Buford was played by Robert Earl Jones, an actor and prizefighter who had been blacklisted by the House Un-American Activities Committee (HUAC) in the 1950s, and the father of actor James Earl Jones. The senior Jones was an early collaborator with poet and playwright Langston Hughes, an important figure of the Harlem Renaissance of the 1920s, as well as having early screen appearances in the all-Black films of Oscar Micheaux. The year before *Cockfighter* he had just turned in a memorable performance as Robert Redford's mentor in Oscar-winner *The Sting*. While Buford's role is not significant in terms of screen time, it is revelatory in other ways, which I'll get into in a later chapter.

Former matinee idol Troy Donahue was cast as Frank's brother Randall (purportedly a late addition to the cast[66]), his star having fallen considerably since the days of *A Summer Place* (1959) — his breakout film opposite Sandra Dee — and *Surfside 6* (1960), the television series that made him a household name. But the loss of regular studio support did open him up to some more interesting roles, such as that of a Manson-esque cult leader in the 1971 film *Sweet Savior*. "To say that Troy Donahue lacks the intensity to portray a messianic death-cult leader is a gross understatement," wrote film programmer Lars Nilsen, "He's so laid back he makes Peter Fonda look like a rabid Gila monster." Shortly afterwards, the actor moved to Atlanta where he lived off-and-on for the next few years, and which may have contributed to his casting in *Cockfighter*. His character's alcoholism in *Cockfighter* also reflected the drinking problem that had led to the demise of his marquee appeal. With a token role in former classmate Francis Ford Coppola's *The Godfather Part II* just completed, Donahue felt he was on the verge of a comeback.[67] "Fame will stick this time," he said on *The Merv Griffin Show*, "I'm better prepared for it now."[68]

The small role of Randall's wife was filled by Hellman alumna and longtime friend Millie Perkins (despite Willeford's misgivings that she was too good-looking for the part), who still had on-again/off-again romance with Oates stemming from their appearance in Hellman's *The Shooting*. But apparently even the occasion of sharing a screen with Warren Oates again was not memorable enough for Perkins to recall anything about the film. "I hardly remember shooting that movie," she conceded, "it had very little impact on me shooting that movie. What was my character? I didn't have much to do in that movie." It is true that for an actor of her stature, she wasn't given an especially meaty part. But it was important to Hellman that he be surrounded by familiar faces. "I like to work with the same actors as often as possible," he said. "It becomes like a family that keeps getting together for reunions."

That said, Perkins does not recall any particular camaraderie on set. "It just wasn't as intimate," she says, comparing it to her experience on *The Shooting* and *Ride in the Whirlwind*. "I only did it as a favor to

66 ***Hollywood Reporter*, April 1974.**

67 **Michaud, Michael Gregg. *Inventing Troy Donahue: The Making of a Movie Star*. Orlando: BearManor Media, 2023. Pg 402.**

68 ***The Merv Griffin Show*, August 27, 1974.**

Monte and it was hardly even anything that I focused in on very much, you know? I really didn't get into it emotionally at all."

Patricia Pearcy, who was cast as Frank's long-suffering love interest Mary Elizabeth, was a Southern-born actress, most active in the East Coast theatre scene.[69] At the time of casting for *Cockfighter* she had a recurring role on daytime soap *One Life to Live*, which was taped in New York City; *Cockfighter* would be her feature film debut. Even though she was far from the only performer never to have worked with her co-stars before, she would remain peripheral and alienated from the bulk of the other cast members in a way that mirrored the seclusion of her character. But Hellman rightly felt that her sensitivity and genuine Southern-ness would be essential for bringing the character to life.[70]

Allman Brothers singer/guitarist Dickey Betts happened to be around the set (due to the close proximity of the Allman Brothers' farm), and songwriter Donnie Fritts (who had appeared alongside Warren Oates in *Bring Me the Head of Alfredo Garcia*) had been recommended by his former co-star for a cameo, so the two musicians were recruited as extras and as robbers in the hotel room pit scene. Willeford was reportedly delighted to see Fritts in a small part, calling him a much better actor than his bandmate (and *Alfredo Garcia*/*Pat Garrett & Billy the Kid* co-star) Kris Kristofferson.[71] According to Willeford's *Cockfighter Journal*, Dickey Betts even offered to score the film, but composing duties fell instead to Michael Franks, later a key figure in the smooth jazz movement of the late '70s/early '80s. New World promotion man Jon Davison said it was likely that Franks came onboard through Hellman, as the choice of composer was usually a directorial decision, adding that, "if Dickey Betts wanted to do the music and Monte turned him down, that was a mistake!" In a 1975 book of interviews with Jack Nicholson, the authors refer to *Cockfighter* as a film "co-starring Millie Perkins and Richard Betts of the Allman Brothers," implying that Betts' presence was its own draw for the film. However Betts does not have much of a memory of the filming, according to his manager David Spero, who told me, "I'm sitting with Dickey and he said all he remembers about this was he was doing acid during the filming and in the crowd cheering. He doesn't recall how it happened that he was asked to be there."

The cast was rounded out by Steve Railsback and Ed Begley, Jr. ("He was a comic at the time, and he had me laughing all the way to the set," says Railsback of Begley, Jr.) as two of Frank's particularly unruly pit opponents. "I did not audition," Railsback recalls. "[Casting director Don] Phillips was a friend of mine and he just asked me if I'd do it. He said Warren Oates is in it, I said of course I'll do it!" Railsback was admittedly a fan of the film's star:

> There was just something about him that attracted me, and what I saw… working with Warren was an incredible experience. And I don't know how it happened, but we just became friends. As a matter of fact when I was wrapped and going back to New York, he took me to the airport in his camper. And he gave me this bottle of sloe gin in a paper bag and said 'just take it on the plane with you!' He was just an incredible man. When I first moved out here to do the miniseries *Helter-*

69 *Cockfighter*'s co-casting director Don Phillips would go on to champion Pearcy's then-romantic partner John Cazale for the role of Sal in *Dog Day Afternoon*.
70 I tried for seven years to get an interview with Pearcy; I left several phone messages for her (on a number that family members verified to be hers) and also offered a bounty to anyone who could get her to talk to me. Her voice is the one I most regret not having in this book.
71 Compo, Susan. *Warren Oates: A Wild Life*. Lexington: University Press of Kentucky, 2009. Kindle. Pg 292.

> *Skelter*, one of the first people that called me was Warren. He was such a great man and an incredible actor, and the two go together — you have to be grounded to be the kind of actor he was. It was just an incredible pleasure just to watch him and be there with him. He lights up the screen. Great actors do that. O'Toole was like that.

Begley Jr., the blond, gangly and (then) hard-partying son of Olympian actor Ed Begley happily accepted the invitation, largely because it allowed him to be on set with Harry Dean Stanton, a familiar drinking buddy from the side-by-side West Hollywood staples The Troubadour and Dan Tana's. "Like my dear friend Harry Dean Stanton, I went to Dan Tana's every night from 1971 through 1978," he recalls in his autobiography, "and like Norm in *Cheers*, we had both earned our seats at the bar there." He continues:

> Harry and I would always stay til last call, then head back to his place on Canyon Drive in the Hollywood Hills, where we'd watch movies on the Z Channel (a precursor to HBO) or simply leave the TV off and listen to a tape of Alan Watts. After years of this, Harry and I got roles in the same movie, a first for us, and we were out of town for some time with Warren Oates and Monte Hellman on *Cockfighter* (If you think that title is about something other than battling birds, I'm sorry to disappoint you).

Though Begley doesn't have much to say about *Cockfighter* in his memoir beyond this passing mention, he did put his photography background to good use by taking a terrific photo of Warren Oates resting in the driver's seat of his personal trailer (Begley had started out in his career juggling camera and acting roles, and even served as stills photographer on the Norman Lear-produced *Forever Fernwood*, a spinoff from *Mary Hartman, Mary Hartman*, in which Begley had a small role as Cathy's deaf-mute beau, Steve).

Oates drove that same trailer across the country and arrived in Georgia — incidentally his ex-wife Teddy and their children had recently relocated to Atlanta — in good time to prep for his role as Frank Mansfield. Most accounts have him staying in his own camper throughout the shoot rather than taking the production up on a hotel room. "Oates off the set was known as a friendly but shy man who was truly a loner," reported Phil Garner for the *Atlanta Journal-Constitution*. He drove himself to the film's various locations, with his dog — a collie mix named J.D. — by his side. The dog was named after John Dillinger, the character Oates was playing when this stray dog "wandered onto the set and into his new owner's heart."[72]

Willeford mentions several below-the-line crew members in his set journal: boom-man Richard Goodwin ("a heavily bearded young man… very dignified… He also plays the guitar and write songs"), production assistant Lois Zeitman ("very vivacious, with an education degree from the University of Tampa"), costumer Patty Shaw,[73] gaffer Hal Trussel, first assistant camera Leslie Otis, chief grip Bill Tharp (who "smiled, even though it is apparently against union

72 Compo, Susan. *Warren Oates: A Wild Life*. Lexington: University Press of Kentucky, 2009. Kindle.
73 He spells it 'Patti' in *Cockfighter Journal*.

rules for a chief grip to laugh or smile") art director/prop man Charlie Hughes ("as fat as an infantry company clerk"), assistant art director Drew Averett and more.

The last person hired on the film was production assistant Steven Gaydos, then a 22-year old Cal-Arts dropout who'd given up film studies to pursue songwriting in Nashville. As a Warren Oates fan, he'd seen Oates and Hellman on TV plugging *Two-Lane Blacktop* back in 1971. "It didn't look like anything I'd ever seen a Hollywood movie look like," he recalls, "and I wasn't all that well-versed in European cinema. I just didn't know what I was looking at." But, inspired by its odd pacing and desert vistas, he reached out to Monte, who invited him to meet up — and it sparked an enduring friendship that lasted until Monte's death. By the time *Cockfighter* started prep in 1974, Gaydos had caught wind of it and started lobbying for a job. "I was the only one who did not get a hotel room, not even to share," Gaydos laughs. "I was the driver of the film production Winnebago, which was this sort of rolling dressing room and green room. And I slept in it. So I wound up being the driver, and doing some set maintenance and set dressing as needed." Gaydos' dogs body job on the film extended to a role onscreen, in the hotel robbery alongside Fritts: "There is a still from the film with my big film debut," he says. "I'm wearing a Nixon mask as one of the gang that robs a cockfight. But I'm also wearing Nestor Almendros' French velvet suit."

Above: Warren Oates on the set of *Cockfighter*, photographed by Ed Begley, Jr.

The 26-day shoot began on Monday April 8, 1974 (there are various shooting schedules in Willeford's papers, and though there are discrepancies between them as the schedule changed, all list April 8th as the first day of shooting). The previous day's Palm Sunday had offered a brief spot of sunshine in an otherwise grim week; only days before, a powerful tornado had whipped through the northern end of the state, killing 16 people. It was part of what came to be called the 1974 Super Outbreak — the most violent tornado outbreak in recorded history, with 100 F4 and F5-level tornados in under 24 hours. Over 300 people would lose their lives in all. Weirdly no one I spoke to remembered the tornado, even though it could have totally derailed the shoot.

The biggest story in the Atlanta newspapers on April 8th was the arrival of baseball star Hank Aaron for the Atlanta Braves home opener that evening. There, Pearl Bailey would sing the national anthem, 1000 doves would be released, and Aaron would hit his 715th home run, beating Babe Ruth's record. All amid racist death threats. On page one of the *Atlanta Journal-Constitution*, the headline "Fussy Feathers" fortuitously accompanies a picture of two squabbling birds — in this case a pair of seagulls engaged in what the paper humourously describes as "a family fuss." And so the stage was set for *Cockfighter* to begin its 28 days in the Peach State.

The most immediate help the fledgling film commission could offer the production at that time was pointing them to suitable locations. "Normally you would hire a location scout and give that person a list of what you need," explained production manager Peter Cornberg, "rush him to get as much material as he can in a short period of time, because you need to make a judgement on his capabilities and his intuition and creativity in terms of doing the location thing, which

SCONSIN
GRAND RAPIDS
CANADA
NEW YORK
JAMESTOWN
MICHIGAN
DETROIT
CHICAGO
TOLEDO
CLEVELAND
FT WAYNE
PENNSYLVANIA
PITTSBURGH
OHIO
INDIANA
INDIANAPOLIS
DAYTON
COLUMBUS
XENIA
CINCINNATI
LINOIS
WEST
VIRGINIA
LOUISVILLE
BRANDENBURG
LEXINGTON
BECKLEY
ROANOKE
KENTUCKY
BOWLING GREEN
CORBIN
VIRGINIA
NASHVILLE
KNOXVILLE
TENNESSEE
NORTH
CAROLINA
ASHEVILLE
CHATTANOOGA
CHARLOTTE
HUNTSVILLE
ISSIPPI
GUIN
COLUMBIA
ATLANTA
SOUTH
CAROLINA
BIRMINGHAM
TUSCALOOSA
GEORGIA
ALABAMA
MACON
MONTGOMERY
SUPEROUTBREAK TORNADOES OF APRIL 3-4, 197
148 TWISTERS IN 24 HOURS
From the FINAL ED COLOR MAP by T.Theodore Fujita, The University of Chic

can make or break a film sometimes if it's not done correctly. So I always wanted to get there as soon as possible. We had a guy down there who I think we got through the Georgia State Film Commission, and he was great. He was a really, really nice guy, very laid back, knew the area very well. I can't remember how much he knew about fighting chickens, but none of us knew much at the beginning!" Cornberg recalls meeting with cooperation at all the locations, which he had scouted a month before everyone else arrived for prep.

Willeford's set diary places Julie and Roger Corman on set at the beginning of the shoot, where the author was also present as a 'technical advisor'. Corman celebrated his birthday in Atlanta in the prep days immediately before shooting began (his birthday is April 5), which was also the day Willeford arrived in Atlanta. Willeford got along well with the husband and wife duo, but he noticed that everyone else on set seemed terrified of Roger. Though Willeford's *Cockfighter Journal* labels production manager Peter Cornberg as "hysterical" (more diplomatically referred to as "very stressed-out" by first AD Don Walters) Cornberg recalls having pleasant, if superficial interactions with the veteran writer. "He was kind of a good ol' boy," says Cornberg, "but he was also an intellectual and he always had interesting things to talk about." This good ol' boy quality in Willeford would serve him well on set, especially with the chicken fighters who recognised and revered him; Willeford finds he has fans among the local cocker population. None of them believed he had never himself raised or fought gamefowl before, given the level of detail in the book. They just thought he wouldn't admit it due to its wavering legality. "Charlie knew a lot of those guys and he had written the book and he had spent a lot of time around that whole area," says first AD Don Walters. "And he was a wonderful guy. Luckily he was on the set all the time, smoking his cigar and tweaking his whiskers, big, big, tall guy and a little portly, but really smart. And he knew the powers and who you had to talk to and who you had to stay away from."

Given their experience with local crews, both Don Walters and Peter Cornberg were hired onto *Cockfighter* immediately after *Moonrunners*, which although completed earlier, suffered distribution woes and wasn't released until 1975. They joined PR man-turned-producer Sam Gelfman, who was making his second picture with Corman (he had also worked on *Caged Heat*, which was released just as *Cockfighter* began production). "*Cockfighter* was a co-production between Sam Gelfman — who I guess brought in some of the money — and Roger," Cornberg explains, "Sam functioned as line producer; he was on location for the whole shoot, as I recall. And because I guess I had impressed the Cormans, they gave me a shot at being production manager. So that's how I got involved."

I ask Cornberg to clarify what a production manager and first AD do. "The production manager is directly responsible to the producer for budget control and is accountable in theory for all the money that's spent," he says,

> The production manager should know where all that goes, and normally has

there wasn't much of that on *Cockfighter*, Monte is pretty laid back and, well, more intellectual. I was going to say benign, but he's not benign because he obviously has accomplished quite a bit in the business. But he's very laid back and he's very graceful and kind to people — which I've learned since then is a bit of an exception.

First AD Don Walters said he also shot second unit, "things like cars going one place or another and, you know, chickens — part of the cockfighting and getting stuff that fills in the gaps." He continues:

> We didn't get enough of the cockfighting itself, which is why they had to fill in, in California. And that was hard because it's hard to get those guys to really let you in on what's going on. And so, if you hire other people to stand in, which they tried to do, it didn't work very well. So it wasted a lot of time. And of course, anything that wastes time with Roger Corman, it's a waste of time and he doesn't want to hear about it. So luckily he was in California for most of the shoot.

Nestor Almendros came to the set straight from Africa where he'd been shooting Barbet

> an accountant who does all that stuff on a picture like that. I didn't have an accountant, most of the first low budget things I did, we never had accountants, there's always somebody back in an office who sent us money on a regular basis, paid certain bills. And I would just send regular production reports back so that Roger and his people would know where we were at in terms of schedule and budget. And generally production manager makes the first schedule.

He continues:

> The first AD basically is responsible for keeping on schedule on a day to day basis. The first AD and the director beat each other up on a regular basis, depending on the film — although

Above: Production manager Peter Cornberg and sound mixer Lee Alexander on the set of *Cockfighter*.

Schroeder's documentary on Idi Amin. "He was suggested by Roger, and I couldn't have been more delighted," said Hellman. "I've had the good fortune to have worked with some of the world's greatest DPs. The DP is always my most important collaborator, along with the actors."

Cockfighter would be Nestor Almendros' second picture for Roger Corman, the first being a 1968 cash-in on the hit film *Grand Prix* (1966) called *The Wild Racers* starring Mimsy Farmer and Fabian. Frances Doel recalls being the one to hire Almendros at that time: "We were shooting in about five or six countries," she explains, shooting the races and then in between shooting the dramatic scenes, moving from country to country. And when I went over to France, Roger told me to meet up with Pierre Cottrell, who had met Roger at some film festival, I think. And Roger liked him and Pierre really wanted to work in movies. He had worked with Eric Rohmer and so he introduced me to [people], in terms of finding a crew, which was part of the job I had to do, as well as finding locations and hotels and all of that. So I had Pierre's help and he introduced me to Nestor Almendros and Daniel Lacambre because, as you know, Nestor is a great cinematographer,

Above: Director Monte Hellman and cinematographer Nestor Almendros on the set of *Cockfighter*.

but his eye problem doesn't make him really well equipped for hanging on the back of a car or shooting like that, which Daniel Lacambre did, and Nestor was the lighting director.

On *Cockfighter* Almendros would serve as both cinematographer and camera operator. Corman knew that having a cinematographer of Almendros' calibre was a huge boost to the film, and as it happened, it even worked out financially for the famously frugal producer. "Nestor was very crucial to the whole thing," Corman recalled. "It's the first picture he ever shot in the United States and I remember I was thinking, I'm gonna have to fly in a cameraman from Hollywood, as there weren't so many good cameramen at that time in the backwoods of Georgia. And I'd worked with Nestor in Paris, and other countries in Europe, and he's the best cameraman I know — it isn't going to cost me much more to fly Nestor to Atlanta, Georgia than it would to fly someone from Hollywood to Atlanta, Georgia."

Of course as a European, getting Almendros the requisite work visa would have been an obstacle outside the budget of the average Corman production, and so he was snuck onto the production without one.

"I called Nestor and told him what we were doing and asked him if he'd like to do it," explains Corman, "and he said 'I'd love to do it, but I don't have a green card!' And I said, Nestor, in the backwoods, the red hills of Georgia, they don't even know what a green card is! Just come in as a tourist, we will meet you at the Atlanta airport, we will drive you straight to the location, you'll shoot the picture, then we'll drive you back to the Atlanta airport and you can go back to Paris. So he laughed, he said, "I can do that!"

It wasn't Almendros' first time trying to get work on American pictures. "Before that he had come to Los Angeles without a visa, hoping to get work as a cinematographer," says Frances Doel, "but he couldn't, he ended up working in a shoe store for a long time.

Above: Camera crew on the set of *Cockfighter*, photo by Charles Willeford.

And then actually the first thing he shot in Los Angeles was kind of a soft porn film that I worked on. I forget what the title was, we shot two versions of it, one that could be cut as an R-rated release, and then one that would be released in the Pussycat Chain. So that was the target, but it was kind of fun. We shot it on weekends. And Nestor was a very good sport about it!"

Almendros was completely committed to *Cockfighter*, accompanying Roger, Julie and Monte on the original scouting trip to Georgia.[74] "I found myself again facing the rather tacky but extraordinarily photogenic image of contemporary Americana," he said in his autobiography, *A Man with a Camera*, "billboards, gas stations, cafeterias, etc; to say nothing of those small Roma circuses, the cockpits."

"I can't remember how much time he had with us in advance," says Peter Cornberg of Almendros, "but I loved him." This sentiment was attested to by the fact that Cornberg teared up in our interview remembering the beloved cameraman. "I haven't thought about him in a long time," he says, apologising for the pause. "One of the most professional, beautiful people I ever met in that business. He was wonderful. We talked about the sun coming up and the sun going down and paid a lot of attention to the weather and light. And he was just an amazing kind of person, that expanded my experience in the business just dramatically."

Almendros is one of the few above-the-line crew who have spoken of *Cockfighter* with fondness and enthusiasm. "For him, I think it was because of the fact that he was functioning on a different level altogether than most everybody else was," suggests Walters,

And the fact that he was European and all the rest of it, everybody was super impressed that he was not highfalutin' or Hollywood or anything like that. He was really down and dirty and could improvise with the best of them. And so I think he had a pretty good time, because he didn't have to put up with all the crap. He just got to get his eye on the camera and go. It was very funny because this is a DP from Europe who was doing this silly stuff, it didn't bother him. He thought it was fun.

His work ethic spoke for itself; Almendros had eye problems ("he was blind as a bat," says Walters) and it was hard for him to work long hours, but he nonetheless pulled 16-hour days on occasion, acting as his own camera operator and setting up the lights for the next day once each day had wrapped. "Nestor's camerawork was crucial to the film, I thought the photography was brilliant," said Corman. Almendros, who had worked with important French New Wave directors such as Truffaut and Chabrol, was a firm adherent of Truffaut's auteur theory — a theory which would be sorely tested on *Cockfighter* as Hellman ultimately came to see the film more as Corman's picture than his own. Still, Almendros always spoke of Hellman in an auteurist capacity, calling him "one of the most interesting personalities among contemporary American film-makers... I knew an artist like Hellman would be able to do something even within severe commercial limitations. The schedule was very tight, particularly for a film with such varied locations and difficult scenes... we had to shoot for twelve, fourteen, even sixteen hours a day."[75]

74 Monte did not recall this trip at all; as a result I am led to believe that what Almendros (and also Roger) referred to as a "scouting trip" was actually just the prep period where they arrived in the area weeks ahead of shooting.

75 Almendros, Nestor. *Man with a Camera*. Farrar-Straus-Giroux, New York, 1984. Pg 134.

Unfortunately Almendros was saddled with an inexperienced crew, which resulted in shots being unusably out of focus, and shooting time being lost due to other errors. "Like most of Roger Corman's productions, it had to be filmed in a very short time," Almendros wrote in his autobiography. "Four weeks — in real locations. The non-union crew was made up of beginners with more enthusiasm than skill." Hellman was sympathetic to his DoP's struggles. "We were slowed down by the problem that the people working with him weren't familiar with his methods," said Hellman in a 1976 *Jump Cut* interview, "and also by the fact that they were really the most inexperienced crew that we could have had. They were fresh out of film school, and some of them were just incompetent, particularly the camera crew. I wasn't happy with the crew except for Nestor; he was terrific."

For his part, Almendros never bemoaned the situation, he just accepted it and moved on — but Hellman was furious. However, he knew it would take his whole salary to replace the crew if he fired them, as according to their contracts they would have to be paid out for the full four weeks either way — in addition to the costs of securing new crew members from LA.

Having no control over the selection of the crew was also unusual for Hellman, but he had gone along with the film's constraints because he liked the material. But despite the lack of an experienced crew, Almendros seemed to appreciate that, at least in a bigger picture sense, Roger's methods served his chosen medium well. "Almost all the new talent of American movies got their start with him," Almendros wrote, "because he is the only anomaly that Hollywood allows."[76]

Almendros always regretted that the quick shooting schedule, combined with the limitations of a novice crew and less-than-stellar equipment, made his work seem "less carefully executed than usual," but

Above: Warren Oates and Charles Willeford on the set of *Cockfighter*.

76 **Almendros, Nestor. *Man with a Camera*. Farrar-Straus-Giroux, New York, 1984. Pg 133.**

said that despite those circumstances, he was pleased with some of his lighting and composition. "Sometimes intuition is a more than adequate substitute for reflection in the creative arts," he wrote in his autobiography, adding that the quick shooting schedule prompted him to adopt the American practice of "asking the laboratory always to print the rushes in one light," so that when the workprint is assembled, more uniform instructions can be given about whether it needs to be lighter or darker, certain colours pulled back or saturated further. It is a practice he continued after *Cockfighter*.

Though Peter Cornberg lobbied for the role of set photographer ("I had made a deal with Roger to shoot stills on the film because I had worked as a photographer"), he lost out to Monte's girlfriend Laurie Bird. While it's possible Bird took a ton of photos that never made it into circulation, the fact remains that official *Cockfighter* stills, not to mention any behind-the-scenes documentation, are hard to come by. "What a shame," Cornberg sighs. "Because we shot in Georgia, which is a very green, lush state and these cockpits, some of the ones that we shot in, could have been there a hundred years. So there was a lot of material, and some of the good ol' boys that we met and worked with, they would have been great photo opportunities for a good photographer."

The actors were all charged with picking out their own costumes, but according to Willeford's *Cockfighter Journal*, Laurie Bird was told to bring hers back, "because they were too expensive." The actress took this as a grievous affront over which she would get the costumer Patty Shaw fired from the film. Shaw had previously worked with production manager Peter Cornberg and first AD Don Walters on *Moonrunners*. When asked if he recalls this incident, Cornberg gives an audible sigh. "Yeah. There was an awful, *awful* bit of stuff there that went on for a period of time. Monte was madly in love with her, infatuated for his reasons and was convinced that she was a great actress [sighs again] and she could do no wrong."

Willeford commented that Hellman was clearly under Bird's influence; while recognizing his talent as a director, the author lamented that he was "weak-willed as a man."[77] Bird was the only person on set that Willeford actively disliked; he saw her as a rude brat at odds with the camaraderie elsewhere on set. Even the extras complained about Laurie Bird. In the *Atlanta Journal-Constitution*, one of the extras — the wife of one of the cockfighters making his acting debut — commented on how nice everyone was, "all except that little skinny girl, what's her name... That Dody, she's snooty. I don't know why. She's just a child. And she doesn't talk to anybody except that boy with the fuzzy head." The boy, of course, being director Monte Hellman.

Still, Willeford admitted she was great in the role.

Another actor — likely a local Southerner, as with many of the smaller parts, according to Roger — was originally cast as the referee Ed Middleton, but Hellman claimed to have fired him the night before the shoot because "something wasn't right."[78] But since Willeford was on set — and already had a planned cameo as Peach Owen, president of the Southern Conference Cockfighting Association — Hellman offered the part to him. It was a significant step up, dialogue-

77 **Willeford, Charles. *Cockfighter Journal: The Story of a Shooting*. Santa Barbara: Neville Press, 1989. Pg 58.**
78 **Hellman, Monte. *Cockfighter* commentary, Anchor Bay edition.**

wise. As of April 9th, the second day of shooting, Willeford had the role. He gave a wholly naturalistic performance.

"There couldn't be anybody who'd be more perfect for it," conceded Hellman.[79] He was reportedly so natural that when his character reprimands Jack Burke, Harry Dean thought Willeford was really reprimanding him, despite Willeford's protests that he was just acting what was in the script. In a June 1974 *Publisher's Weekly* article talking about authors appearing as actors in films based on their work, Willeford joked, "If I'd known I was going to wind up *playing* Middleton, I'd have made him more important."

The first scene in the final shooting schedule[80] was that of Frank with Ed and Martha at the Middleton couple's house (which is why the first actor cast to play Ed was able to be fired so soon into filming). The location used in the film was the home of Ank Carlton, the owner of the cockpit in Toccoa, Georgia where the Plant City fight was shot. Carlton had been a cockfighter for 65 years, so no set dressing was needed.

The world of the film inevitably required that the cast members learned how to handle roosters well enough to bluff their way through a staged fight. Surprisingly they weren't given much time to get acclimatised to the particularities of the sport — in some cases only a few hours — but Oates took to it pretty quickly. Conversely, both Willeford and Hellman noted that Harry Dean Stanton remained uncomfortable holding the birds, but points out that this was within character, since the more prosperous Jack Burke has an occasional handler. "I wasn't crazy about that," Stanton said of the film's subject matter. "I don't like to see two chickens trying to kill each other. The only thing worse would be dogfights. Those aren't my cup of tea."[81]

"What the movie's about is something I had never seen," Steve Railsback says. "As an actor I was interested, but as a person I'm not." He had held chickens before — his grandmother had a farm — but nothing like the tough fighting birds in *Cockfighter*. He remembers training for one day and being told things like "to rub their backs and try to get them under my arm, and stuff like that. It was the technical advisor — he wanted me to get the feel of the rooster, I remember something about him telling me to kiss the rooster, having to hold the rooster close. It wanted to get away; roosters are tougher than chickens and it's hard to hold them." The cockfight with Railsback's character was shot with five cameras. "The trick," Hellman offered, "was not shooting another camera!"

On April 14th, Ed Begley Jr arrived on set, anxious for a couple reasons. Chief amongst them, he'd just come from a crime scene in LA… in his own back yard. A few days earlier, on April 9th, a neighbour was alarmed by a malodorous stench emanating from the (usually empty) trash can in the alley behind Begley's rented bungalow at 11059 ½ Fruitland Drive in Studio City (as a hardcore environmentalist even then, Begley boasted that he could fit a month's refuse in his glove box). Turns out the source of that odour was the dismembered body of the 17-year old Taunye Lynn Moore, who had been missing for a year. "The denial is so strong the first time you see something like this," Begley offered in his autobiography. "I'm staring at it all, and I was thinking 'Is that a

79 Hellman, Monte. *Cockfighter commentary*, Anchor Bay edition.

80 An earlier shooting schedule reflects an opening gas station sequence that was in the script but ultimately cut from the film.

81 Love, Damien. "The Wanderer: Harry Dean Stanton" in *Supporting Features: Writing ad Interviews on Movies and Moviemaking*. 2016 Kindle edition, Loc 4208.

large leather ottoman, surrounded by some smaller pillows...?'" When he realised what he was looking at, he says it "filled me with a sadness I had not yet known."

Secondly, Begley was concerned about having to do his own stuntwork in the scene where he goes after Oates with an axe, especially since, as he tells it, "I'm not certain that there was a stunt coordinator on the set. Warren called a halt to the sequence for a while until they made the axe safer with some tape. I believe he had cut his hand on it." As Oates' biographer Susan Compo says, the prop man had given them a fully sharp axe to use instead of a dulled one.

Everyone on *Cockfighter* had their own reason for being there, and the motley crew did their best to make a solid picture despite wildly varying levels of experience, baggage carried over from previous projects, and expectations that were at times at odds with each other. "It was a bad working situation because everybody was out of step, and it sort of remained that way all the way through," recalls Walters. "So I'm not surprised that Monte was not happy." He remembers some friction between Hellman and Oates in particular, which Millie Perkins confirms. "Warren used to fight with Monte and had arguments with him," she concedes, "Warren always spoke up and decided, you know, argued with him if he didn't agree with what Monte wanted him to do, he fought back. They really respected each other, but you couldn't tell Warren to do something that he didn't want to do. He wouldn't do it. He was his own person, very much so... they had a very volatile kind of creative relationship." Despite this, Hellman claimed that he and Oates only ever had one argument throughout their entire friendship (a brief difference of opinion on the set of *The Shooting*); which seems to indicate some disagreement about what constitutes a disagreement.

Out of everyone, Charles Willeford seemed to be enjoying himself the most, and as his

Above: Contact sheet depicting the CECO truck in a ditch toward the end of shooting.

Cockfighter Journal attests, he functioned as a sort of observant drifter, who kept himself safely above the drama of an often heated set. He flew home on May 3, "back to mundane reality, teaching D.H. Lawrence to bewildered strangers."

The last day of shooting was May 3, and was supposed to end with the motel flashback sequence, which would be shot in the Lithonia Holiday Inn where the crew was staying (although an earlier version of the shooting schedule places it on April 9th, along with gas station restroom and highway payoff scenes that were ultimately dropped entirely), but a location snag with 'the Place' led to the two scenes being swapped in the schedule (Behind the scenes contact sheets shared with me by AD Don Walters reveals the 'snag' was a production truck landing in a roadside ditch).

In a letter from producer Sam Gelfman to "Charlie" dated May 15, 1974, he tells Willeford he just watched eight hours of dailies and enthuses about how good they were — especially the scene at 'the Place'. He mentions it was an "extraordinarily trying day." They had to change locations at the last minute because they couldn't get the CECO-Mobile anywhere near it — this meant the scene got moved and shot the next day, thus the change in the shooting schedule. Gelfman continues that "Warren and Pat were terribly hesitant" to play the scene nude but they did it. "There wasn't a whole lot of chemistry between the two of them," admits Walters. "Everybody is supposed to get naked and roll around on a blanket by the lake. And Warren didn't want to do that. I don't think he was too happy with the way his body looked at that point. So there was a standstill and we couldn't figure it out. And I finally said, 'Wait a minute, what if it's the end of the love scene and they're getting dressed and talking.' And that seemed to appeal to Warren, because all he had to do was take his shirt off and put it back on. And Patricia liked that because she didn't actually roll around naked in the bushes. And that one worked out pretty well."

Sam Gelfman's letter to Willeford continues: "For once in Monte's career, the scene was shot in one take and one setup, and it's absolutely beautiful."

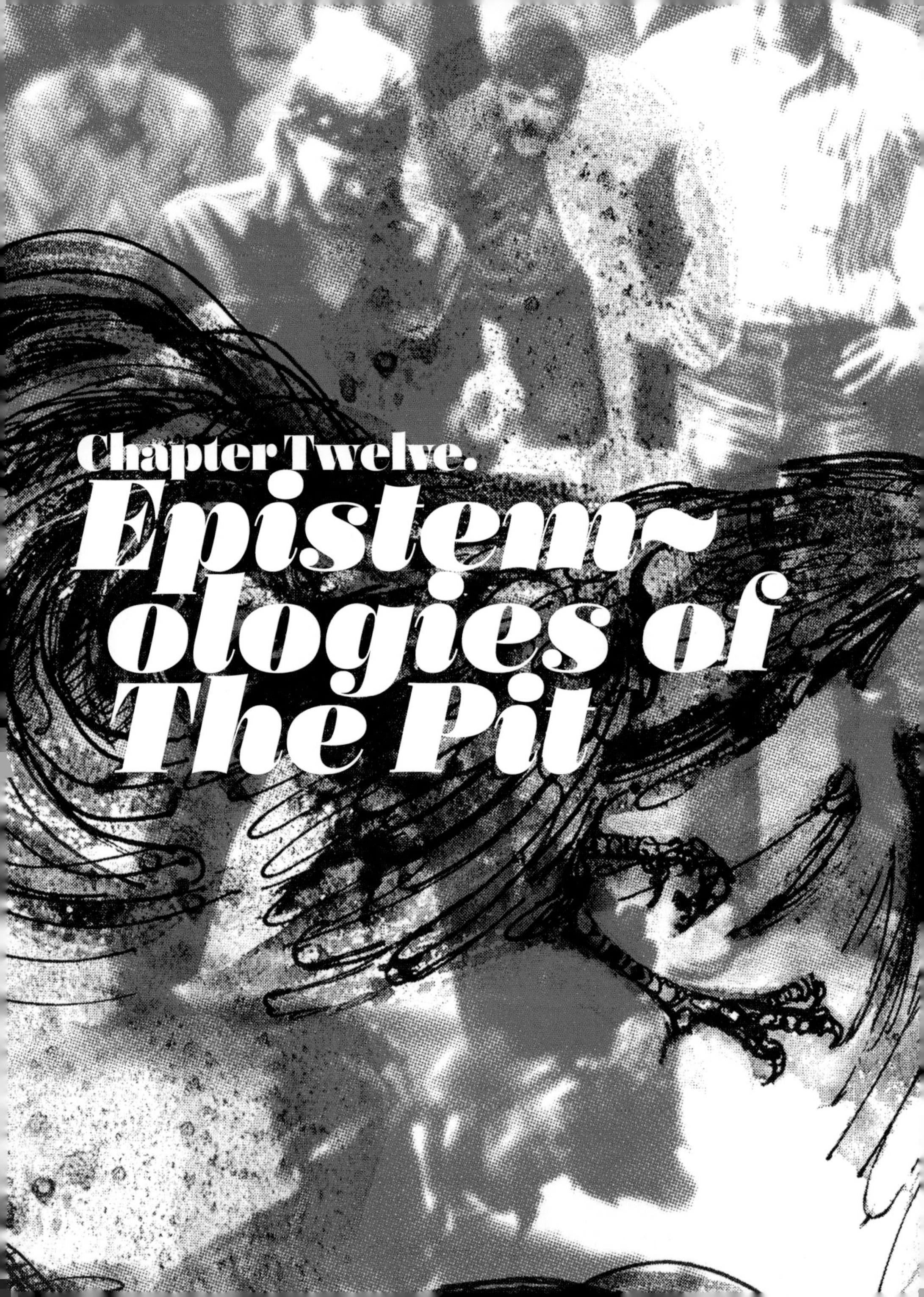

Chapter Twelve.

Epistem~ologies of The Pit

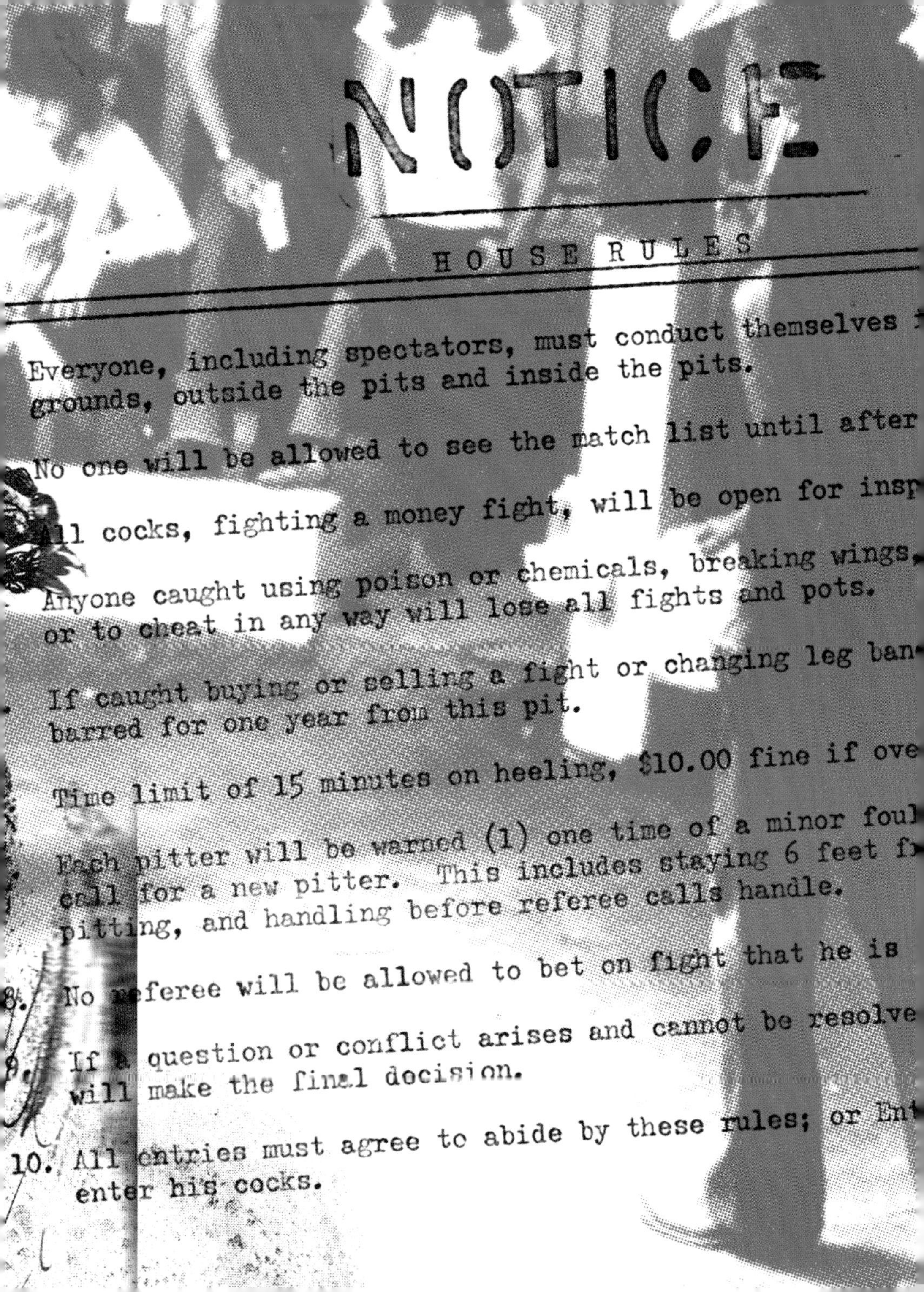

NOTICE

HOUSE RULES

Everyone, including spectators, must conduct themselves
grounds, outside the pits and inside the pits.

No one will be allowed to see the match list until after

All cocks, fighting a money fight, will be open for insp

Anyone caught using poison or chemicals, breaking wings,
or to cheat in any way will lose all fights and pots.

If caught buying or selling a fight or changing leg ban
barred for one year from this pit.

Time limit of 15 minutes on heeling, $10.00 fine if ove

Each pitter will be warned (1) one time of a minor foul
call for a new pitter. This includes staying 6 feet fr
pitting, and handling before referee calls handle.

8. No referee will be allowed to bet on fight that he is

9. If a question or conflict arises and cannot be resolve
will make the final decision.

10. All entries must agree to abide by these rules; or En
enter his cocks.

Did I tell you about the first time I went to the fights? We walked in, got our memberships — you had to be a member to enter but they were like $5 or something. I cannot remember the name of the first place we went. It was not The Bayou Club. But it was crowded, a circular pit with plexiglass all around it and bleachers on all sides. The stench of urine was overpowering, my nostrils were practically bleeding, that smell alone I thought would make me pass out. I didn't think I'd be able to stay in there five minutes. As we were looking for seats I walked past the pit and WHACK, a chicken smacked against the other side of the plexiglass right beside my head and left a bloodstain and I thought, holy shit, I am not going to be able to take this. I felt really gross, and it stank and I was like, what am I doing here. Why did I want to do this. And then we found a spot and I watched a couple matches and I found it so violent and barbaric. And when the fight would slow down they'd move those chickens into the drag to keep fighting while they brought a new fight into the main pit. Everyone was flashing hand signals at each other from across the pit, acknowledging each other when they won or lost because they'd have to settle up after, it was all on honour system, people bet against strangers.

So then Karrie said to me, "do you want to make a bet?" And I said "I only brought $10." And she said "that's ok, we can just bet each other a dollar." So I said ok, and we each picked what bird we wanted. We didn't do odds because I didn't know how that worked. And as soon as we shook on it, it was like a switch went off and I just wanted my bird to kill her fucking bird.

FOR A DOLLAR.

This is the price of humanity. Haha.

- Email from me to Jimmy McDonough, May 3, 2021.

The agility of this "switch" became the core of my obsession on a personal level. What preoccupied me was trying to discern how the disconnect happens. The compartmentalisation. How the barbarity of the sport — I hesitate to use the word cruelty, because I really don't think it's that — is rationalised, codified, and made acceptable to one's value system.

The fact is once the surface revulsion has passed and the physical sensation of burning nostrils is overcome it becomes obvious that what is at play in a cockfight is not just a group of sadists sitting around goading two birds to kill each other. There are thousands of years of history propping up this sport, the import of which is clung to by modern-day adherents, whether or not they could cite the specifics of that history.

Modern game cocks are descended from the red jungle fowl of what is now India and Pakistan, and evidence of human-engineered cockfighting has been found on seals and figurines in the region dating from over four millennia ago. One of the earliest recorded cockfights was in China in 517 BCE, at the same time that cockfights were being carried out in Dionysian theatres in Ancient Greece. The sport was carried around the world on trade routes, and by the 19th century, cockfighting was in practice globally. In the 16th century most manor houses had their own cockpits and trainers, and the Globe Theatre (where Shakespeare famously staged his plays), was "first and foremost a battleground for chickens rather than a stage for actors."[82] It was brought to North America through the colonising forces of England, France and Spain, but the greatest influence on the spread of cockfighting in the American South was the English, whose enthusiasm concerning the sport also prompted the first movements to ban it.

After attending his first cockfight — either in Palm Beach or at the Orlando Tournament, depending on which of his writings one references, Willeford spent 18 months doing extensive research on the ins-and-outs of cockfighting and interviewing those who made their living at it. Based in Florida as he was, many of his research documents stem from that region, including a one dollar booklet *Modern Tournament and Derby Rules* (1950 Revised edition) by cocker and promoter Henry D. Wortham that Willeford picked up at the fights — and which remained for many years the Southern

12.—Dead cocks. A dead cock is a cock that in the opinion of the referee is actually dead and not dying, he loses immediately to the live cock that is not a runaway. If a cock dies during Rest, he shall not be declared dead until pitted. If both cocks are dead the fight is a draw and each entrant receives one-half fight. If both cocks are mortally wounded when Time or Count is given, the referee will not stop to see which cock will die first, but will continue to the end of Time or Count before rendering his decision.

(11)

82 Lawler, Andrew. ***Why Did the Chicken Cross the World?: The Epic Saga of the Bird that Powers Civilization.*** **Atria Books, 2014. Kindle edition. Pg 102.**

standard, as supported by trade magazines such as *Grit & Steel* and *The Gamecock*. The magazines in Willeford's papers date from 1958, indicating that this was the period he was doing his research. An empty folder in the Willeford archive indicates the onetime location of a 30,000 word document called "A Cocker's Guide" which Willeford originally wrote as a manual for the book, and later loaned to the film production.[83]

His surviving papers also include a "House Rules" sign he swiped from the pit (no date or location indicated), which include things like:

- Limit to 15 minutes on heeling, subject to fine
- No one can see the match list until after the derby
- If caught changing leg bands, owners and handlers will be barred for one year
- Must stay six feet from cocks at all times after pitting, and no handling until the referee says 'handle'
- Referees cannot bet on any fight they are calling

And so on. As dictated by Wortham's rules, the match list refers to the fact that cocks must be of equal weight (or within 2 ounces of each other) to be pitted, and though it is common practice for cockers to cut feathers off to make a weight class (as can be seen in in Hellman's film), even the location of feathers that can be pruned are governed by rules (the weight classes established for cockfighting were later adapted into boxing, in the mid-18th century).

Wortham's rules also state that the score lines have to be eight feet apart, thus dictating that an official pit can't be smaller than 16 feet across (though smaller pits make appearances in films and likely in unofficial hacks, including those in the 12-minute 1973 PBS documentary *Feathered Warrior* — which depicts a fight in a parking lot, its only boundaries determined by the crowd of spectators circling the fight); rest between pittings is 20 seconds, and that if a cock dies during rest, he can't be declared dead until pitted. He also makes clear the distinction between a tournament and a derby; in a tournament, a stated number of entrants show a stated number of cocks at previously determined weights in such a way that every entrant would meet each other (a system devised in 1908 by Sol P. McCall, a Louisiana-based cocker and author of the 1926 book *Conditioning Cocks Correctly*, still widely in print). A derby is a smaller event than a tournament, and one can show any cock that meets the weight as opposed to one specific determined cock (which is where the idea of "changing leg bands" comes in — once weighed, the cock gets an identifying leg band, and in the case of a tournament this would be for a specific bird, and can't be changed to another cock even if of the same weight.) You'll often see cockers shearing off feathers at the last minute trying to get them to fit into a certain weight class. In the pit the handlers stand on their starting lines, holding their birds who are "billed" (their beaks placed close together three times) and flushed (allowed some wing movement) so that they are riled up and recognise their opponent. Then the handlers hold their birds (often by the tail) on their starting line until the ref calls for them to "pit" — when they are let go to fight.

As Harry Crews noted in his 1977 *Esquire* article, the fighting season starts at the

83 ***A Cocker's Guide*** **is variously referred to in archival documentation as "The Cocker's Guide" and "The Cockfighting Guide." Hilariously, the surviving table of contents is written partially in the world's most despised font, Comic Sans. I followed the guide through three sales to various collectors, and was told through an intermediary that the current owner had plans of his own and would not allow me to access it for my book.**

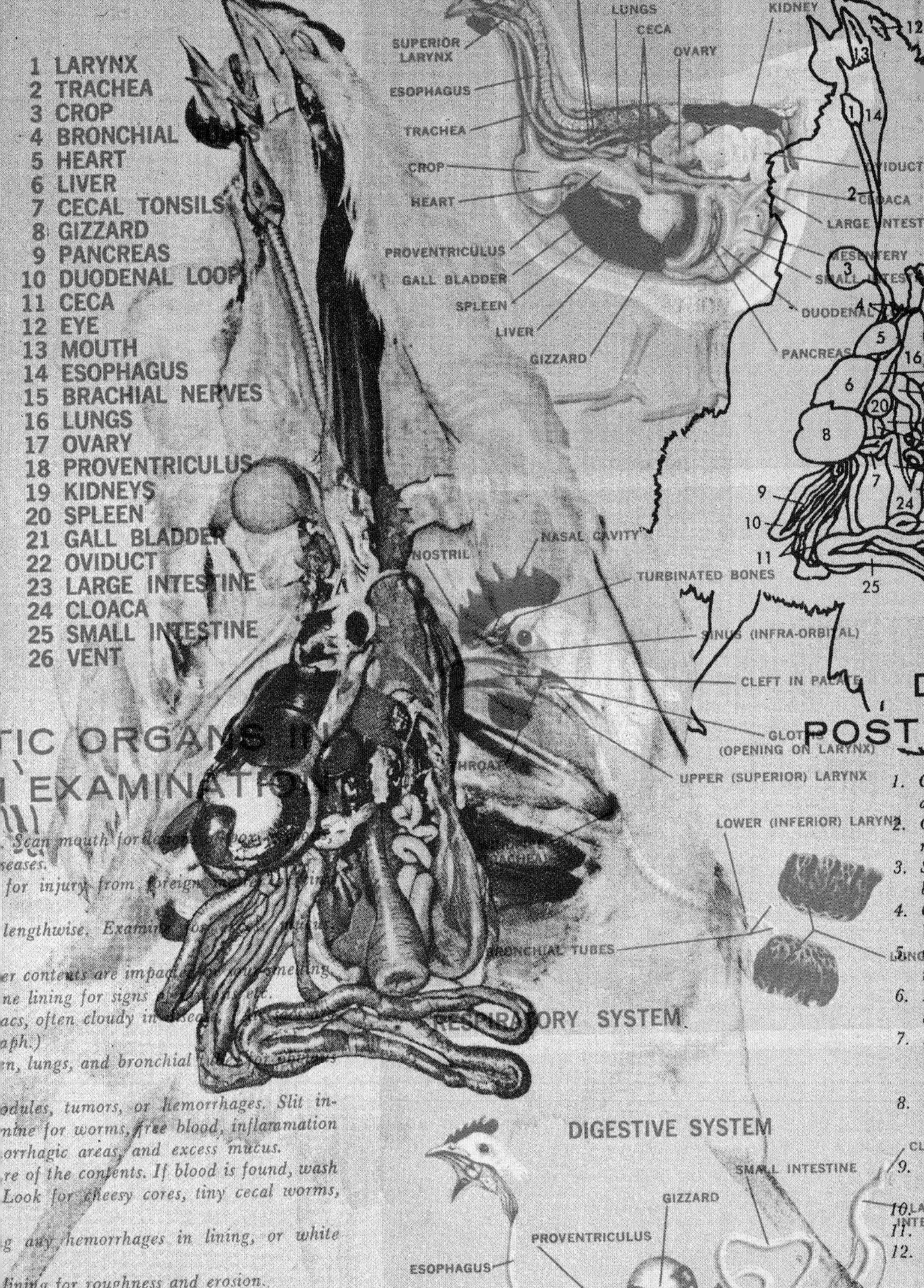
1 LARYNX
2 TRACHEA
3 CROP
4 BRONCHIAL
5 HEART
6 LIVER
7 CECAL TONSILS
8 GIZZARD
9 PANCREAS
10 DUODENAL LOOP
11 CECA
12 EYE
13 MOUTH
14 ESOPHAGUS
15 BRACHIAL NERVES
16 LUNGS
17 OVARY
18 PROVENTRICULUS
19 KIDNEYS
20 SPLEEN
21 GALL BLADDER
22 OVIDUCT
23 LARGE INTESTINE
24 CLOACA
25 SMALL INTESTINE
26 VENT
LUNGS
KIDNEY
CECA
OVARY
SUPERIOR LARYNX
ESOPHAGUS
TRACHEA
CROP
HEART
PROVENTRICULUS
GALL BLADDER
SPLEEN
LIVER
GIZZARD
PANCREAS
NASAL CAVITY
NOSTRIL
TURBINATED BONES
CLEFT IN PALATE
(OPENING ON LARYNX)
UPPER (SUPERIOR) LARYNX
LOWER (INFERIOR) LARYNX
BRONCHIAL TUBES
RESPIRATORY SYSTEM
DIGESTIVE SYSTEM
SMALL INTESTINE
GIZZARD
PROVENTRICULUS
ESOPHAGUS
POST
TIC ORGANS
EXAMINATION
seases.
for injury from
lengthwise.
ne lining for signs
acs, often cloudy in
aph.)
n, lungs, and bronchial
odules, tumors, or hemorrhages. Slit in-
nine for worms, free blood, inflammation
orrhagic areas, and excess mucus.
re of the contents. If blood is found, wash
Look for cheesy cores, tiny cecal worms,
g any hemorrhages in lining, or white
lining for roughness and erosion.

dawn of winter, as the roosters are moulting all summer. Their combs are clipped tight, because they contain enough blood that it would be an extreme handicap in a fight for the comb to get slashed. Curiously, Crews describes the trimming (or "dubbing" as it's most commonly referred to) as taking place "when the moon is in Pisces, the sign of the feet, since cockers believe a cock will bleed to death if it's trimmed at any other time." While I haven't come across this specific astrological reference anywhere else, it is true that dubbing a cock is better in cold weather due to the reduced blood flow. Either way, the cocks are given Vitamin K to help their blood coagulate more quickly, which is not only apparent in the many, many ads in cockfighting magazines advertising Vitamin K and other nutritional solutions, but also mentioned within Willeford's *Cockfighter* itself.

In a subplot excised from the film version, following the loss of his car and trailer to Jack Burke, Frank cycles through a series of money-making schemes to try to get back on track. The first of these is to hit up his friend Doc Riordan in Jacksonville, who owes Frank 800 dollars. Frank describes Doc as "another man like myself, riding along on an inborn, overinflated self-confidence and a wide outward smile. Deep inside, I knew he was worried sick about being unable to write me a check for my money." When Frank approaches him, Doc is in the midst of trying to mass-market his new miracle-product, Licarbo, a licorice-based indigestion aid. He tries to convince Frank that his train is a-comin' in and they're both gonna be filthy rich when Licarbo hits big! But as Frank says, he "wasn't about to ride another man's dream; I had a big dream of my own." He instead offers to erase the debt in exchange for a ten-year supply of various medicinal cocking supplies, which includes conditioning powder (a mixture of iron and Vitamin B1 for muscle-enhancement); dextrose capsules (an energy booster to be used just before a fight); Doc Riordan's patented Blood Builder (containing Vitamin K, whole liver and other secret ingredients); disinfectants (soda, formaldehyde, sulphur, sassafras, creosote, camphor and others) intended to ward off lice; and turpentine — a few drops of which will cure any number of ailments from asthma to distemper, cholera and more.

Many cocker magazines operate as platforms for advertising more than anything else, and such medicinal blends sit alongside gaffs and heels, notices of upcoming derbies and offerings of pedigreed gamecocks themselves in the publications' smorgasbord of advertisements. An issue of *Gamecock* in Willeford's personal collection features an article on long versus short heels, and defines four types of fighters: shufflers, rough & tumble, sparrers and combination fighters. The shuffler is nearly always a body-cutter, while the sparrer is nearly always a head-cutter. According to the piece, shufflers and rough & tumble do better in long heels and sparrers do better in short heels. Frank Mansfield states that he prefers short 1 ¼" heels — his ace cock at the start of the story, Sandspur, is a head-cutter — but his gaff case is armed with everything he might need depending on what a certain competition requires (or based on a coin toss in the event of unofficial hacks), up to 3" Texas Twisters and even a set of slashers he was given as a gift by a Puerto Rican breeder. Frank communicates his disdain for slasher heels in the book — arguing that they are too deadly and thus leave too much to chance, as a lucky hit can end the fight instantly — and in *Cockfighter Journal* Willeford explains that "Slashers are fought mostly in Louisiana, South America, Puerto Rico, and in the Philippines. Georgia is "Long Heel Country," with large roosters, mostly from 4.5 up to 6.5 pounds, and they fight in 2 6/8th-inch up to 3-inch spurs, round from base to point, and needle-sharp. The wicked slasher blades, although they are tied on one leg only, are sharp enough to shave with."

My own personal experience with cockfighting was in Louisiana, the only state in the South to adopt the slasher style of fighting, which as Willeford notes is more popular in the Philippines and Latin American countries. Why Louisiana (especially South Louisiana) should be the one state that diverges from the more widespread tradition of Southern cockfighting has been assigned to its "curious cultural milieu, involving Spanish, Indian, Chinese, German, Anglo-Irish, and perhaps most important, French roots," writes scholar Jon Griffin Donlon, who continues: "It was largely Cajuns, in that essential, creolized and hybridized meaning who concretized the notion of *joie de vivre*, a mentality which maintained the cockfights..." This touches on an important characteristic I encountered in my own travels in Southern Louisiana, namely this idea of *laissez-faire*, or staying out of people's business (while offering a detached politeness). The fight to keep cockfighting legal — as mentioned earlier, Louisiana held out the longest, until 2008 — is just one manifestation of the pushback against increasing pressure by the government "to impose organized management methods on contemporary people in the state."[84] In this battle to preserve their individualism, cockfighting served as a potent symbol. The push to ban it was equally symbolic: as Collin Levey noted in the *Wall Street Journal* in 2003, "with a world full of intractable problems, banning various kinds of animal entertainments is a cost-free exercise in cultural superiority designed mainly to offend on a class basis."[85] More on that later.

I attended my first cockfight in 2003 — it was in fact one of my bucket list goals when I moved to Texas earlier that year (the others were to meet Roky Erickson and visit the house from *The Texas Chain Saw Massacre*, both of which I did) — and throughout 2003-2004 I made several trips with friends over the border to Louisiana, where we'd camp out for the whole day, or sometimes the whole weekend, to watch the fights. Since you can sometimes see 20 fights in a single day due to the turnover in the main pit, I probably saw well over a hundred cockfights in those two years. Our most frequent pit was the closest one: The Bayou Club in Vinton, just a hop over the border from Orange, Texas. Some weekends we hit several places, including Hébert's in Abbeville (the game club may not be there anymore but the nearby

Above: The Atchafalaya Game Club.
Note the two drags on either side of the centre pit.

84 **Donlon, Jon Griffin. *Bayou Country Bloodsport: The Culture of Cockfighting in Southern Louisiana*. Jefferson: McFarland & Company, Inc., 2014. Kindle. Pg 15.**
85 **Qtd. Donlon, Jon Griffin. *Bayou Country Bloodsport: The Culture of Cockfighting in Southern Louisiana*. Jefferson: McFarland & Company, Inc., 2014. Kindle. Pg 17.**

BAYOU CLUB
MEMBERSHIP
THIS CARD CERTIFIES THAT :
Rier-LaJanisse
IS A MEMBER IN GOOD STANDING
EXPIRES 6-1-04
SPONSOR: Mark Johnson
This is to certify that
Kier-LaJanisse
(non-transferable)
registered with the
Bayou Club • Vinton, Louisiana
This card is good through December 31, 2004
No 2421
Atchafalaya Game Club, Inc.
2003-2004
Membership Card
SUNSET
LOUISIANA

BAYOU
CLUB
SUNSET

COMMON COCKFIGHTING IMPLEMENTS

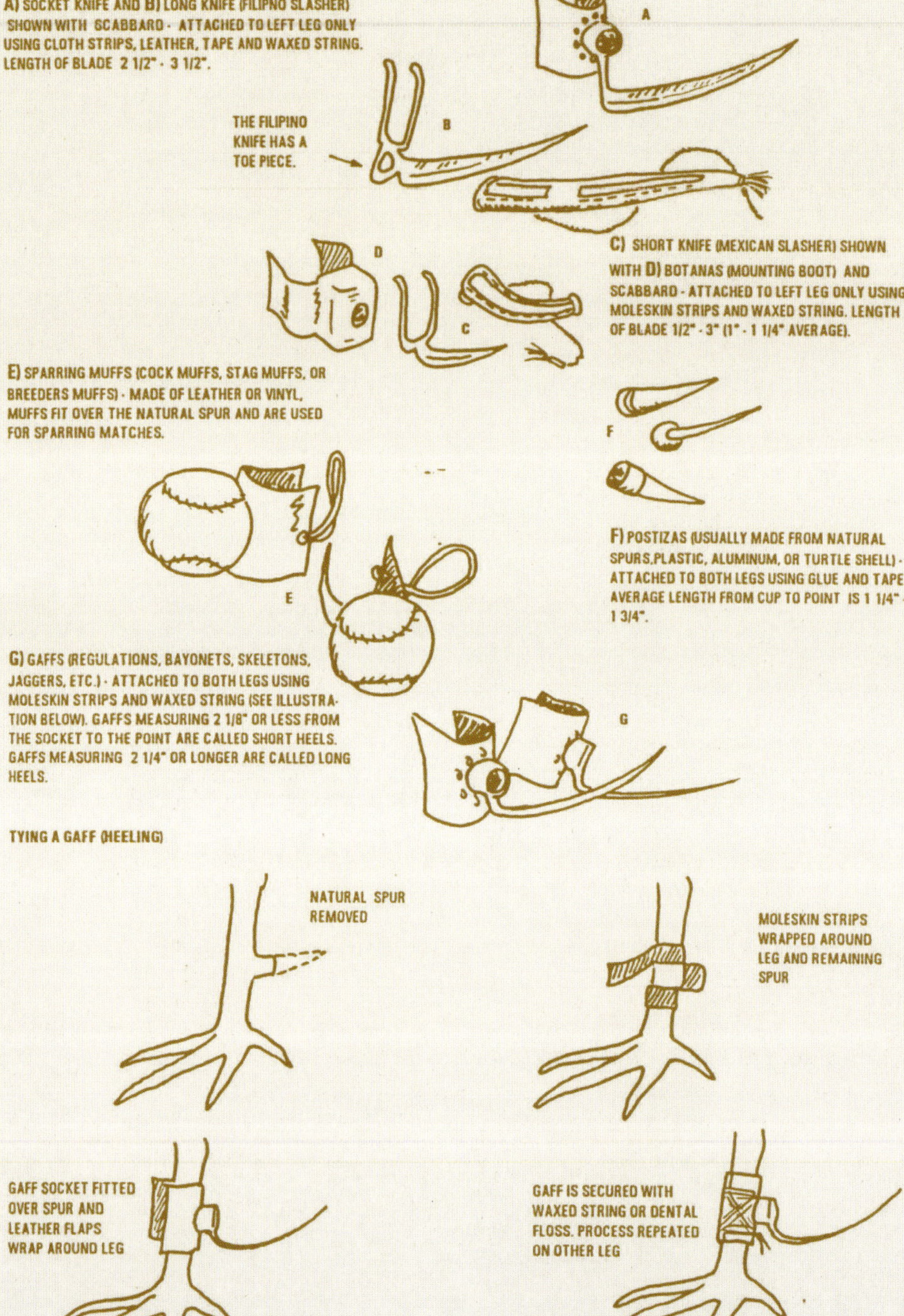

Hebert's Meat Market is run by the same family), a pit called Mom's that doubled as a flea market (we assumed the grouchy-faced woman parked behind the concession stand was "Mom"), and the prestigious 600-seat Sunset Recreation Club, which had been around since the 1940s and hosted the annual *Grit & Steel* Breeders Cup. One of the biggest pits I went to was Atchafalaya in Henderson, LA — which had two levels of spectators looking down on the main pit, flanked by drags on either side. It may have been a fluorescent-lit stadium cobbled together out of chipboard and chicken wire, but it was a stadium all the same.

Eventually I stopped going — not due to my own disinterest, but the disinterest of anyone I knew who drove a car.

The multigenerational audience (there were small children running around, as well as grandmothers selling crafts) made it atmospherically more aligned with any rural family-oriented activity, like a hayride or a jamboree, where people attended as much to escape boredom as anything else. Outside of those there for the hobby or the business of it, many people form the spectatorship who have a limited engagement with the sport; they'll be privy to the practicalities and ethics of the betting, but not necessarily the arcane practices that inform them. I could never get a handle on the odds and hand signals enough to bet against anyone other than whoever accompanied me to the fights, but the ethics of it were clear. As scientist and jazz musician William Loughborough (collaborator of Chet Baker, Harry Partch and others) explains on his website, at one point he found himself staying at the Texas farm of country star Ray Price, who raised racehorses and gamecocks. Loughborough had a side hustle as a card shark and took quickly to cockfighting. About the betting, he says,

> Someone stands and shouts "I'll lay 100 to 80." It is bad practice to ask which rooster he is selecting; if you lay the odds you pick the bird. Also you might be favorably surprised when he picks the bird you don't want. If you lose the bet, form dictates that you seek out the winner and pay him. Very seldom is this protocol violated. Another convention is when you are in a position to win a big purse by winning one final match. In this case you are expected to "hedge" by betting against your own chicken because if you lose you will at least get some consolation money; if you win, the purse makes the loss of one bet insignificant.

It was important to Willeford that the book retain as much of this practical detail as possible, and the film likewise sought to capture the cockfighting world in near-documentary form; there is even a letter in Willeford's papers from producer Sam Gelfman requesting use of his *Cocker's Guide* for reference in making the film. Cinematographer Nestor Almendros' documentary background would serve him well in capturing the minutiae of the cockfighting milieu. "The camera lies in wait, like a hunter, for an image of reality," he wrote in his autobiography, and these documentary elements of *Cockfighter* were always integral to Hellman; they remained the parts of the film he was most proud of. Again summoning Kracauer's *Theory of Film*, Hellman said his motive was "not to transform reality and thereby make it art, but merely to record reality."[86]

86 **Hellman, Monte in Joyce, Paul.** ***Plunging on Alone: Monte Hellman's Life in a Day*** **(1986).**

In his review of *Cockfighter*, critic Jonathan Rosenbaum cited the authenticity of the film as its greatest quality. He commends Hellman for his "uncanny talent for directing rural speech to make it sound like crazed ritual incantation... Suffice it to say that in both his direct use and his paraphrases of the look and speech of local yokels, Hellman has an infallibly witty and accurate ear and eye."

Clearly the three weeks of prep Hellman did in Georgia, during which he met and interviewed the many real-life cockers whose jargon would form the basis of Oates' offscreen narration (written in after the film was already shot, partially by Oates himself) was time well spent. "I didn't have any experience with it, but I'm always interested in doing a film about a subculture," explained Hellman on the Anchor Bay commentary, "because I like getting involved with people who are so intensely involved with some activity that they're passionate about... I really was a little repulsed by the actual cockfights but I fell in love with the people who were doing it. I really enjoyed delving into their characters and discovering who they were." Noting their superficial similarity to the protagonists of *Two-Lane Blacktop* in terms of their relationship to gambling, Hellman admitted that "The real-life counterparts, many of whom appear in the movie, were much more complex, and provided a texture, making my job much easier."

"They were a very cheerful lot," recalls Frances Doel, describing the real-life cockers who made up the film's background. "They were basically enjoying what they do. I mean, to me, at first I found it difficult. I was a little put off by it, but I knew that I had to get over that because this was their world and it was important to them and they have their own sense of honour about it."

"You know, I probably should say that I was disgusted by it, but I wasn't," says Steven Gaydos. "I took it at face value that it was part of a culture all over the world that people did this. I don't think I really got it, but I wasn't so terribly disgusted and offended as I probably should have been. I remember around that time, Laurie Bird's brother Donnie was married to a very spiritually-inclined woman who's good friends with Bob Dylan and his wife out in Malibu. And she said that Monte was going to pay karmically for making a movie about something as vile and evil as cockfighting."

The film's gamefowl advisor, who provided all the game cocks for the film, was Billy Abbott, assisted by fellow Lithonia, GA-based enthusiast John Trotter. Abbott was a third-generation cocker who had been breeding since he was a high school student in the 1940s. Abbott established "Rooster Village International" — a 10 acre, 1000-bird game farm — in 1963. While cockfighting had long been illegal in the state, breeding the birds was not, and Abbott "took advantage of Georgia's soil and climate, which are excellent for cock-rearing"[87] in order to raise cocks for export to international buyers. He was proud of the fact that each bird had a personal space of 30 square feet[88] (as opposed to two square feet which is the standard in the poultry business). Oates allegedly adopted Abbott's manner of walking for his depiction of Frank Mansfield — quite convincingly too, according to Willeford.

Opposite bottom right: Technical advisor Billy Abbott as he appears in *Cockfighter*.

87 **Billy Abbott obituary in *Atlanta Journal-Constitution*, March 1999.**
88 **Fay, Tim. "Farmer Keeps Tradition of Breeding Gamecocks" in *Atlanta Journal-Constitution*, Feb 3, 1994 Pg J1.**

"Billy Abbott was just a gem," says Peter Cornberg,

> He had a farm out in the woods someplace with all these beautiful little houses, like, you know, a metre by a metre which all had their own roof and everything with these fighting cocks all on tethers. And there could have been 50 of them in this big pasture. And that was his business was raising these chickens and fighting them. We got to know him quite well and he was a lot of help — you need people like that when you're talking about something that's totally documentable, you can't start pulling punches and inventing things. Just like when I did *Moonrunners*, we had old time moonshiners who knew where to put the best still, depending on the purity of the water in the stream that was close by, you always need experts like that.

Above: Various real-life cockers who appeared in *Cockfighter*.

"He was a pretty heavy-duty guy and I guess he made a lot of money at it," continues Don Walters,

> And he was a good ol' boy kind of, you know — very skinny, rangy. And he was typical of the guys, he was making money and drove a really nice truck and a really nice car. And all those guys were fine. It was once you got into a cockpit situation with the cameras and it got very difficult because those are usually very jammed with people. And when the cockfights are going on, everybody is screaming and hollering and making bets. So it was a little hard to control all that. And I don't think Monte was quite ready for it, for that particular kind of improvisation.

The cockfights were all filmed at real, active cockpits — there would often be real fights between setups — owned by cockers who appeared in the film as extras, with the exception of 24-year old A.B. Greeson, the long-haired blond kid memorably costumed in a headband and tuxedo, who took on the role of the book's sole Native American character, Pete Chocolate, and had several lines in the film. "He was one of my favourites," says Peter Cornberg of their youngest chicken fighter. Greeson's own farm acted as Frank's game farm in the film, where the birds are raised and conditioned.

"We had two or three cockpits," recalled Peter Cornberg, "which were circular things about 20 feet in diameter or something. And then there's bleachers all the way around and, you know, we shot in two or three of those. Fascinating stuff. But we set it up to be as real as possible. And although we were shooting a movie, the money going from hand to hand was real, and I mean, every couple of minutes one of the chickens would hurt the other one. And then all of a sudden all the odds would change and all of this cash would be going back and forth as people won or lost."

Don Walters, who was charged with shooting some of the second unit said of the cockfights that "it was fairly easy except for the fact that the cameras are intrusive and it was much easier to handhold than it was to put them on sticks. But they loved the idea of being on camera — the problem was keeping them from looking *in* the camera!" But setting up the fights that weren't just background atmosphere — where a specific bird had to win or lose — often required working backwards: "You can't plan who's going to win it," says Walters. "You have a pretty good idea that that one is a whole lot better than the other one just from talking to the owners and the cockfighters. But you

Above: A.B. Greeson who played Pete Chocolate in the film.

pretty much have to just play it as it lays and see who wins, and then back out from there with the other scenes that lead up to it." They also could sub in a bird of the same colour, as they would be virtually indistinguishable to the viewer, especially in a fast-moving flurry of flying feathers. But one thing they couldn't do was try to manipulate the chickens. "It just doesn't work," says Walters. "They don't listen."

Cook's Hollow (where Frank meets the Begley Jr. character) and the Allmont pit (where various Allman Brothers band members make an appearance as extras)[89] were both shot at the farm of Jimmy Williams, 25 miles from Forsyth, Georgia. Williams was interviewed by the *Atlanta Journal-Constitution* during the film's climactic cockfight between Icarus and Little David. He explained to journalist Phil Garner the complex process of training a cock for pitting — including a strict regimen of daily physical exercise, especially in the two weeks leading up to a fight, after which he is put in a dark cage by himself to wait, so that when he emerges, he is at his fighting peak. "This timing is critical," reports Garner, citing what the cockers have told him, "If the peak of readiness has passed, they say the rooster has 'gone over.'" Williams stresses this as well: "A cock that goes over couldn't whup the hen that hatched him."

One reason the film is rarely celebrated on the big screen is the contention over whether or not the cockfights in the film are real — a question that has invited different answers at different times. "I gotta tell ya, none of those roosters were hurt," Steve Railsback assured me. "We couldn't have real cockfights because we had to predict the outcome," Hellman explained to Dennis Bartok in the commentary for the Anchor Bay edition. "We had to know which bird was going to win. So all the fights are staged… the birds are usually wearing rubber gaffs instead of steel gaffs." The word "usually" is an important modifier here. Because later in the same commentary, Hellman admits that the cockfight in the hotel room flashback — the one over which Frank vows to keep his mouth shut until he wins the coveted Cockfighter of the Year Award — was real: "One is killing the other in that particular case, I'm embarrassed to say." The birds used were all trained fighting cocks, so the decision was justified in that they would have been in a fight the next day anyway. But they didn't just allow the birds to fight for real — they fixed the fight. Warren's losing cock had rubber spurs while his opponent did not. The losing bird was unfairly pummeled.

In his *Cockfighter Journal*, Willeford describes art director/props man Charlie Hughes having to make realistic three-inch rubber gaffs for the film, the usage of which is also corroborated in the 1999 obituary of technical adviser Billy Abbott. "A lot of this was underground at the time," explains his son Reg Abbott in the obit. "He was willing to make it as right as possible for the film." Of course, it's still possible that insisting the fights were staged is part of an ongoing mythology meant to cover up for illegal activity. That said, even in the 1990s, the animal cruelty-related fines for cockfighting (as opposed to gambling fines) were only $250 — hardly a deterrent for what could be a $100,000-a-year side business, considering the rarity of police raids. Some regional legislators have been reluctant to actively prosecute cockfighting because they acknowledge its "authenticity as a form of folk life."[90]

89 As Willeford relays in *Cockfighter Journal*, the Allman Brothers apparently had a farm nearby and agreed to be part of the crowd. Note Willeford variously refers to this pit as the "Allston pit."

90 Hawley, Fred. "The Moral and Conceptual Universe of Cockfighters: Symbolism and Rationalization" in *Society and Animals*, Vol 1, No 2 (1993): Pg 167

GRIS GRIS

15¢

Volume 3, No. 31
June 8-14, 1976

COCKFIGHTS
Are They Really That Bad?

Is There a Head Louse Epidemic in our Schools?

The Private Lives of Louisiana Legislators

Who is *Grassroots Gus*?

2-A THE ATLANTA CONSTITUTION, Thurs., April 18, 1974

End to Cockfights For Film Demanded

By FREDERICK ALLEN

The Atlanta Humane Society has demanded that Gov. Jimmy Carter stop a film company from staging apparently illegal cockfights near Toccoa for a movie about the bloody sport.

Dr. David W. Dreesen, executive director of the society, asked Wednesday, "Why put a rooster through that kind of torture just for human entertainment?"

In a letter to Gov. Jimmy Carter, Dreesen said, "We deplore the filming and exploitation of such a cruel and illegal activity in our state and call upon your office to withdraw support of this particular film and to ask (the producer) to take leave of our great state and produce his bloodthirsty film in some less enlightened area."

Dreesen said he has also asked Stephens County Superior Court Judge Robert H. Harris to issue an injunction blocking the cockfights.

Production officials admitted Wednesday that they have staged a number of cockfights in which birds were injured.

The film, called "The Cockfighter," stars veteran actor Warren Oates and deals with a man who makes his living betting on cockfights.

Sam Gelfman, coproducer of the movie, said rubber spurs have been used on the roosters to cut down on injuries.

However, asked by a reporter if he could give assurances that the birds have not been hurt, Gelfman replied, "I can't tell you that at all. When you have two roosters that go at each other, they go at each other. (But) none have suffered to the extent that they've been killed."

In Toccoa, Stephens County Sheriff Bill Wilkinson said Wednesday his office has been in contact with the film producers and has concluded that "there's been no law violated."

According to Wilkinson, "I think some of them (roosters) did get pecked on the head, but none of them lost an eye or anything. There's nothing we plan to do."

The sheriff said he talked with an agent of the film company, Rio Pinto Productions, and was told permission for the staging of the fights had come from Gov. Carter's office.

A spokesman for the governor said that a letter had been sent to the company, but that it merely offered governmental cooperation during the filming of a simulation of illegal activity.

"In no way," the spokesman said, "did Gov. Carter intend to condone in any way an actual cockfight, which is in violation of Georgia law."

Carter's letter states, in part, "So that nobody will misunderstand your mission, I urge full governmental cooperation during the filming of what is usually considered an illegal activity."

The governor's letter went on to compare the situation with the filming of a staged bank robbery.

In the meantime, Carter Wednesday approved a letter to Rutherford Phillips, executive director of the American Humane Society, requesting that an observer be sent from the society to the filming site.

The governor's spokesman said Carter has not yet received the letter from Dreesen in Atlanta.

Cockfighting is illegal in Georgia for two reasons. It violates gambling laws, in most cases, since wagering is the customary purpose of staging the fights.

Secondly, it violates section 26-2802 of the Georgia Criminal Code, which states, "A person commits a misdemeanor when his act, omission or neglect causes unjustifiable physical pain, suffering or death to any living animal."

The section goes on to exempt activities such as slaughtering animals for food, hunting within legal limits and medical and scientific projects.

Corman was more straightforward, saying without hesitation that "It was real. Totally real. Lew [Teague] shot the actual fighting and then we cut it in such a way that the right bird came out on top. Lew directed the cockfighting scenes, and as editor he was able to edit them. He put it all together." What Corman was referring to are additional cockfighting scenes shot after principal photography had wrapped — which will be addressed in more detail in a later chapter — but his conviction is shared by production manager Peter Cornberg, who says that "there were dozens and dozens of chickens and they were always dying right and left. The political correctness business… when we went down there and we were responsible for killing all these chickens — for all I know they all got into the stew pot every night as well — but trying to clean up the idea of cockfighting, saying, 'Oh no, they weren't real fights.' That's utter nonsense."

The feisty Melhorn Black who chases Frank at Omar's farm — a spontaneous performance — was one such casualty. When Oates cuts its head off for being too "high-stationed" (meaning his natural spurs are too high up on his legs, which is considered a handicap in a fight), Hellman conceded that it was real, saying that "We killed the best actor in the movie."[91] Oates had to psych himself up for the scene, and worse, the head didn't come off straight away and the bird took several minutes to die.

In his article, Phil Garner describes the final fight in which White Lightning — what one of the referees calls "a dead-game chicken"— finally defeats Little David. Both birds lie limp in the pit, White Lightning slightly more conscious, but just barely. According to Garner, at this point Hellman shouted, "Cut! Let's do it again before they're really dead." But the journalist claimed that, since the filmmakers weren't using real gaffs, they just fought the birds to the point of exhaustion to make them appear dead, or nearly so. "Oates' rooster is trembling violently," Garner reports. "He walks on the bent under-joints of his feet, wobbling and bedraggled." "I think he's going into shock," Oates says. Hellman calls to resume, "quickly before the roosters pass out!" Once the shot is captured, Oates runs off to get the bird some coffee, fearing it's going to die.

Garner mentions that the production company had been troubled by the SPCA a week prior to the shooting of this scene, and thus had to assure them that they were using rubber spurs for the fights. "The Georgia Film Board, successful in enticing moviemakers to the state, responded with a timid defense," Garner wrote, "pointing out

91 Hellman, Monte. *Cockfighter commentary*, Anchor Bay edition.

the humane measures being taken by the moviemakers." Garner does not elaborate on what these humane measures might be.

He reports that an extra at the Plant City fight (who was paid ten dollars cash and free beer) told him that the fights at that location were real. According to an April 18th article in the *Atlanta Journal-Constitution*, it was this location that prompted the SPCA to demand that the Georgia film commission stop the filming. In a letter to Jimmy Carter, the head of the Atlanta Humane Society David Dreeson wrote: "We deplore the filming and exploitation of such a cruel and illegal activity in our state and call upon your office to withdraw support of this particular film and to ask [the producer] to take leave of our great state and produce his bloodthirsty film in some less enlightened area." Dreeson also appealed to a Superior Court Judge for a legal injunction against the cockfights. "Production officials admitted they have staged a number of cockfights in which birds were injured," the paper reported. *Box Office* reported on the controversy as well, citing Dreeson's letter and confirming that Stephens County Sheriff Bill Wilkinson stood up for the producers, asserting that no laws had been broken and that they would not take action against the film.[92] Jimmy Carter was brought into the argument when it was claimed that his office had condoned the fights, which his office denied. The day before the article appeared, Carter's office claims to have sent an invitation to the American Humane Society to observe activity on the set. Peter Cornberg doesn't recall the production having any issues with the SPCA, but concedes that "the Georgia film commission could have been running cover for us. They may have taken on the SPCA before we ever heard about it."

For the final SCT fight at Senator Foxhall's mansion (filmed at Bulloch Hall in Roswell, on the other side of Atlanta from its setting in Milledgeville), the cockpit was especially built 100 feet from the house. While the tourney has a spectatorship in the hundreds in the book, the onscreen counterpart appears comparatively modest. According to an *Atlanta Weekly* set visit article, the crowd was comprised of recruited extras from the Roswell Boosters Club and other civic groups who "had never seen a cockfight, but they had cheered with bloodthirsty exuberance, needing little prompting."

If *Cockfighter*'s eventual audience weren't quite so enthusiastic (the cockfighting would prove both its greatest handicap and its greatest asset), at the very least the film's devotion to realistic detail and complex characters inadvertently fostered a shift in attitude towards the sport among some of the film's participants — due largely to their real-life counterparts and the rich, fascinating and honour-bound world they occupied. "Dick arrived in Toccoa three weeks ago, dead set against cockfighting," Willeford says of Richard Shull near the end of his journal. "After talking to him today, I think he is now neutral about the sport, as I am myself — neither for nor against it. Dick's change of attitude is because of Billy Abbott and John Trotter. If two outstanding men like them could be into the sport full time, it simply could not be a reprehensible pastime. I have never met two finer men in my life; they are truly Southern gentlemen in every respect."

92 *Box Office*, May 20, 1974.

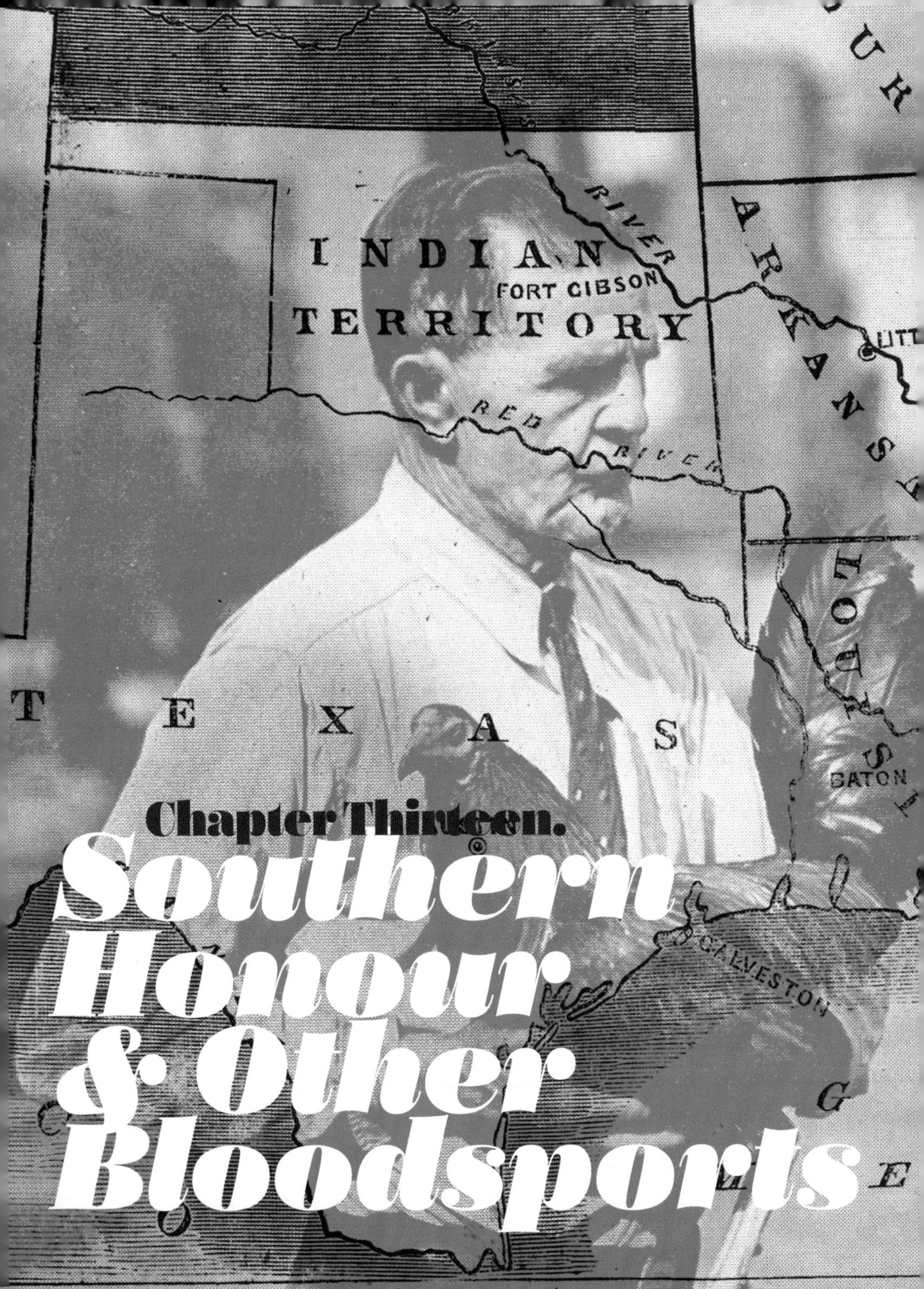

Chapter Thirteen.
Southern Honour & Other Bloodsports

KENTU
TENNESSEE
NASHVILLE
NORTH
SOUTH
COLUMBUS
CAROLI
MISSISSIPPI
ALABAMA
GEORGIA
MILLEDGEVILLE
SAVANNAH
MONTGOMERY
JACKSON
MOBILE
TALLAHASSEE
NEW ORLEAN
TORTUGAS I.
KEY WEST

"In a strange way, the cockfights imbue these people with poignancy rather than ugliness — their frame of experience is small and circumscribed, their desires so ritualised, it is as if their existence depended on the framework of winning and losing in order to have meaning."

Kent Jones, writing about *Cockfighter* in *The Last Great American Picture Show*

In his set visit for the *Atlanta Journal-Constitution*, Phil Garner interviews the various real cockers who came to play versions of themselves onscreen. One of them, named "Jimmy" — likely Jimmy Williams (whose strains are highly sought after on game fowl forums even today) — says to the writer: "In the jungles of India, that rooster would just go about his business taking care of his hens until he happened upon another rooster and then there'd be one hell of a fight. One rooster would always kill the other rooster. That way, the strongest, most aggressive rooster always won and those traits were preserved through a natural breeding process." Garner then muses on Jimmy's theorising: "Jimmy's smile, his pause to wait for a reaction, indicated that was the way he thought nature always worked."

What's interesting — not only about Jimmy's story, but also Garner's own reaction to it — is what it says about perceived class differences in the American South. As ubiquitous as it once was in some areas, cockfighting is generally understood as a low-class sport for low-class people. A violent remnant of a since-evolved South. But as Willeford himself estimates, there is more to this violence when it is so intertwined with the historical culture of honour that permeated *all* classes in the South.

Bertram Wyatt-Brown, who wrote the Pulitzer-nominated study *Southern Honor: Ethics and Behavior in the Old South*, defines honour as:

> the cluster of ethical rules, most readily found in societies of small communities, by which judgements of behavior are ratified by community consensus. Family integrity, clearly understood hierarchies of leaders and subordinates, and ascriptive features of individuals and groups are guides for these evaluations… it cannot be too strongly emphasized that honor is not confined to any rank of society; it is the moral property of all who belong within the community, one that determines the community's own membership. Even those who rebel against the society and its conventions or who stand outside or below the circle of honor must acknowledge its power… Thus honor served all members of society in a world of chronic mistrust, particularly so at times of crises, great or small. The ancient ethic was the cement that held regional culture together.

Commentators of the American South often cite violence as a defining feature of the region (in 1920, sociologist H.C Brearly cheekily referred to the South as "that part of the United States lying below the Smith and Wesson line"[93]) but point out that it's often paired with a "contrasting cultural trait"[94] like religion, manners or hospitality. Though other types of organised violence exist throughout the US, there is a distinctiveness to Southern violence that I feel is still very steeped in notions of personal honour. Most of us would consider violence to be anti-social, but this is not typically how it functioned in the South. Scholar Amy Louise Wood considers Southern violence to be "performative," a necessary means of constructing identities and forging communities — the flip side of Southern hospitality.

It's also important to remember that cockfighting was actually one of the more *genteel* of Southern bloodsports. As Elliott Gorns' illuminating article "Gouge and Bite, Pull Hair and Scratch" explains, there is a rich tradition of violent brawling in the South, notably from the late 18th century through the Antebellum era. "How men fight," he writes, "who participates, who observes, which rules are followed, what is at stake, what tactics are allowed — reveals much about past cultures and societies." Throughout the 18th century, various laws had to be installed to curb the more extreme aspects of pre-determined brawls, such as stomping, biting, eye-gouging, and cutting off tongues and noses. But as with cockfighting today, those laws were not necessarily heeded.

The reasons for fighting were often deemed "trifling and ridiculous" to those who cared to document them, whose shock was compounded by those fights having fixed dates and times so to ensure an audience, like organised sport. Thus the hazy boundaries between spontaneous eruptions of violence (invariably triggered by insults to one's honour), pastime and sport that characterised such activities in the American South. Whereas Broughton's Rules of the British ring (what is broadly considered

93 Qtd. in Wood, Amy Louise, Ed. *The New Encyclopedia of Southern Culture*, Vol 19: Violence. Chapel Hill: University of North Carolina Press, 2011. Pg 4.
94 Wood, Amy Louise, Ed. *The New Encyclopedia of Southern Culture*, Vol 19: Violence. Chapel Hill: University of North Carolina Press, 2011.

Top: Eye-gouging illustration by Albino Hinojosa from Robert William Mondy's book *Pioneers & Preachers: Stories of the old Frontier.*

a 'fair fight') specified that the fight ended when the first person fell, Southern bruisers kept going, like a cockfight, until one party could no longer fight. This style of fighting became known as 'Rough and Tumble,' with an emphasis on maximum disfigurement. Some repeat brawlers even filed their teeth and fingernails to points. As Gorns observes, "'Saving face' was not just a metaphor."

Cockfights acted as a ritualised, arms-length version of this kind of violent dispute. "Society is built on the impulses of aggression controlled by ritual," says classical studies scholar Walter Burkert, echoing Freud's similar assertions in *Civilization and its Discontents* (1930). Likewise, in his 1977 book *Violence and the Sacred*, René Girard posits that all religions were created to protect humans from their innate violent tendencies. While there was much cyclical, reciprocal violence in the early South, the cockfight was a deliberate distillation of that violence into a proxy battle that protected the community from its own destructive impulses. The cockfight is, as Alex Vernon says (in his discussion of Nathaniel West's *Day of the Locust*), "community stability in ritual space." Accordingly, fighting among cockers and audiences within the confines of the cockfighting arena is typically forbidden as it compromises the group and their endangered custom (there is usually no alcohol permitted at the events to support this).

The cockfight's heavy internal regulation rendered it more palatable than other types of bloodsports across classes as a means of displaying prowess. "Honour," "integrity" and "gameness" — the latter of which can be described as a defiant courage, and is the most important characteristic a fighting cock can have — are the most common words in a cocker's vocabulary. "Cockers know exactly what they are doing and they call it by its right name," wrote Harry Crews in *Esquire*. "When they bring cocks to a pit, they bring along with the cocks their own breeding skill and feeding skill and handling skill. Perhaps most of all, they bring their integrity."

But in order for cockfighting to be understood symbolically as a sacrificial act, there has to be enough of a correlation nurtured between the cocks and the cockfighters themselves — and frankly, the double entendre takes care of that. The fighting cock is the totem animal of this closed society, and represents the cocker's extended self, through which he hopes to demonstrate proficiency and grit. "The subcultural themes which constitute the *Weltanschauung* of the cockfighters is built around the following notions," writes Fred Hawley in his essay "The Moral and Conceptual Universe of Cockfighters," listing "gameness, individualism, authoritarianism, teleological totemism and vitalism, sexual animism, excitement, rationalization and proselytism" with teleological totemism and vitalism and sexual animism deduced to be the most significant of these. "Totem in this context refers to an animal, bird or sacred object that serves as a central point of reference to those in a tribe, group or society," he continues. "The transcendent symbol for the cockfighter is, of course, the gamecock." Cockfighting derives its mythology in part from the purported character of the gamecock itself, which is considered an emblem of courage and resistance. In the cockfighting press, the same adjectives are used to describe both the cocker and his gamecock, thus aligning their character and bonding them as surrogates for one another. "It seems to me that the cocker undergoes a brief transition, carried on the hammering wings of a mere chicken, toward the primordial essence of life," writes scholar Jon Griffin Donlon, "For a moment, and via fowl proxy, the Trickster is amuck."

Hawley writes of cockers who have shrines glorifying gamecocks past and present, and points out the care pre-Columbian Meso-American civilizations would lavish on human sacrificial victims prior to their slaughter, which we can see mirrored not only in the superior treatment of the fighting cocks as they prepare for battle, but also in the countless depictions of sacrifice in genre films of all stripes. As with other types of sacrifices, the sacrificial blood appeases the gods and ensures a new season of fertility and abundance. As Hawley writes: "The beloved bird must die for the sun to rise and set."

"The intimacy of men with their cocks is more than metaphorical," writes Clifford Geertz in his essay "Deep Play," describing how these men look upon the birds "with a mixture of rapt admiration and dreamy self-absorption." When Frank first sets eyes upon the bird soon to be known as Icarus, he reflects that "If there is anything more beautiful than the sight of a purebred game cock in the morning light, I do not know what it is." This comment conveys a profound love of these birds; they are not disposable property to the cocker — even though the categorisation of fowl as property rather than animals in certain state laws is the one thing that long allowed him to fight them.

The cockfight carries with it a strong sense of ritual, fostered by the strict choreography, the prescribed set of movements and the perceived collaboration between the fighting cock and his handler. We can see such choreography in *Cockfighter*, through the circular movements, the billing of the cocks (one-two-three), the repetitive foundation of predictable gestures that is pierced by the bird's sudden, wild improvisation. This facet of the cockfight — its potential as a dance loaded with signifiers — is not limited to *Cockfighter*, but is discernible in all artistic representations of the cockfight, from ancient pottery to contemporary films. Whether you look at the fusing of man and cock as a spiritual symbiosis or a creative partnership, the totemic purpose of the bird is realised.

Cockers will also be quick to tell you of the sport's aristocratic lineage, a lineage they believe directly links them to the early British settlers who populated the South during a time when cockfighting was at its peak of popularity back in England. There is a strong

Above: 19th century engraving of a British cockpit by G. Presbury; from the original by Hogarth.

emphasis on the gamecock — like the Southerner who conditions him — having made a long journey across the world over centuries, inherited from the noble kings and emperors of antiquity. This distinction — that these are not just any "dunghill' chickens, they are of royal stock — buttresses the mythology around the sport.

But as W.J. Cash (born in Gaffney, SC, the home of longtime cockfighting magazine *Grit & Steel*) writes in his influential 1941 book *The Mind of the South*, it was not British nobility, driven out of England by Cromwell, that most Southerners descended from, despite this enduring myth. "Such men do not embark on frail ships for a dismal frontier where savages prowl and slay, and living is a grim and laborious ideal," he writes,

> The laborer, faced with starvation; the debtor, anxious to get out of jail; the apprentice, reckless, eager for a fling at adventure, and even more eager to escape his master; the peasant, weary of the exactions of milord; the small landowner and shopkeeper, faced with bankruptcy and hopeful of a fortune in tobacco; the neurotic, haunted by failure and despair; and once in a blue moon some wealthy bourgeois smarting under the snubs of a haughty aristocracy and fancying himself in the role of a princeling in the wilderness — all these will go. But your fat and moneyed squire, your gentleman of rank and connection, your Cavalier who is welcome in the drawing-rooms of London — almost never.

As scholar Amy Louise Wood has noted, their ethics derive more directly "from the honor-bound culture of their Scots-Irish ancestors who dominated European migration to the Southern colonies" and brought the self-reliance of the Border regions with them across the Atlantic. And this is important because it imbues their honour codes with the baggage of class distinctions (as determined by ethnicity) in place at the time of these migrations. Connected to the social function of violence in these communities is an emphasis on "breeding" or "pedigree" which was often the baseline for one's social standing, and for those with limited social mobility, the pedigree of their fighting cocks and their arcane knowledge of Old World aristocratic traditions became leverage, at least in their own minds.

According to Wyatt-Brown, three types of events gave "meaning to life and strength to reputation" in the Old South: hosting, gambling and dueling. All three were integral in determining community standing and establishing membership in certain social circles. Even the concept of Southern hospitality was a display of power and standing: "Great planters and small shared an ethos that extolled courage bordering on foolhardiness, and cherished magnificent if irrational displays of largesse." Of the importance of gambling, Wyatt-Brown affirms that it "dramatized vicarious triumph and misfortune within a structure of strict rules... the point of play was the distribution of honor and status." What's interesting here is the implication of social mobility.

These diversions had social meaning, and although the winnings conferred status, they were not merely about making money and in fact, there was a strict division in perception between those who gambled leisurely

Cockfight.

and those who lived off it. Honour was readily attributed to "high-minded, liberal gentlemen" who placed no great value on the money that changed hands, which was seen as largely symbolic. And in fact, such "high-minded, liberal gentlemen" used their status to get laws enacted that prohibited professional gambling. Such laws frequently went unenforced because gambling events made for exciting spectatorship, but could be used on a complaint-basis to punish those who transgressed social boundaries. But the idea was that "the *compulsion* to gamble was as unmanly as failure to play." So while the cockpit had its codes of conduct, the social mobility implied only went so far, and the "honour" that is still frequently cited by cockers as an indelible part of their lineage would not have been socially applicable given the dependence of many on their winnings. This may be my saddest discovery in terms of deconstructing contemporary cockers' sense of value and their allusions to regal ancestry — that if their ancestors fought cocks as a means of subsistence, their esteem would be diminished within the very tradition they claim to uphold.

As Daniel R. Hundley noted in "Social Relations in our Southern States," there was a distinction between the controlled violence of the gentlemanly duel and sportsmanship of their own gambling events, and those of the lower economic classes, whose violence and impropriety were seen as inherent to their social status. He referred to a character type of "The Southern Bully," which he described as "a swearing, tobacco-chewing, brandy-drinking Bully, whose chief delight is to hang about the doors of village groggeries and tavern taprooms, to fight chicken cocks, to play Old Sledge, or pitch-and-toss, chuck-a-luck, and the like, as well as to encourage dogfights, and occasionally to get up a little raw-head-and-bloody-bones affair on his own account."[95] Such transparent double standards allowed those with wealth and class to better their social standing via the sense of honour they accumulated while competing in such activities, while among the lower classes, the very same activities were characterised as sources of shame and debasement that both reinforced their lower status, and were policed more rigorously. Southern author Walker Percy (*The Moviegoer*) once wrote to Bertram Wyatt-Brown that Southern honour was "an ethic so overloaded with moral contradictions that its twists and turns could tax anyone's sense of objectivity."

When looking at the apparent contradictions in Southern rituals of violence — and how they can co-exist with concepts of gentility and hospitality — it's important to consider that honour was tied to reputation and social standing and was not the same as *conscience*. Provided one operated within the rules of honour, there were no pangs of conscience.

Honour codes declined after the late 19th century Revival movements; Wyatt Brown maintained that only a fifth of all Southern whites were churchgoers before the Civil War, and that this mass evangelising and conversion served as a new means of holding communities together and keeping people in line. In mainstream society, honour codes are no longer used as a means of reward and punishment, although its language survives in military culture. The 'ethic' of personal honour has largely gone underground, as a governing factor in criminal organisations, and illegal sports like cockfighting. In the

95 Qtd in Bruce, Dixon B., Jr. *Violence and Culture in the Antebellum South.* Austin: University of Texas Press, 1979. Kindle. Pg 76.

which provided the fertile ground for the reliance on violent private justice."[96]

There's also an interesting connection to be found in the literary habits of Southerners, and surviving stereotypes that insist only the leisurely classes were/are literate are belied by not only evidence of reading among all classes, but by what they chose to read. Wyatt-Brown writes that the roots of the Southern honour codes go back centuries, claiming that in the Antebellum South, "the philosophy of the Emperor Marcus Aurelius' *Meditations* was nearly equal to the Bible as a source of moral wisdom." This Southern obsession with the guiding principles of classical antiquity is corroborated in Walker Percy's writings (in a posthumously-published essay collection he highlights the words of Marcus Aurelius as capturing the best of the South: "Every moment think steadily, as a Roman and a man, to do what thou hast in hand with perfect and simple dignity, and a feeling of affection, and freedom, and justice"), and in the pages of *Cockfighter* itself, Frank Mansfield refers to his brutal game-test as the "Roman method," among other references to ancient texts. Aside from such Classical references, it's still easy to find a copy of what was purportedly the first book about cockfighting, George Wilson's *The Commendation of Cockes, and Cock-fighting; Wherein is shewed, that Cocke-*

cockpit, all betting is on the honour system — no one is paying attention to anyone else's bets, which are all conducted across the pit via hand signals. Honour and reputation are everything, and the more illegal the activity, the more valuable a currency honour becomes. It's also worth noting that in the North, strong formal institutions were in place to maintain social and political order in the 19th century, which made honour codes less valuable. Whereas in the South, a reason for the continued persistence of such codes over the centuries has been cited as "weakness of the institutional environment,

96 **Grosjean, Pauline. "A History Of Violence: The Culture Of Honor And Homicide In The Us South" in *Journal of the European Economic Association* 12, no. 5 (2014) Pg 1286.**

fighting was before the coming of Christ (1607) — which likewise aligns the sport with antiquity — and if you go on gamefowl supply websites today (or even just Amazon) you'll find an abundance of centuries-old books still in print, such as *The Royal Past Time of Cockfighting* (1706), *The Cocker's Manual Devoted to the Gamefowl* (1878) and *Cock Fighting: Sport in the Olden Time* (1912). The fact that these books are still available (many in budget versions) clearly indicates that cockfighters, far from being anti-literate, are in fact reading antiquated forms of English in their spare time — and simultaneously absorbing some outdated values peripheral to it.

What these combined activities — the cockfighting, gambling, honour codes, stoic philosophy, and the prescriptive manuals for all of the above — imply, is a culture centred on propagating traditional ideals of masculinity. It was this very culture that Hellman's film sought to replicate, which is part of why it posed a challenge to its comparatively passive, progressive director. "They are part of a very male-oriented society," *Cockfighter* co-producer Sam Gelfman said to the *Atlanta Journal-Constitution* of the real-life cockers who worked on the film. "Most of these guys are typical male chauvinists. They hunt, they gamble, and yet they are very good family men." And those families will often find themselves upholding those traditions even after their patriarch is gone; many game farms remain family enterprises through succeeding generations.

Probably the last cockfighting narrative film made before the sport was finally banned in all 50 states was *The Grey* (2004) based on Frank Manley's 1998 novel *The Cockfighter*. It was filmed in Kentucky where, at the time, cockfighting was technically only classed as a misdemeanor (despite being a felony on a federal level). Enforcement of cockfighting and related gambling activities was notoriously lax in Kentucky up until 2020; as conveyed in the film, consumption of alcohol was significantly more regulated.

The Grey stars (and was co-written and co-produced by) Mark Boone Junior (later elevated to household status via *Sons of Anarchy*) as a gruff and violent rural cocker bent on making his 12 year-old son a third generation cockfighter. While its low budget shows, it is easily the best American cockfighting movie since Hellman's and is clearly indebted to the latter's languorous pacing, slow-motion visuals and emphasis on authentic locations and dialogue.

While the young son is eager to impress his father and clearly values their family's cockfighting tradition, his mother fears he doesn't understand the emotional impact that the death of his rooster (which he has named and tends to like a pet) will have on him. Not only does the mother challenge the cherished family tradition, but when the boy gets in the pit, his opponent is a woman, much to the chagrin of his father: "Championship cock, gonna lose to a goddamn woman!"

The woman is seen as a disrupter, both inside and outside the pit. As far as these guys are concerned, cockfighting may have lasted centuries, but there's always a woman hovering over its precarity, threatening to tear it all down.

Chapter Fourteen.

Junk Fowl: The Women of Cockfighter

"With its blatant double entendre, cockfighting constitutes the ultimate macho sport," says Woody Haut, writing about Willeford's *Cockfighter* in *Neon Noir*. According to Jesse Pearson's intro to the 2011 reissue of the book, when Willeford's biographer Don Herron took Willeford to address the Maltese Falcon Society he explained the straightforward naming of the characters — Frank's name was such because he was straightforward and honest (he's not really), and his last name "Mansfield" was due to the fact that cockfighting is "a man's field." Of course both of these points are contentious and, I think, too facile to be true.

It's made clear in both the book and the film that for Frank to partner with Omar — even temporarily, for a single season — is a massive step for someone who rejects companionship of any kind. But it is a mathematically-calculated decision; at least, that's how Frank can justify it to himself. Sharing his time, his life (his cocks!) with a woman — that would be another matter entirely. There's just no place for that kind of distraction in his world. And while there are exceptions, this largely reflects attitudes about women in the cockfighting community in general.

It's fair to say that women are in the minority — whether as spectators or active participants — in the homosocial spectacle of cockfighting. Needless to say some heads were turned when my friend Jasmine and I, both then in our late 20s, walked into a tiny rural cockpit in Louisiana with smiles on our faces and less than $30 in betting funds. It was 2004. I'd been to the fights before, but to bigger pits and with numerous male friends, where my presence was less conspicuous. Though we ambled in ahead of him — thus the strange looks — we were accompanied by a well-known Louisiana cocker named Jim, and that eased the suspicion. Jasmine had found him in a cockfighting forum online, where she posted that two women were looking for a host to show them around some cockpits — and not just the more high-profile ones, but some real down-home, out-of-the-way places.

There was a ramshackle quality to the place, with a dirt floor and a pit roughly 12 feet across (it looked smaller than official regulation) that was surrounded by just a double bench around each side, seating maybe 40 people all together. The place seemed crammed and claustrophobic and

everyone was speaking French. "This is a real Cajun pit," our host said proudly. It was so small I can't even recall if there was a drag — those tiny secondary pits the cocks get moved to one the fight slows down, to allow for a new, more energetic fight to move into the main pit. We noted one cocker with straggly hair wearing a black satin jacket with two embroidered cocks fighting on the back, flanked by the words "Til Death do us Part." I leaned over to Jasmine: 'I *want* that jacket."

We were the only women there, aside from the woman running the ticket booth, and one of the guys asked, facetiously, in an accent straight out of *Southern Comfort*, if I wanted to hold his cock. "I sure do!" I said, unruffled by the double entendre. I took the white fighting cock on my lap and held it tight — it was hard as a rock. "They're pure muscle," Jim explained. "That's why you can't eat 'em." It seemed one of the most wasteful and depressing parts of cockfighting to me, that gamecocks are bred and conditioned with so much care and yet at the end of the day they're good for nothing but the trash. I've been told in the Philippines and Malaysia they eat them anyway, and in the 1908 collection *Histories of Game Strains* (still widely available in print), Mrs. O.I. Payne — whose father Captain J.D. Mayberry created the Black Roundhead strain in the late 1800s — notes that "there is no chicken so good to eat as game — when you have game chicken dressed, you have something to show for your trouble." In years of subsequent research I've turned up as many references to eating them as not eating them, so this precept seems regionally-specific.

As I was holding the bird, I overhead the man in the satin jacket whispering to Jim,

Above: At the cockfights circa 2004.

"Where did you meet these girls?" "On the internet!" Jim answered. "Damn," the guy said, scratching his head beneath his baseball cap. "I gotta get me that internet." (If I sound like I'm flippantly describing a Southern hick stereotype, that is unique to this fellow, who really did seem like some kind of cartoon character.)

But even with the Jim's endorsement, our presence had obviously changed the vibe in the room. There are rarely women present who are not tied by blood or marriage to the men who make their living there. In America, the wives and daughters of professional cockers often work the ticket booth, the concession stand, and tirelessly hand-make cockfighting-related crafts to sell at the merch stands. I once bought a baseball cap bearing a pair of hand-painted fighting cocks from a grandmotherly type who would paint them and pass them off assembly line style to another woman who would then blow-dry them for quicker turnaround. We found that when you see women in American cockpits, they are usually someone's relative, participating in a support role as a matter of course, and almost always sublimating their own interests to those of the men in their lives. Many of them came to refer to themselves as "chicken widows" because their partner's obsession with the sport was so all-consuming.

Harry Crews apparently had a different experience; he noted in his *Esquire* article that there are "a great many ladies who are avid, even rabid cockers," continuing to say that they "seem to do extremely well at all levels of the sport." At the turn of the last century — aligned with the peak of

the suffrage movement, unsurprisingly — women were alleged to be showing more of an interest in the sport, and in April 1906 a woman wrote into cocker magazine *Grit & Steel* looking for other "female fanciers" of the sport. In my research I've encountered references to women-only contests, facetiously dubbed "powderpuff derbies," but the only evidence I've seen of one is a photograph in Tim Pridgen's longstanding classic *Courage: The Story of Modern Cockfighting* (1938) that shows two women handlers and a gaggle of young women looking on. Looking through decades of gamefowl magazines — which typically include photos of tournament and derby winners — images of women as anything other than cover models are rare.

But there are perhaps a surprising number of women working behind the scenes, in less visible roles. Industry magazines *Grit & Steel*, *The Gamecock*, and *Feathered Warrior* all featured long-running female editors. Harry Crews mentions Gamecock editor Sally E. Marburger in his *Esquire* piece, citing her magazine as "the finest journal devoted to game fowl published in the country" (indeed a copy of *The Gamecock* is visible on the table in Frank's trailer in the opening shots of *Cockfighter*). In the 1950s and '60s when Charles Willeford was doing his research for *Cockfighter*, the editor of *Grit & Steel* (based in Gaffney, South Carolina, founded in 1899 and in print until 2009) was also a woman: Miss Sara Ellen Culbertson. Note she is identified as "Miss" — she later married a fellow named John M. Gruber. It's possible she fell into the role because she was simultaneously a linotype operator at the Greenwood, SC newspaper *The Index-Journal*, which did not mention her cockfighting publishing history in her obituary on April 17th, 1975. She may have just squeaked in a screening of *Cockfighter* before her death.

But she wasn't the only female editor of *Grit & Steel*: there was also Ruth DeCamp-McMillan (daughter of its founder Edward Hope DeCamp) and later Ruth Thompson Skinner. Though she had worked at *Grit & Steel* in some capacity since at least 1950, Ruth DeCamp-McMillan did not take over as editor immediately after her father's death in 1952 — instead, Sara Ellen Culbertson became the editor, it seems until she got married and started a flower shop (Jon-Ellon's in Gaffney, still in operation), at which point Ruth DeCamp-McMillan took over and ran the magazine until her death in 1971.

Rival magazine *Feathered Warrior* (founded 1903) also had a female editor, Verna Dowd, who saw the magazine through its end in 2009 when it finally succumbed to threats from the SPCA. That women had such prominent roles in the official communications related to the sport is a distinct contribution that warrants its own study.

Ruth DeCamp McMillan

Mrs. McMillan Wins S. C. Press Awards

Ruth DeCamp McMillan was winner of an Award for the Best Magazine Edited by a Woman at the S. C. Press Association meeting, First Place for Display Alvertising and First Place for Publicity Writing for Direct Mail also were won by Mrs. McMillan and the Grit and Steel.

Mrs. McMillan has won the award for the "Best Magazine Edited by a Woman," five times since 1963.

But there were occasional telltale signs that the editors were women: in the headlines section of the April 1968 issue of *Grit & Steel,* there is a notice that the "Gaffney Strangler" has been indicted on four counts of murder. In a rare departure from cockfighting-related news, the capsule relates that Lee Roy Martin, age 31, has been charged with the strangulation deaths of two women and two young girls in the community over the previous year, and that "we are all breathing easier in Gaffney now."

In the Philippines, where cockfighting is a billion-dollar national pastime and home of the World Slasher Cup (which draw 25,000 spectators biannually), women cockfighters exist, but make up a minority; the biggest presence women have at the cockfights is in the beauty pageants often accompanying them. There is a lot of suspicion around women in the pit; partially because, for centuries, women have historically been behind much of the public policy aimed at discrediting and outlawing the sport — as Andrew Lawlor points out in his book *Why Did the Chicken Cross the World?,* the associated "gambling and drinking often meant poverty and abuse for the women left at home" — but also because of older folk beliefs that have carried over from Southeast Asia where they were established thousands of years ago. A cock

Above: Ann-Margret (top row) at the cockfights in *The Cincinnati Kid* (1965).

touched by a menstruating woman is sure to lose. A cocker cannot have sex the night before a fight. There is even a belief that the reason women can't be cockfighters is because if male and female cockers pit their birds against each other and the woman loses, she'll end up pregnant. Even roosters are not allowed access to hens in the period leading up to a fight. There is a strong association between femininity, weakness and corruption that cockers aim to avoid costing them a fight, so these old superstitions are heeded and female participation therefore discouraged or even banned outright.

In Alan Dundes' essay "Gallus as Phallus: A Psychoanalytic Cross-Cultural Consideration of the Cockfight as Fowl Play" he notes that French women often ridicule their cockfighting partners, with the common exclamation that "he holds his cocks more often than he holds me!" asserting that women's disdain for the sport is seen as diluting its symbolic significance. "The whole point of the phallic competition is to 'feminize' one's opponent," he says. "This symbolic feminization becomes less meaningful in the presence of actual women." Harry Crews commented on the implicit sexuality of the cockfight and the multiple layers of embarrassment suffered when a cocker loses his match: "when a man's Kelso or Blueface or Gray or Whitehackle or Allen Roundhead quits — when a man's cock quits in the pit, he suffers a profound humiliation. *When a man's cock quits.* Yes, that's part of the ritual, too. Perhaps the biggest part." Women don't rate very highly in the libidinal economy of the cockfighter.

In film, cockfights have been occasionally used as sites of female pleasure; in *The Cincinnati Kid* (1965), Ann-Margret accompanies title character Steve McQueen to a cockfight and clearly gets erotically charged by the spectacle. As the crowd gets riled up into a frenzy, there is a quick cut to actor Rip Torn, in a hotel shooting range, shooting a gun aimed at the viewer and emphasising the orgasmic finale of the fight. In the Manila-set *Too Hot to Handle*, Cheri Caffaro (erstwhile action star and wife of director Don Shain) plays an heiress and contract killer who loves her work... maybe a little too much. Her sadistic hits ("It's better to kill something that takes a long time to die") are complemented by a recreational visit to a cockfight, where from the very first peck she is so turned on that she starts undoing her top ringside, and launches into a masturbatory fantasy that cross-cuts red satin with bloody feathers.

But in Hellman's *Cockfighter* and *Two-Lane Blacktop*, women are just seen as an obstacle to the antihero's goal, and in the case of Laurie Bird's characters in both films, she is literally traded from one male character to another, an irritating piece of luggage.

As film critic Molly Haskell pointed out in an interview with the *Supporting Characters* podcast, these early 1970s halcyon days of Hollywood, where highly personal films were being made with studio resources, were largely beneficial to the male vision. In her book *From Reverence to Rape*, she talks about the roles for women in this period as something that had to be asserted constantly in a milieu that prized the male worldview — which is especially interesting when you consider that this was also the height of radical feminism in America.

The Roger Corman-produced pictures of the 1960s and 1970s directly engaged with progressive politics and the zeitgeist of second wave feminism in asserting their female leads' erotic agency — despite the fact that Corman alumnus Joe Dante has synopsised them dismissively as "women would take their clothes off and get in trouble and say left-wing things." When I pointed out to Dante that I disagreed, he did concede that their sexual politics were still more considered than many other exploitation films. "And it was Roger who encouraged that there was always one plot line that was 'the issue,'" continues fellow alumnus Allan Arkush. "I remember being really surprised when I saw, like my first day at work, *Caged Heat* and how the lobotomies and the treatment of prisoners — even though they were naked in the showers — was an issue. And I was really taken by that."

Not to mention that Corman productions had more gender parity on the crews than almost any other movies being made at that time, whether they were exploitation or major studio films. "You've probably heard the line from many, many people," offers Beverly Gray, who worked in the script department at New World,[97]

> that Roger likes to hire women because he feels they're smarter, work cheaper and are more loyal. And he had a female attorney, Barbara Boyle who became quite a powerhouse in her own right, he started people like Gale Anne Hurd. Some people feel that he's more comfortable with women. And you can go into all sorts of psychological reasons for that, but he also very pragmatically has these women who have sort of dual attributes — that this woman is strong and tough and has got a mouth on her and sometimes is sexually powerful, but she also takes her clothes off and that's for the guys in the audience. And I've always found that really, really interesting. Roger took great pride in being progressive.

Frances Doel agrees that Corman always found a way for his progressive views to be foregrounded even in an exploitation film context. "Roger always insisted that the women — like in the *Student Nurses* and *Student Teachers* films and so on — that the women couldn't just be somebody's girlfriend. They each had to have their own ambition, and they had to have their own story. And that was Roger. I mean, that was Roger responding to the rise of feminism, but also I think it was, on his part, genuine that he really hated women being *just* girlfriends." So in some ways the sexual politics of *Cockfighter* are surprising given that track record.

But with *Cockfighter*, Corman was adapting a ten-year old pulp novel whose characterisations of women were comparatively old fashioned, reflecting that of the unique subculture that served as Willeford's backdrop. It was going to be a hard sell and potentially a disappointment to audiences and critics used to a certain type of 'Corman girl.' Even Corman's other 'Southern' films were centered on a female protagonist. "One could say in its defence that its presentation of women, in both the

97 Corman's stock reference to Siegfried Kracauer plays out again here: "He interviewed me and said, if you come to work for me, I would like you to read Siegfried Kracauer's *Theory of Film* and we'll discuss it. So of course I said, well, I'd be glad to do that. I got the job. And I read Siegfried Kracauer and I kept waiting to have this literary intellectual conversation, which never happened."

novel and the movie, was true to that world," offers Frances Doel. "In the very parochial world of cockfighting, that is the way women were perceived, certainly at the time — but probably also in the seventies."

"There's one really silly thing from the script that I've never forgotten," recalls Beverly Gray, whose first official task at New World was to give notes on the latest revision of the *Cockfighter* script. "And that is where they are leading into a sex scene, she's topless, I think it's outdoors, and it said something about how 'she's approaching her mid-30s, but her breasts have not yet prolapsed.' And I said, *prolapsed?* What the heck does that mean? This idea that, my goodness, she's remarkable enough to not be sort of a sagging old lady, even though she's almost 35. I was younger than 35 when I read that, but it's always stayed with me, like "gee, have I prolapsed yet?"[98]

But Monte Hellman's relationship with his female characters was never aligned with the Corman school of tough, sexy women, nor those to be found in Willeford's back catalogue, who are minor irritations at best and persistent distractions from the hero's ambitions at worst. But there is never an aching need in Willeford's protagonists for a lady love. This left the director with a particular challenge in adapting the story, because woman are more important in his films and in his life — despite his noted struggles to connect with people on a social level (his short bio on his AirBnb host page unashamedly stated that he was "still looking for the mother of my next five children").

"Hellman considers himself 'as asocial as it is possible for a social being to be,'" Aljean Harmetz stated in a 1971 *New York Times* piece timed to the release of *Two-Lane Blacktop*. "In four years at Stanford he never once had a date. He has been married twice. Both his marriages were the result not of courtship but of 'instant rapport.' He remembers that early in his second marriage 'we would trade off dinner with a few friends. But that got rarer and rarer in recent years. Now I maintain the few friends I have with an occasional phone call.' Still, he admits, 'As much as I'm a recluse, I need another human being around.' The other human being he is seeing at the moment is Laurie Bird." It was on the set of *Two-Lane Blacktop* — featuring Hellman's then-wife Jackie in a small role — that he began an affair with the teenaged Laurie Bird, leading to what Hellman's friend Deanne Mencher called "a very, very ugly divorce." Hellman and Bird even showed up at Mencher's house appealing to her to testify on Monte's behalf. "I remember being on the stand and just saying that I felt Monte could provide a great *intellectual environment* for his children," she says with a cackly laugh, noting that it was the only thing she could think of to say in his defence. "But Jackie was devastated by people vouching for Monte more than they vouched for her."

In *Cockfighter*, Frank's disdain for women is obvious throughout the film and is even more flagrant in the book, beginning with the character of Dody White, a leggy 16-year old who's attached herself to Frank. The character is perfectly embodied by Laurie Bird. Though she and Monte had become a couple on *Two-Lane Blacktop*, when it came to *Cockfighter*, it was actually Corman who suggested her for the role of the innocent, freewheeling Dody White.

98 See Pg 43 of the script; Mary Elizabeth is noted as being just shy of 30 years old.

Dody White is a pouty bumpkin who's all arms and legs, and Bird's character here, as in *Two-Lane Blacktop*, has a rambling quality, she sort of goes where the wind blows her — something Hellman said reflected her real personality. "Your description of Laurie is pretty exact," he commented, "so I guess I achieved my usual goal in capturing the actual personality of the actor… The job of the actor is not to become the character, the character has to become the actor." One of the only surviving on-camera interviews with Bird depicts her at the time of *Two-Lane Blacktop*, with a tousled shag and a striped shirt that looks straight from the department store kids section, evading questions and offering up ridiculous statements about how the worst day of her life was when she broke her headphones, and the best day of her life will be when she buys an island and owns all the people on it. She is a hard person to like, and yet she became an object of fascination for many, including director Monte Hellman, who eventually married her.

As noted in his *Cockfighter Journal*, Charles Willeford thought Laurie Bird was perfect for the part of Dody White, but despised her personally — a sentiment that was supposedly shared by everyone else on set. He claimed she was the kind of obnoxious person who could clear a room, and even the extras on the set noticed something off-putting about her; the *Atlanta Journal-Constitution* quoted the wife of one of the real-life cockfighters employed for the film describes all the cast and crew as nice and friendly, "All except that little skinny girl, what's her name. She's from New York, you know."

"The girl [Hellman] was with was giving him lots and lots of trouble," recalls first AD Don Walters. "She was a pain in the neck. She was terribly insecure, she didn't have very much experience at that point. She just made a fuss about everything. It was just bullshit. You know, if she stepped in something, it became a thing. If she didn't have the right clothes that day, it became a thing. If somebody looked at her funny… She was just terribly uptight and that made him more uptight. So his mind was not really on the film so much."

When I asked him about this, Hellman shrugged. "Laurie was very opinionated," he said. "But she wasn't mature enough to realise that not everyone shared her opinions."

"He was actually very protective of her," says Frances Doel of Monte's handling of Laurie on set. "I know he was aware that she wasn't liked. I mean, she was just obnoxious, really. She basically would put everybody down. She needed to be the centre of attention, I think. And she also felt she had a special position as Monte's girlfriend. And because Warren smoked, Willeford smoked and I did — we all smoked and she was always bitching about that. 'I've just washed my hair!' Things like that. 'Take her away, make her go, *make her go*!' Looking back, I can better appreciate it, now that I've given up smoking, but at the time… she just never made friends with anybody."

Beverly Gray remembers Laurie being around the office with Monte, "carrying the books and things like that, carrying his script," and gives Bird the benefit of the doubt. "She seemed nice and eager and young. I think the fact that she was his girlfriend was gonna put her in a complicated position in any case."

Left: Laurie Bird as depicted in a spread for *Show* magazine, March 1971.

"She was a lovely young lady," says Monte's longtime friend Steven Gaydos in Laurie's defence. "She was incredibly bright. She was creative, but she was about 21 or 22 years old. And she probably flounced around like a privileged little princess and people weren't going for it. I don't think it was that extreme, but I could see that people thought that she wasn't everything that she thought she was. You know, people on a film set, it's a little microcosm of society and you've got buffoons and you've got sad cases and you've got heroes and you've got, you know, slugs. Everybody's true nature comes out in the making of a movie."

But he also felt that her role in *Cockfighter* did not allow her to shine as she had in *Two-Lane Blacktop*. "She had just been the heart and soul of this poetic perfect masterpiece where she was central to the story," offers Gaydos. "And there was a great arc to her character in that story and great scenes for her to play. Maybe that's the secret of why Monte was not happy with the *Cockfighter* script. The movie's romance is between a man and his girlfriend, and they're never really together in the whole movie. There isn't really a kind of Monte Hellman relationship there at the heart of the movie. Laurie played Harry's wife, so sort of a comic extra part. I think that it was a little bit of a comedown for her where suddenly she was just a character performer."

Gaydos tries to chalk up Laurie's petulance to her inexperience; that she was perhaps over her head as an actress when the role didn't just require her to play a version of her free-spirited self. "I'm sure people thought, boy, you know, she's with the director. Great. And she's 20 and he's 45. Great. Welcome to Hollywood. She was a bit neurotic and her behavior really got worse once we got back to LA because she was just deeply troubled. It was not going to turn out well for her and Monte. And it didn't."

Dody White ends up marrying Jack Burke, Frank's friendly rival who had essentially "won" Dody in a hack with Frank. Though she complains about Burke's age ("He must be 40 years old!"), he's much more of a pushover than the obstinately mute Frank, and she gets accustomed to Burke's wealth, and the smart outfits he buys her for when she cheers him on from the sidelines.

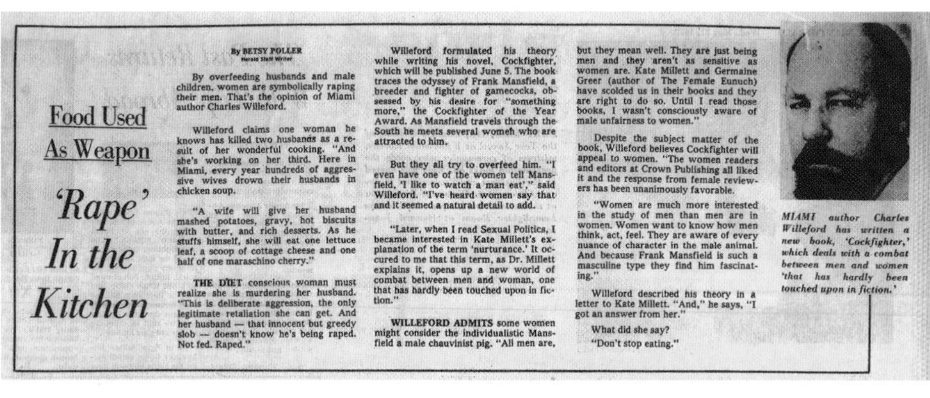

Food Used As Weapon

'Rape' In the Kitchen

By BETSY POLLER
Herald Staff Writer

By overfeeding husbands and male children, women are symbolically raping their men. That's the opinion of Miami author Charles Willeford.

Willeford claims one woman he knows has killed two husbands as a result of her wonderful cooking. "And she's working on her third. Here in Miami, every year hundreds of aggressive wives drown their husbands in chicken soup.

"A wife will give her husband mashed potatoes, gravy, hot biscuits with butter, and rich desserts. As he stuffs himself, she will eat one lettuce leaf, a scoop of cottage cheese and one half of one maraschino cherry."

THE DIET conscious woman must realize she is murdering her husband. "This is deliberate aggression, the only legitimate retaliation she can get. And her husband — that innocent but greedy slob — doesn't know he's being raped. Not fed. Raped."

Willeford formulated his theory while writing his novel, Cockfighter, which will be published June 5. The book traces the odyssey of Frank Mansfield, a breeder and fighter of gamecocks, obsessed by his desire for "something more," the Cockfighter of the Year Award. As Mansfield travels through the South he meets several women who are attracted to him.

But they all try to overfeed him. "I even have one of the women tell Mansfield, 'I like to watch a man eat'," said Willeford. "I've heard women say that and it seemed a natural detail to add.

"Later, when I read Sexual Politics, I became interested in Kate Millett's explanation of the term 'nurturance.' It occured to me that this term, as Dr. Millett explains it, opens up a new world of combat between men and woman, one that has hardly been touched upon in fiction."

WILLEFORD ADMITS some women might consider the individualistic Mansfield a male chauvinist pig. "All men are, but they mean well. They are just being men and they aren't as sensitive as women are. Kate Millett and Germaine Greer (author of The Female Eunuch) have scolded us in their books and they are right to do so. Until I read those books, I wasn't consciously aware of male unfairness to women."

Despite the subject matter of the book, Willeford believes Cockfighter will appeal to women. "The women readers and editors at Crown Publishing all liked it and the response from female reviewers has been unanimously favorable.

"Women are much more interested in the study of men than men are in women. Women want to know how men think, act, feel. They are aware of every nuance of character in the male animal. And because Frank Mansfield is such a masculine type they find him fascinating."

Willeford described his theory in a letter to Kate Millett. "And," he says, "I got an answer from her."

What did she say?

"Don't stop eating."

MIAMI author Charles Willeford has written a new book, 'Cockfighter,' which deals with a combat between men and women 'that has hardly been touched upon in fiction.'

She becomes a cocker's wife, which is presented as a pretty joyless existence.

"Outside of taking care of a man's needs, women don't get much pleasure out of life anyway," Frank says in the book. His view of women is so limited, he sees them only as appendages to men, and in fact, he pities them for this. Pity is one of the few emotions he reserves for women in the story (the other is outright disdain). In those moments in the book where he digresses into reflections upon womanhood, his proclamations are borderline ridiculous. "Women really do like to see a man eat," he observes, "especially if they are fond of the man concerned, and he's eating food they have prepared for him. I have never denied any woman the dubious pleasure of watching me eat."

Tangentially, this is actually a sentiment Willeford repeated on occasion, and not just in his fiction. An article called "Rape in the Kitchen" (with the subtitle "Food Used as Weapon") appeared in the May 31, 1972 edition of the *Miami Herald*, written by Betsy Poller, about a decade before she married her interview subject and became Betsy Willeford. "By overfeeding husbands and male children, women are symbolically raping their men," it begins, "That's the opinion of Miami author Charles Willeford." In what plays like a straight-faced debate, Willeford pronounces things like, "This is deliberate aggression, the only legitimate retaliation she can get. And her husband — that innocent but greedy slob — doesn't know he's being raped. Not fed. Raped."[99] This hilarious if inflammatory tirade ends with Willeford claiming that he wrote superstar feminist Kate Millett a letter, sharing his theory with her.

Dear Mr Willeford
Thanks for your fan letter.
My address is 307 Bowery NYC 10003. I look forward to reading your novel.
Don't stop eating.
Millett

Millett responded with a postcard, which stated simply, "Don't stop eating."

After he loses everything in his match against Burke, Frank ends up at the home of fellow cocker Ed Middleton, where the two enjoy a meal prepared by Ed's wife — who says not a word in the presence of the men she feeds. But her presence is felt behind the scenes; it is from Ed that Frank buys his ace cock Icarus ("White Lightning" in the film) after Ed's wife forces him to give up cockfighting, causing Frank to assume that she is perhaps "going through her menopause, and, as a consequence, losing her mind."

99 **Poller, Betsy. "Rape in the Kitchen" in *Miami Herald*. May 31, 1972. This article was later plagiarized in the September 10, 1972 issue of *The National Enquirer*, with the charged R-word changed to "attacked."**

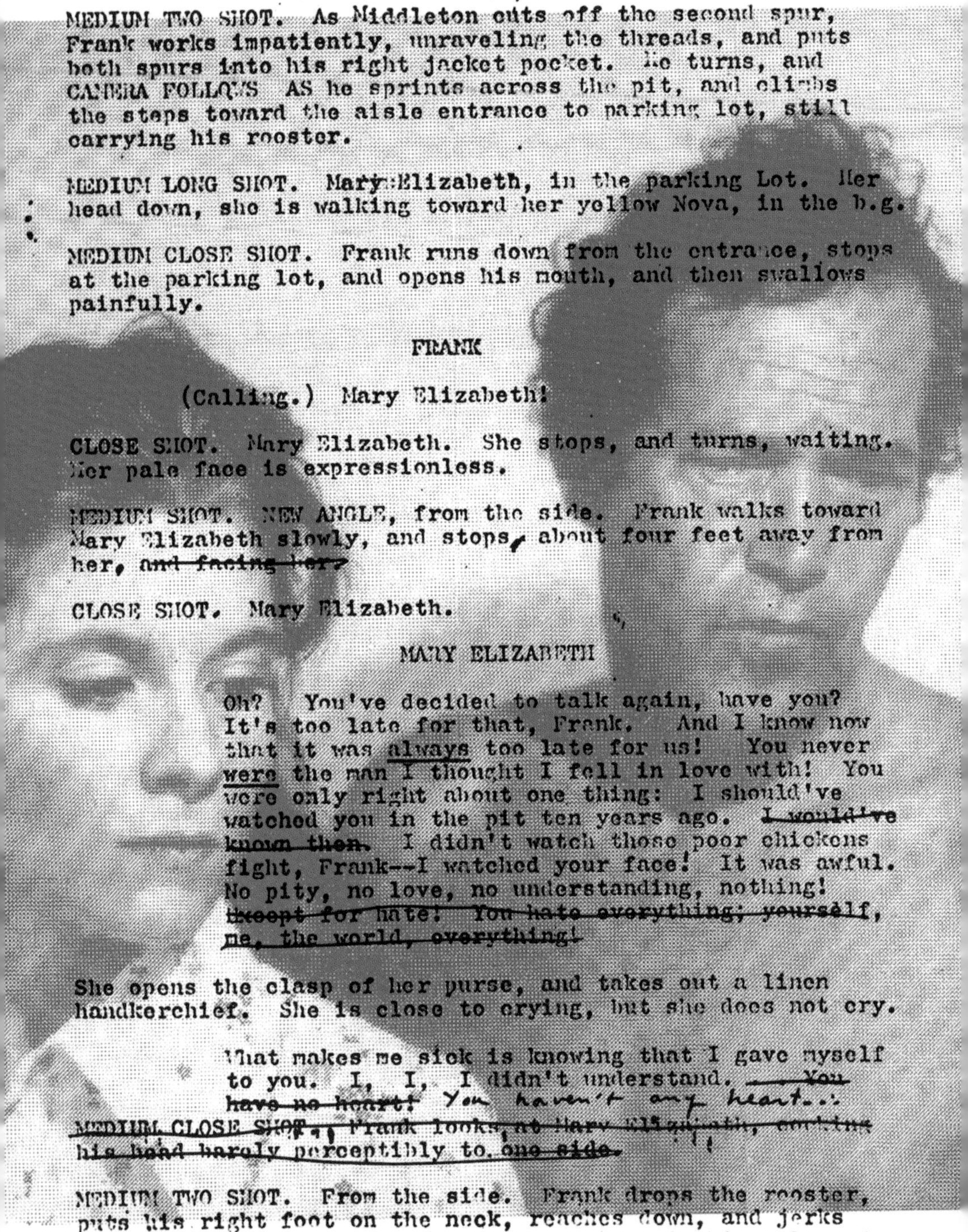

MEDIUM TWO SHOT. As Middleton cuts off the second spur, Frank works impatiently, unraveling the threads, and puts both spurs into his right jacket pocket. He turns, and CAMERA FOLLOWS AS he sprints across the pit, and climbs the steps toward the aisle entrance to parking lot, still carrying his rooster.

MEDIUM LONG SHOT. Mary Elizabeth, in the parking Lot. Her head down, she is walking toward her yellow Nova, in the b.g.

MEDIUM CLOSE SHOT. Frank runs down from the entrance, stops at the parking lot, and opens his mouth, and then swallows painfully.

FRANK

(Calling.) Mary Elizabeth!

CLOSE SHOT. Mary Elizabeth. She stops, and turns, waiting. Her pale face is expressionless.

MEDIUM SHOT. NEW ANGLE, from the side. Frank walks toward Mary Elizabeth slowly, and stops, about four feet away from her, ~~and facing her.~~

CLOSE SHOT. Mary Elizabeth.

MARY ELIZABETH

Oh? You've decided to talk again, have you? It's too late for that, Frank. And I know now that it was <u>always</u> too late for us! You never <u>were</u> the man I thought I fell in love with! You were only right about one thing: I should've watched you in the pit ten years ago. ~~I would've known then.~~ I didn't watch those poor chickens fight, Frank--I watched your face! It was awful. No pity, no love, no understanding, nothing! ~~Except for hate! You hate everything; yourself, me, the world, everything!~~

She opens the clasp of her purse, and takes out a linen handkerchief. She is close to crying, but she does not cry.

What makes me sick is knowing that I gave myself to you. I, I, I didn't understand. ~~You have no heart!~~ You haven't any heart...

~~MEDIUM CLOSE SHOT. Frank looks at Mary Elizabeth, cocking his head barely perceptibly to one side.~~

MEDIUM TWO SHOT. From the side. Frank drops the rooster, puts his right foot on the neck, reaches down, and jerks off the rooster's head. He holds the head in his palm, offering it to Mary Elizabeth.

All the women in the film are wives, save for Frank's hometown sweetheart Mary Elizabeth — who desperately wants to be one. Mary Elizabeth is a real Southern Belle, who keeps trying to rope Frank in with the dowry her father's offered to put up, describing herself as "a real bargain." Frank repeatedly humours her, leaves her hanging, his silence allowing her to project her fantasy of married life onto him without dispute.

In the film, the riverbank scene where Frank and Mary Elizabeth make love was filmed in a single master shot, the two lovers silhouetted against a wall of beaming sun. But although Hellman can recognise the beauty of Mary Elizabeth's devotion to Frank, amply expressed through Nestor Almendros' breathtaking cinematography, Frank himself remains emotionally alienated from her in a way he does not from his brood cocks — he likes playing with Mary Elizabeth, as though they were still teenagers fooling around, but she has grown up in his absence and he resents that.

Aligned wholly with Frank's perspective, Willeford's book does not permit Mary Elizabeth the same consideration that the film adaptation does; the novel pities her, whereas in Hellman's eyes, she is a noble and patient emblem of redemption that Frank stupidly rejects. But there's no way Mary Elizabeth would make it as a cocker's wife, a fate unbefitting the real lady she aspires to be.

In the film, even her secondhand knowledge of what it is Frank does is so limited; she has never seen a cockfight and has no understanding of the violence and chaos that is such a prized part of her beloved's existence. In the book Mary Elizabeth is far less ignorant about cockfighting — decrying it as "morally wrong, legally wrong and every other kind of wrong!", but during the film shoot, Hellman didn't let actress Patricia Pearcy see a cockfight until the climactic Milledgeville Tournament where her character has to see one for the first time, in order to capture her real reaction.

The director's biggest regret was not having a second camera to film her horrified face as Frank tears his ace cock's head off and hands it to her.

With this grisly offering extended to a disgusted and bewildered Mary Elizabeth, Frank is announced Cockfighter of the Year, the long-awaited impetus to end his two-year long silent protest. He speaks for the first time. As previously asserted, Hellman maintained that Frank's last line, "She loves me, Omar" — practically the only line of dialogue he has in the film that isn't voiceover — drove producer Roger Corman over the edge. "It's not a logical ending," Hellman admitted. "Roger has a scientific mind, and he needs things to be logical and very precise, and what we had was a very poetic line that can be taken many different ways." The evocative line reinforces Frank's idealistic notion of himself as a lone wolf with a higher purpose than marriage or a conventional life or job. It is an acknowledgement of what he could have, if he wanted it — which boosts the potency in rejecting it.

Nonetheless, the announcement, heard from a distance over a loudspeaker, feels anticlimactic compared to the very clear symbolism of the imagery onscreen; instead of sharing in Frank's catharsis, at the end of it all is just a limp cock with no head.

Writing of various modes of gambling (including cockfighting) in the Old South, scholar Bertram Wyatt-Brown noted that, "the narcissism involved in gambling and the frequently related sexual problems and inability to establish mature relationships all seem part of the magical thinking in which the gambler is engaged, especially when caught up in the passion of the play." Frank's relationship with women is even more removed than that of his predecessor in Willeford's *The Woman Chaser*, whose protagonist Richard Hudson also questions his sexuality, since his sex drive is completely subsumed by his drive for creative perfection. Hudson's burn-it-all-down response to any suggestion of compromise is not that different from Frank Mansfield tearing his prizewinning cock's head off at the end of *Cockfighter*.

But this ending has a slightly different significance in the book — and in early drafts of the script. The fact that Frank calculates his personal relationships in much the same way as he calculates his odds in the pit is most apparent in Willeford's novel, where he has romantic ties to not one, but two women.

There is another female character in the book — the widow Berenice Hungerford — who appeared in the earliest version of Willeford's script but was excised for time constraints ("Charles told me that Roger Corman told him that his first draft of the script would make a ten-hour film," says Betsy Willeford). Interestingly, Berenice is a character name Willeford returns to multiple times throughout his work, most notably in *The Burnt Orange Heresy*. "I asked Charles about the several Berenices," Betsy Willeford told me. "He and his wife had an apartment in Coral Gables and a condo in Fort Myers beach. When you drive across the state on the Tamiami Trail, you pass by a big stucco building, painted teal if I remember correctly. *Berenice's Bar-be-que*."

But Berenice adds another dimension to Frank's callousness; at the novel's close, Frank hedges his bets by playing off the two women against each other; he's been conditioning both of them all along, and only one of them will win, while the other will be destroyed. He even describes their clothing the way he would describe a bird's plumage (Willeford's book *The Black Mass of Brother Springer* even features a taste of the misogynistic analogue between women and chickens that colours *Cockfighter*'s prose: "The outside of the chicken was a beautiful colour — the shade of a two-day bruise on the tender side of a woman's thigh."). While Mary Elizabeth expresses her disgust at Frank's passion and means of income ("If I'd seen you in the cockpit ten years ago, I would've known then. I didn't watch those poor chickens fight, Frank, I watched your face. It was awful. No pity, no love, no understanding, nothing! Hate! You hate everything, yourself, me, the world, everybody!"), her rival Mrs. Berenice Hungerford shows only delight and curiosity. Hungerford wins.

"It was something interesting about the book," says Frances Doel about Frank's alternate paramour in the source text, "because I felt that it made a lot of sense in a way, to have him treat the women the same way he treats the fighting cocks, to have to see who wins at the end. But at the same time I could see how that would just completely add a whole extra half hour to the movie. And so it's probably one of the easiest things to cut."

One thing that distinguishes Berenice from her rival is that Mary Elizabeth is young, she wants to get married, wants children, and she's been waiting for Frank so that her life can begin. That's why she feels like it's all been a waste. Berenice on the other hand, is a widow — she's had a full life already, and her grief made her believe there wouldn't be anything else. So she's surprised at the pleasure she gets from Frank, she puts no expectations on it, at least not within the confines of this story.

I visited the Willeford archive in Fort Lauderdale on several occasions over the course of writing this book. Though initially I didn't find a version of the script featuring Berenice, there was peripheral evidence — letters, script reader feedback etc — that she appeared at least in the first draft. In a July 5, 1972 letter from Frances Doel to Willeford, she points out that Roger doesn't want Frank to invite both Berenice and Mary Elizabeth to Milledgeville, that it would be better if Bernice showed up unexpectedly. Presumably the first draft contained just this turn of events, and Corman's suggestion would have added suspense and stakes in a more conventional way. But it undermines Frank's calculating nature; it's very important that in the book he deliberately invites them both, knowing that it will invite a confrontation. He is unconcerned about the prospect of any social awkwardness — not because he is romantically oblivious, but because he wants to see which of them will win.

But in the cockfighting world, such wins are precarious and temporary. Berenice is still just a stand in for his real love — and the real love he has lost at the end of the book isn't Mary Elizabeth, it's Icarus, the white cock. As Jesse Pearson says in the intro to the 2011 reissue of Willeford's book:

> But then, yes, Frank does have tears in his eyes at that final fight. Is it love? Is it an acknowledgment of the end of his quest, for better or for worse? It could be that Frank, the sensitive troubadour amidst cockfighters, sees more clearly the parallels between men and fighting roosters. There is also a deep intimacy between Frank and his birds, as when he sucks away the blood from his rooster's wounds in the book's first fight. As Frank says, 'A chicken's brain is about the size of a BB, but within those tiny brains there is an infinite variety of character and personality traits.' Perhaps the love that Willeford sees from a cockfighter for his birds is like the love that a good general has for his troops

Moreover, the film's controversial punchline "She loves me, Omar" diminishes the contempt signified by the offering of the bird's head — "the beaten, bloody, but never bowed head" — as a memento. In the book, Frank is overjoyed to close that nagging chapter of his life: "After thirty-three years, I was a mature individual. I had never needed Mary Elizabeth, and she had never needed me. Finally, it was over between us — whatever it was we thought we had. My last tie with the past and Mansfield, Georgia was broken. From now on, I could look toward the future, and it had never been any brighter."

In August 2022 I revisited the Willeford archive to check on some details in the shooting schedule I'd not properly documented the first time around. It was during that visit I discovered a folder labeled "Shooting Script" which I thought I had perused previously, but upon opening the folder I realised it had been mislabeled: I was stunned to find the (259-page!) early version of the screenplay featuring Berenice that Frances Doel had referred to in her various correspondences with Willeford. And not only that, but at the end of the script were *two alternate endings* totally different from what ended up in the film.

There are other notable differences to the script: it includes Stephen Hooker's songs "Empty Pockets" and "Georgia Gal"; incorporates the character of Doc Riordan who tries to ply Frank with a get-rich-quick scheme in the book; depicts the brutal sequence of cutting off a chicken's legs and setting it on fire (thus Doel's note that the character is too unsympathetic); the romantic scene at 'The Place' is written to be shot in high contrast black & white; and most outrageously, the motel room flashback is conceived as an experimental sequence in which male characters crow instead of talk (and the female characters cluck)!

But the presence of Berenice (confusingly crossed-out and renamed 'Irma' in the last 10 pages of the script) and the bearing this has on the plot and the ending is much more significant. After the final fight, with both women present, Frank accepts his award and leaves for Puerto Rico with Berenice when Mary Elizabeth proves to have no stomach for the sport. In this way the original script ending reflects that of the book.

In the alternate ending — presumably written as backup in case Corman wanted something more "exploitation"-style — Mary Elizabeth returns to the pit and shoots Frank, he pulls out a knife and lunges at her — the two of them literally facing off in the cockpit! Frank dies in the pit holding the knife, as Icarus' decapitated head is dropped on the ground beside his dead, limp hand.

One last thing about Frank Mansfield and women: Frank does eventually get married… but not in this book. In Willeford's 1984 breakout hit *Miami Blues*, after the female lead Susie Waggoner leaves her psychopath boyfriend Junior in the dust, she goes to Ocala and marries a man named Frank Mansfield. And though Willeford does have a habit of recycling names for different characters, he confirmed in an interview with Don Herron that this Frank Mansfield is one and the same… presumably beguiled by an award-winning vinegar pie.

Over: The alternate 'exploitation-style' ending from Willeford's early draft of the *Cockfighter* screenplay.

CLOSE SHOT. Bernice's eyes widen with astonishment.

BERNICE

Oh! You--you've got your voice back!

CLOSE SHOT. Frank.

FRANK

Yeah, and you'll probably wish I hadn't."

CLOSE SHOT. Bernice.

(Puzzled.) I- -I don't know what you mean.

CLOSE SHOT. Frank.

FRANK

You'll find out that I'm quite a talker, Bernice. How'd you like to go to Puerto Rico for a few weeks?

MEDIUM SHOT. ~~Bernice~~ Mary Elizabeth enters the pit from parking lot entrance, and pauses. A FLASH Shot.

MEDIUM CLOSE SHOT. Bernice. A few other spectators, smiling, are listening in on the conversation.
MUSIC. "Empty Pockets." SNEAK IN.

BERNICE

Right now--I'm so confused that the only answer I can think of is "Yes."...

MEDIUM CLOSE SHOT. Frank. At pit level. He laughs, pushes his hat back,
MUSIC: Music up stronger, building gradually.
MEDIUM LONG SHOT. From Judge's table POV. Frank, grinning, walks toward the table with a slight swagger. The camera lifts, and we see Mary Elizabeth walking down the steps into the pit.

CLOSE SHOT. Frank's happy, grinning face.

MEDIUM LONG SHOT. Ed Middleton, Senator Foxhall, Peach Owen. smiling behind the table, and coming closer as Frank walks.

MEDIUM CLOSE SHOT. Mary Elizabeth. As she steps off last step into pit, she reaches into her purse and takes out ~~the~~ her .38 pistol.

MARY ELIZABETH

(Calling sharply.) Frank!

MEDIUM SHOT. Frank, from Mary Elizabeth's POV. He turns around, sees the pistol, apparently, and starts toward her.

CLOSE SHOT. Mary Elizabeth. She points the pistol and fires it. AAquick FLASH SHOT.

MEDIUM SHOT. Frank, falling to his knees. As he falls, he reaches into his right hand pocket, and comes out with his knife. He pushes the button, the blade comes out, and he struggles to his feet.

MEDIUM TWO SHOT. Frank and Mary Elizabeth. New Angle, from the side. He lunges for her, striking out with the knife, and she fires again as he dives, arm straight out, and falling headlong.

MED SHOT CUTTING ON ACTION – FRONT view of his diving Lunge,

MEDIUM CLOSE SHOT. Frank's arm, making and arc, holding the knife like a dagger, as he comes down. The knife blade cuts througs Mary Elizabeth's polo coat.

CLOSE CLOSE SHOT. Point of blade cutting through Mary Elizabeth's coat, continuing after the slash into the ground.

AUDIO. There is another shot.

CLOSE CLOSE SHOT. Frank's hand, gradually relaxing its grip on the knife handle. It stops moving, falls away from the knife.

CLOSER CLOSER Shot of unmoving fingers and knife in ground. Into the shot, in SLOW MOTION, the head of Icky falls beside the hand, loosely wrapped in the handkerchief. As handkerchief falls open, to expose the head beside the fingers,

MUSIC OUT ABRUPTLY.

FADE OUT TO BLACK.

CRAWL FOR CREDITS.

Chapter Fifteen. The Great (White) Cock

In 1959, Charles Willeford published the short story "A Genuine Alectryomancer" in the February issue of *Alfred Hitchcock's Mystery Magazine*, which later appeared as "The Alectryomancer" in his 1963 collection *The Machine in Ward Eleven.* Alectryomancy is a form of divination that utilises a chicken — most commonly a white rooster — attached to a table of letters or symbols as fortune-telling device.

Rooster augury of this type was very common among ancient Romans, where — according to the author of *Why Did the Chicken Cross the World?* — "no major decision was made without using the animal in divination rites." As the chicken migrated around the world through international trade, it assumed a symbolic role in almost every culture it encountered. In the Zoroastrian tradition it opposed demons and sorcerers; in Greece it became the sacred animal of multiple deities; in Rome it predicted the outcome of battle; the Egyptian cults of Mithras and Isis sacrificed it in temples; Islam believed it communed with angels; Shinto belief held it as sacred to the goddess of the sun; Daoist priests used it to ward off evil spirits; and in Christian lore, it announced the apostle Peter's betrayal of Jesus on Good Friday. "Gods, creeds, and dogmas appeared, vanished, and transformed," writes Andrew Lawlor, "but the chicken became a constant and essential part of our worship." In many of these cultures, it is a white animal — most commonly associated with purity and holiness — that is required for ritual and/or sacrifice.

Rooster divination also formed the basis of the 25th episode of the Boris Karloff-fronted American anthology series *Thriller* (broadcast March 14, 1961) which featured a segment called "The Extra Passenger," written by August Derleth and directed by Ida Lupino (and starring her own brother as the victim of his uncle's deadly fowl totem). This form of divination is closely related to Ouija, orniscopy (bird divination) and gyromancy (in which the diviner is within the circle themselves) but its legacy

survives in the relatively young Texan tradition of "chicken shit bingo" (in which a chicken is placed on a numbered platform and its droppings indicate the winner of the collected pot of cash).

In Willeford's story, a writer living on the island of Bequia is surprised to learn that the eponymous rooster diviner knows things about him that he has not shared with anyone: namely, that he left Oxford and moved to the West Indies on the advice of a pure white game cock (he ate the game cock that night, and departed the next day). The writer is drawn to return to the alectryomancer's mountaintop shack again and again, but in each reading, the rooster only spells out M-O-R-T — the French word for "dead." The writer loses weight, can't sleep, and becomes paranoid that death could take him at any moment, by any means — even though he swears he is not superstitious. Even when a colleague warns him that the alectryomancer is a huckster and the rooster has been trained to always spell out the same word, a brush with death in the ocean causes the desperate writer to seize the Obeah prepared for him by the alectryomancer as a good luck charm. The writer survives the fatal prediction and holds the Obeah responsible for saving his life — after which, his writer's block dissipates and he gets to work on the novel that's been eluding him. The beginning of *Cockfighter* is here.

Cockfighting can be seen as a surviving component of this strange tapestry of chicken rituals. As modernity overtakes and alienates, the cockfight serves as a link to what the cocker perceives as a heroic and mythic past. As scholar Fred Hawley asserts, the moral universe of the cockfighter is a dualistic one; both pagan and Judeo-Christian belief systems co-exist symbolically, the blood sacrifice deriving support from both the hierarchy of living things as established in the Bible, as well as the animism of pre-Christian ritual practice.

"To victory at Milledgeville!" Omar shouts, stacking three plastic champagne glasses on top of each other, "Life passes this way but once, not withstanding the Hindus, and I say celebrate a victory twice — once before the magic event, and once after it. A ritual is what it is — religious. Mystical in its power to evoke the gods of lightning victory.

As the top glass fills, it overflows into the next. And on down into eternity: the mystic realm of the Great Cock!"[100] He laughs and passes a glass to each Frank and Buford. And though Buford is not named as a partner in the "Anglo-Polish team of Mansfield and Baradinsky," he shares in their salutary drink nonetheless. There is still acknowledgement of Buford's difference within the world of *Cockfighter* — Frank refers to him as "my negro helper" — but Frank and Omar do their best to bridge it… within the limits of the Southern culture they are part of.

Compared to much Southern writing, where the spectre of slavery and segregation is wired into every narrative and sowed into the very landscape upon which these narratives unfold, *Cockfighter* (like its silent protagonist) has little to say — at least, directly. But the haunted preoccupations of the Southern Gothic do not escape *Cockfighter* completely, and one can scarcely find a better emblem of antebellum notions of purity than the film's choice of the pure white game cock. In the book the ace cock Icarus is described as the most 'brightly colored" gamecock Frank has ever seen; he then goes on to detail the configuration of various colours on the bird's plumage. In other words, in the book, the bird is not white. Choosing a white cock for the film may have been a practical consideration, to aid in audience identification of the "hero" bird, but inadvertently or otherwise, it brings cultural baggage with it.

100 **This monologue is not in Willeford's earlier script (although the scene itself is), and was likely an addition of Hellman/Rauch.**

Above: Omar and Buford share a moment in *Cockfighter*.

That many documented forms of rooster divination and/or sacrifice specify a white rooster as the sacred animal resonates with the elevated position of the pure white cock Icarus (or "Icky") — although changing his name to "White Lightning" in the film somewhat diminishes the classical resonance of the bird's original sobriquet (one who flew too close to the sun and got burnt).[101] "Another literary allusion lost," Willeford laments in his set journal.

The author spoke of the influence of classical mythology on *Cockfighter*, but also admitted that he didn't apply it beyond a surface level, so any analysis of the story in those specific terms tends to fall apart. However the symbolism in its most basic sense is there, and it is deliberate. But by eschewing the name Icarus, and instead imposing mythological status on the bird through the use of colour, the film makes a very different symbolic choice; one that triggers a more direct resonance with the film's geographical history.

Apart from its sole Native American character Pete Chocolate (played by the Caucasian real-life cocker A.B. Greeson in the film), *Cockfighter* has one Black character: Buford the kindly farm hand and occasional cock trainer. In the film, Buford is played by the 6'2" Robert Earl Jones, a gentle giant with that kind of performative simpleness that is aimed at disarming prejudice in his white counterparts. Frank is wise to it ("As soon as I looked at him he laughed the professional laugh of the American negro") but he also knows Buford is there by choice. Buford has his own farm with a wife and four kids, and still elects to spend most of his time at Frank's, despite the irregular pay — because, like Frank, Buford lives and breathes for gamecocks. "He loved gamecocks," Frank says, "And I believe he would have sacrificed an arm or a leg for the opportunity to fight them. Because I knew this much about the man, I was well aware that his rich and easy laughter was insincere. What the hell did Buford have to laugh about?"

There is an ongoing gag about Buford continually finding where "Mr. Frank" has hidden his booze, and helping himself to it — "he thought that finding my bottle was some kind of a game" — but nights on the farm are quiet and Frank and Buford routinely share a drink as friends. "Before Buford had finished the cupful of whiskey he got mellow and sang for us — old time blues and field hollers. When he held a note long enough for me to catch it, I would hit the corresponding chord on my guitar. I might have been a little drunk, but I thought Buford had the greatest voice I had ever heard." I always find myself wishing we could linger in this moment longer. It is the book's only real acknowledgment of the generational pain that comes with Buford's difference, how it is still there underneath "the big white smile shining in the middle of his ebony face."

Although it could be argued that he infantilises Buford, Frank's measured approach to racial difference is one of his more redeeming qualities: in the book, when he finds out his brother has joined the White Citizen's Council he makes sure that the Black tenant is allowed to live out his days on the family property after it's sold, while leaving his brother homeless. In Willeford's script, Buford asks if he can accompany Frank to the Milledgeville tournament, and Frank shakes his head no. Given Frank's

101 This also reflects what happened to Frank in that motel room with Jack Burke. In the end, Icarus' head is snapped off by his own 'father' (Frank) after doing him proud and winning the match. In classical mythology, Icarus' father, the inventor Daedalus was also embroiled in a fiasco (one of many) involving the theft of a pure white bull intended for sacrifice — the colour white for a sacrificial victim reinforced as a cultural norm.

somewhat fraternal relationship with Buford, one might presume he is merely shielding Buford from any prejudice he may encounter at the Senator's home (the shooting location of which had been a plantation with enslaved workers). But the fact is *Cockfighter* was written at a time when the deeply segregationist Jim Crow laws installed after the Civil War were still fiercely upheld in the South. African-Americans were not welcome in official Southern pits. "Unfortunately, because of his color, he was barred from almost every white cockpit in the South," Frank laments in the book, "He would have been an invaluable assistant for me on my trips to circuit cockpits, but I couldn't take him along."

Things hadn't always been that way. African-Americans were a key demographic in Southern cockpits in the antebellum era, and even laid the foundation for the ubiquity of chickens in the North American diet; Andrew Lawlor points out that turkey, goose, pigeon, partridge and duck were the fowl most commonly eaten by European settlers, while chickens were the only animal enslaved people were even legally allowed to own, and thus became a key ingredient of meals, entertainments and folk magic.

Of the Louisiana cock pits, writer Ralph Dempsey of *New Histories* wrote: "In a state where many people were commonly isolated in ethnically separate groups such as Cajun, Creole, Hispanic and African American and where racial animosity was not uncommon, cockfighting had appeared a unique activity. Amongst the gambling, drinking, blood and feathers these people had felt a welcomed common bond; as one commentator noted 'the pit serves its historical function of cultural middle ground, meeting- and melting-point of southern subcultures, ethnic groups and economic classes.'" Frank echoes this sentiment in *Cockfighter*, asserting that

> Members of the cockfighting fraternity are from all walks of life. There are men like myself, from good Southern families, sharecroppers, businessmen, loafers on the county relief rolls, Jews and Holy Rollers. If there is one single thing in the world, more than all the others, preserving the tradition of the sport of cockfighting for thousands of years, it's the spirit of democracy.

That the cockpit acts as at least a superficial equaliser of class and race is borne out even in early documentation, such as a *Harper's New Monthly Magazine* article of May 1857, whose illustrations depict a racially and economically diverse crowd. In the post-civil rights American South, cockpits again became more diverse, especially as the number of Mexican enthusiasts — Mexico being a country where the sport remains legal to this day — grew exponentially. "Especially considering the rural, working-class character of contemporary cockfighting in the South, for many participants the

TRIMMING.

Above: Illustration from *Harper's New Monthly Magazine*, May 1857; Right: An article by *Roots* author Alex Haley in *Writer's Yearbook '73*.

The author's search for his own African ancestors took imaginative research, seven years and luck. The result: "Roots", will be published by Doubleday this year and movie rights have been sold to Columbia.

RESEARCHING THE UNKNOWN

by Alex Haley

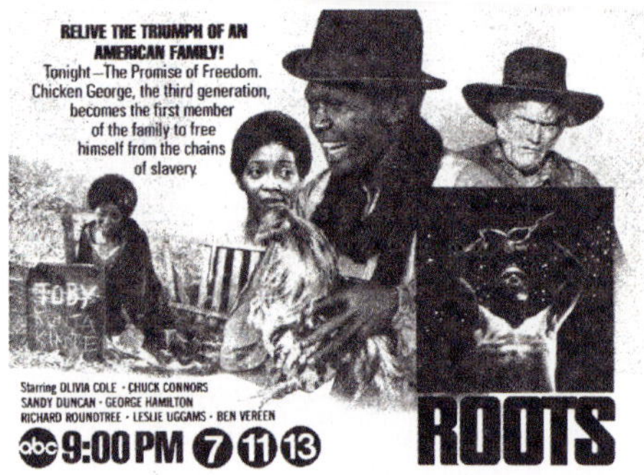

pit has created a unique forum where their predominant notions about cultural demarcations blur, at least temporarily," writes scholar Marko Maunila, noting that outside the pit is a different story altogether.

What is not often commented on is that America's preeminent narrative concerning the journey of a Black family from Africa, through slavery to emancipation — Alex Haley's *Roots* (1976) and its 1977 television mini-series — sees that family's first legal acknowledgement of freedom determined not by the outcome of the Civil War, but by cockfighting.

In the first episode of the miniseries, Kunta Kinte — having been captured on the banks of the Gambia river — sits starving, sweating, sick, crammed into the bowels of a slave ship bound for America and tells another stolen 'passenger' of a nightmare he's just had:

> I dreamed I was hunting.
> Running faster than I ever ran before, spear in my hand.
> I was hunting a great, huge bird whose wings stretched from one river bank to the other.
> It turned and flew towards me.
> And I saw it was all white.
> All white.
> Its great flapping wings swallowed me up and choked me.
> I opened my eyes, and I was here…
> In the belly of that terrible bird.

With its obvious reference to the slave ship personnel who captured him, the dream challenges the positioning of whiteness as "pure" or "good" in spirituality and myth, and instead reveals it as corrupt and ruthless pretension, which the series will aim to strip away and expose over its subsequent seven episodes.

As the story passes through succeeding generations of the family, there emerges a character named "Chicken George" (played by Ben Vereen in the miniseries) who is the

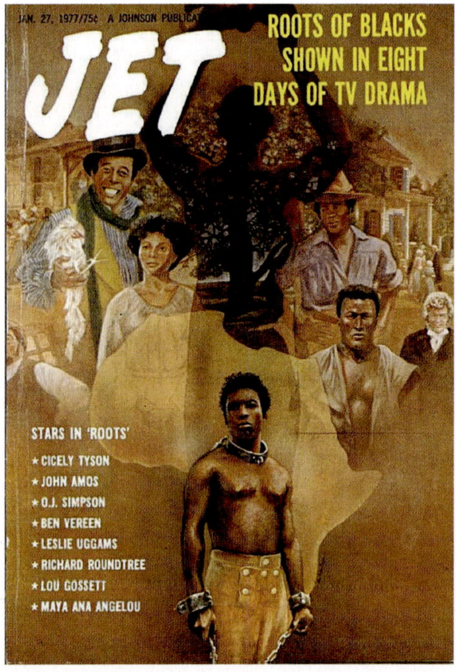

Right: The two faces of Chicken George: in the 2016 remake of *Roots* (top) and the 1977 original (bottom).

son of Kunta Kinte's daughter Kizzy, the result of a rape by slave master Tom Moore (Tom Lea in the book) who also happens to be a cockfighter. Tom (played by Chuck Connors) is also — according to the social hierarchy of the South — a "cracker." The self-made owner of a modest farm, he is incredibly sensitive to the arrogance of his more affluent neighbours. Tom has enslaved farmhands who train and fight the birds, in exchange for the incentive of a small share of the winnings. Growing up in this milieu Chicken George becomes an ace cockfighter, and a mutual dependence develops between Tom — desperate to be accepted into "the South's most elite gamecocking circles" — and George, who has started saving up to buy his own freedom. The cockfights allow him to interact and share news with slaves in other parts of the South — and he has heard of precedents where slaves from other plantations have been successful in raising enough to buy their autonomy. It's important to note that though *Roots* makes frequent reference to free Black men active in cockfighting, they are always referred to as "hackfighters" — which means they are holding fights outside of the official tournament circuit, even though they may be following the circuit itself in pursuit of worthy opponents. Chicken George, on the other hand, so long as he is working in tandem with his white master, is able to enjoy notoriety and esteem within accepted gamecocking circles.

It's interesting to note that the sport, as practiced by Connors' character, aligns with previously noted class distinctions; when Tom first appears in the series he is dining with plantation owner Robert Reed, who expresses a clear disdain when Tom tells him about his profession. Because to the wealthy, cockfighting is a hobby, a leisure activity where the associated gambling has little effect on their cache of wealth — while Tom's reliance on cockfighting as a profession is depicted as pathological and degenerate. This is reinforced later when Tom makes the bet that will set Chicken George's freedom into motion; he bets (and loses) 20,000 dollars against a visiting British aristocrat (Ian McShane), who observes Tom's drunken boasting — among a disorderly, white-trash local fanbase — and comments that, "If I said 'a sport for kings,' I stand corrected; this chap and his friends would disqualify it as even a sport for gentlemen!" But Tom's over-betting — which sends him teetering into the dangerous terrain of Bentham's "Deep Play" — is fuelled by his need for class revenge: "If he could win this fight it would make him forever a heroic legend for all poor crackers," writes Alex Haley in the book, "a symbol that even the snobbish, rich, blueblood massas could be challenged and beaten!" But in the end, even Chicken George will have more social mobility than a cracker like Tom.

Upon winning, the aristocrat demands the use of Chicken George as a trainer overseas for a limited time as a means of covering Tom's debt. Tom assures Chicken George that if he follows though — thus saving Tom from insolvency — he will grant him his freedom upon his return, which he does. According to Alex Haley's own research, George Lea, or "Chicken George", was the first member of Haley's family line to be granted his freedom, and he won it by his skill in cockfighting. It must be noted that Haley's research and the accuracy of his historical timeline in *Roots* has been questioned by even his most ardent supporters; but taken purely as historical fiction, it is still significant that cockfighting is given such a pivotal role in the emancipation of Haley's ancestors.

Right: Jocelyn (Alex Descas) in Claire Denis' *No Fear, No Die* (1990).

The motif of the white bird is also centralised in Claire Denis' cockfighting film *No Fear, No Die*, where it represents the unspoken longing for self-determination that whiteness implies. Bob Marley's song "Buffalo Soldier" is a constant refrain throughout the film. The title of the song refers to the post-Civil War Black cavalry who served an army that continued to segregate and abuse them even after emancipation, and was written as a Black resistance ballad. Here it becomes the anthem of two displaced Black men brought from the West Indies by a white gambler, who intends to exploit their skills to create a lucrative underground business. As with Tom in *Roots*, the French gambler Ardennes invests in a co-dependent relationship with the two immigrants, who do the brunt of the work training and handling the birds.

As Catherine Wheatley points out in her essay "La Famille Denis," the cockers' kinship is based on their marginality, which is also tied to their transient status as immigrants. In *No Fear No Die*, the illegality of underground cockfighting is likened to racial exclusion as well as the low social status of migrant workers, which is why Denis' decision to open the film with a quote from African-American pulp writer Chester Himes is especially fitting; aside from his Harlem Detective novels — the famous Coffin Ed and Gravedigger Jones series that began with *A Rage in Harlem* (1957) — Himes' earliest novels depicted the experiences of black migrant workers during the Second Great Migration of 1940-1970. Himes himself had emigrated to France in the 1950s.

Robert Earl Jones had himself been a part of the First Great Migration of 1910-1940; he was a Mississippi sharecropper who moved to Chicago and became a boxer, billed as 'Battling Bill Stovall.' He moved on to New York for a job with the Works Progress Administration in the 1930s, which is where he met poet and playwright Langston Hughes. There is a 1995 video recording of Jones at the Foundry Theatre performing a Hughes poem called "The Negro Speaks of Rivers":

> I've known rivers:
> I've known rivers ancient as the world
> and older than the flow of human
> blood in human veins.
>
> My soul has grown deep like the rivers.
>
> I bathed in the Euphrates when dawns
> were young.
> I built my hut near the Congo and it
> lulled me to sleep.
> I looked upon the Nile and raised the
> pyramids above it.
> I heard the singing of the Mississippi
> when Abe Lincoln went down to New
> Orleans, and I've seen its muddy
> bosom turn all golden in the sunset.
>
> I've known rivers:
> Ancient, dusky rivers.
>
> My soul has grown deep like the
> rivers.[102]

Published in W.E.B. DuBois' magazine *The Crisis* in 1921, it was Hughes' first published poem, written when he was a teenager crossing the Mississippi River to live with his estranged father in Mexico City. In talking about the poem Hughes has noted that the river acts as a strong metaphor for the African-American experience during the Great Migration. In the context of this

102 From *The Collected Poems of Langston Hughes*, published by Alfred A. Knopf, Inc. Copyright © 1994 the Estate of Langston Hughes. The recording of Robert Earl Jones can be seen at https://vimeo.com/83780808.

SEVEN MOMENTS OF LOVE

An Un-Sonnet Sequence In Blues

by

Langston Hughes

To Carl Jones —
These monologues,
Sincerely,
Langston
1939

"vast uprooting of population" scholar William Hogan notes that it "recognizes the need for a new kind of rootedness, one that embraced a history of migration and resettlement."

Stories of Black mobility also carry the implication of Black rebellion, and while the denial of Buford's potential for travel on the cockfighting circuit speaks to this, such tensions exist more explicitly throughout both *Roots* and *No Fear, No Die*. The white man needs the Black employee to perform, but not well enough that they can leave him. A programme of verbal abuse ensures their codependence.

When Jocelyn's favourite cock, the eponymous 'No Fear No Die', falls in battle, he becomes despondent and begins to drink heavily. He lets all the cocks loose and they begin to kill each other while he lies crumpled on the floor amidst the melee. Ardennes is furious, and again, Jocelyn's race is employed as a cheap shot: "You West Indians are all assholes! Good only to sweep up crap! You deserve to get screwed over by whites!" Instead of fighting Ardennes directly, Jocelyn turns his aggression on his friend Dah; the lateral violence mirroring that of the released fighting cocks.

But the larger environment of the cockpit — including the stands that house the audience — simulates what Clifford Geertz called "the social matrix, the involved system of cross-cutting, overlapping, highly corporate groups — villages, kin-groups, irrigation societies, temple congregations, "castes" — in which its devotees live." The cockfight is a reflection, a reenactment, and sometimes a temporary inversion of social hierarchies. Geertz refers to those gathered around the ring as "a superorganism in the literal sense," and indeed, the pit or arena — as in antiquity — is a sacred space. Only the handler, the referee and combatants can enter its confines. It is the "magic circle," as deployed in centuries of spiritual practice from the ancient Mesopotamians to Judaism to Wicca.

There is also something interesting about the closed society of the cockpit being an ostracised society outside of that space, and the subversion of normal social hierarchies that can manifest within the confines of that space. It recalls the medieval Charivari and Carnival, a complex of rituals and social practices at the center of which is often a mock-procession targeting a designated community scapegoat — sometimes represented by a non-human effigy, but which generally involved rowdy and violent roleplay. Playing the role of such scapegoats, marginalised people normally excluded from the discourse of power were temporarily endowed with some political attributes, much as the cockfight facilitates the crowning of a perceived fool as "king for a day." French historian Marie-Yves Bercé writes that "the normal sanctions of the youth kings and kings of fools — burlesque tribunals, charivaris, skimmingtons, and mock sacrifices — were endowed with obvious aggressive potential. These burlesque weapons could offer passages from carnival to revolution and appear as subversive."[103]

Jocelyn picks a pure white bird as his replacement champion and names it

103 Qtd in Christol, Florent. "Christmas Evil and the Cultural Myth of the Fool-Killer" in *Yuletide Terror: Christmas Horror on Film and Television*. Eds. Paul Corupe and Kier-La Janisse. Spectacular Optical 2017. Pg 50.

after Ardennes' girlfriend Toni (Solveig Donmartin). "Did anyone ever see a cock like this?!" Jocelyn brags as he parades the white cock around the pit, recalling Frank Mansfield's beatification of his own white cock, Icarus. When the rooster is nearly killed in a fight, Jocelyn approaches the real Toni who is watching pitside and begins rubbing the bloodied cock on her white dress in a sexual motion, until Ardennes' son — who also covets Toni himself — stabs Jocelyn and kills him. Jocelyn collapses into the pit, undone by both woman and whiteness.

Both *Roots* and *No Fear No, Die* address complicated issues of race in the cockpit in a way that *Cockfighter* never does. While there is an identifiable residue of traditional Southern racial hierarchies in the relationship between Frank Mansfield and Buford (unlike every other male character in the book, Buford does not get a surname), and early versions of the script attempt to give Buford's character more prominence (as well as occasional quips by other African-American characters), most of this was cut out of the final shooting script. Only the pure white prize cock 'White Lightning' remains, a steadfast symbol of all the things left unsaid.

Chapter Sixteen.

Hatched to Kill:

Post-Production & Release

Filming on *Cockfighter* wrapped on Saturday May 4, 1974, brought in on time and within its $400,000 budget.[104] In his set report, Phil Garner cites the film's co-producer Sam Gelfman as predicting that *Cockfighter* was "going to be a sleeper." He didn't know it was going to go to sleep and not wake up for several decades.

Lewis Teague (later to direct animals-run-amok classics *Alligator* and *Cujo*) was enlisted to help Monte edit the film. Teague had first come to film as a programmer, running one of the many theatres owned by theatre chain owner Bob Lippert — who coincidentally had also produced Monte Hellman's early Philippines-shot films *Backdoor to Hell* and *Flight to Fury* (both 1964). "Lippert was Roger Corman before there was a Roger Corman," says Teague. Like Corman, Lippert gave a leg up to many filmmakers who later became celebrated in their own right, including Sam Fuller, Hellman and Jack Nicholson, and exploitation-turned-evangelical director Ron Ormond. Says Teague:

> He had a theatre chain and he made real cheap films to put in the theatre. He had a little movie theatre on Sunset Strip that was supposed to show what they called 'Nudie Cuties' back in that day. The Nudie Cuties opened up in '65, the same year that hippies took over Sunset Strip. So his audience was not coming to Sunset Strip at that time. So I know the guy named Fred Roos. He's a producer, produced all of Coppola's films. Anyway, he knew Lippert. Fred called me and asked me if I wanted to do something with this little theatre, because it wasn't going to make it as a sex venue. It had 16mm projection, and I wanted to show retrospectives of some of my favourite old directors. And so I took it over and ran the Cinematheque 16 for several years for Lippert.

Teague had been angling to move over to the Corman camp after getting a raw deal on a film called *Dirty O'Neill: Loves of a Cop* that was distributed by AIP. "*Dirty O'Neill* did not set the world on fire," he admits. By the early '70s he was working for the local LA PBS station KCET in the documentary department, but was searching for something bigger. He knew Corman's reputation for giving many young filmmakers their first shot in the director's seat. Ironically he had earlier turned down an editing gig for Corman — on the recommendation of Martin

104 *Box Office*, May 20, 1974.

Scorsese, with whom Teague had been in the same class at NYU — in order to focus on the ill-fated *Dirty O'Neill*. Recalls Teague:

> I wanted to figure out some way of getting to Roger Corman so that I might be able to direct a film for him eventually. So I'm trying to figure out some way I access Roger. And I heard that Monte Hellman was going to be directing a film for him and I had met Monte socially. We knew each other. We had mutual friends. So I called Monte and said, 'Hey, Monte, I hear you're doing a film for Roger… and I wanted to find out if there's any chance I could work with you' — because I knew Monte liked to edit his own stuff. And Monte said, sure, you can help me edit it. If it's okay with Roger, it's okay with me. So then I got Roger Corman on the phone and told him that Monte wanted me to help edit his film. And Roger said, if it's okay with Monte, it's okay with me. So that's how I got on board.

Although Teague is credited onscreen as sole editor of the film, both Teague and Hellman have asserted that they edited the film together. Hellman's first professional role in film was as an editor at ABC television and he cut many AIP pictures before directing his own — which he also usually edited himself. For a director as particular as Monte, it wouldn't have been easy to delegate responsibilities like this, but the schedule required it. Teague was brought on as an additional editor due to time constraints. "Roger wanted the picture ready in an impossibly short period of time," commented Hellman. "The only way to accomplish this was to bring on a second editor." That said, Hellman came to appreciate having a second editor to work with, and not only due to the time constraints. "He's an excellent editor," Hellman said of Teague in a 1976 *Jump Cut* interview. "We hadn't worked together before, but we saw eye to eye on most things and he made suggestions about the scenes that I had cut. We really worked as a team. Essentially what he cut were the most difficult scenes, the cockfighting scenes. His major experience had been in the documentary field, so I felt that he was better qualified to do those scenes than I was."

"Monte is a terrific editor and he edited all the dramatic stuff in the film," says Teague. "He basically just asked me to cut the cockfighting scenes. So that worked great for me because I didn't consider myself nearly as good an editor as Monte was, but I love cutting action stuff. And so that's what we did… I cut the action footage under Monte's supervision, Monte let me exercise my creative impulses as much as he could, and then would come in and mould it a little bit to suit the story. So I really enjoyed that connection a lot."

But Corman saw Lewis Teague's role as being somewhat more substantial — at least as far as the former's commercial interests went. "Well, actually Monte shied away from shooting the fighting cocks," Corman said, "which came as a little bit of a surprise, because having been a director for so many years myself, particularly when I'm shooting on location, I'm there for pre-production planning and the first few days, and then at that point I leave it to the director and the production manager. [When I saw it], the picture was paced a little bit slower than I thought, and there wasn't enough cockfighting."

"I know that normally Roger gives his directors an enormous amount of latitude," says Teague, who went on to direct *The Lady in Red* for Corman in 1979, "but when it comes to having to make a commercial decision, he can put his foot down." And it seems that this was one of those times when Roger was going to put his foot down.

Recalls Teague:

> In the final stages of the editing, I assume that [Monte] and Roger had some differences of opinion. I wasn't privy to them. I didn't hear them or witness them, but I do know that Monte at one point left town with his girlfriend. He went up to San Francisco, I think it was. And Roger came into the editing room and we talked a little bit about the action sequences, especially the final sequence. And Roger wanted to know if there was any way we could spice it up, make it a little more exciting. And I volunteered to go out and shoot some extra shots of chickens fighting, no additional dramatic footage or anything that really changed the story. But just to try to give me a little more action footage to work with in the final cockfighting scene. So I got a tiny crew and some chicken wranglers and went out for a day and shot some additional cockfighting footage, which I then cut into the film. And I don't think it made much difference at all, but it satisfied Roger.

"Monte didn't want to direct the cockfighting — in a picture called *Cockfighter*!" said Corman, who was apparently still incredulous over this fact decades later. "So I sent Lew Teague with a cameraman to — I think it was Arizona where cockfighting was legal — and Lew shot most of the cockfighting scenes and that enabled us to bring the action that was supposed to be in the film."

It turns out those pick-ups were shot a little closer to home. In the middle of Los Angeles, California, in fact — the very first state to ban cockfighting in the 1920s, thanks to the lobbying of William Randolph Hearst himself — in a residential driveway.

When prompted by this recollection, Corman acceded that his barber — a California-based cockfighter — may have provided the fighting cocks for the inserts. "They're just a few close shots," Teague points out, "Put up a few hay bales, keep the camera angles so that you don't see above the hay bales in the background, have a few people's hands in the ring, that kind of stuff."

"Well, I'll tell you the story," says production manager Peter Cornberg. "It was shot in MY driveway in Laurel Canyon because I lived at the end of a dirt road and we were able to fabricate some little thing that faked the walls of the cockpit, and Lewis — who was an old friend of mine — was available. I got him and Bill Kaplan to come up to my place." Bill Kaplan is mainly a sound guy, who worked on many exploitation films in the 1970s but also was a camera operator on *Gimme Shelter*. He is not credited on *Cockfighter*. "We had two cameras and it was all close up stuff," Cornberg continues,

MOVIOLA
J&R
SERIAL NO.
MOVIOLA

like beauty shots of chickens, more than anything. I arranged the whole thing with Billy [Abbott]. I think it's possible that he had never been in an airplane before and here he is flying from Atlanta to fight chickens.[105] I don't know anything about the legalities, or what he did to get them in, or if anybody ever questioned him, he had probably a half a dozen. And it seems to me the day before, I picked him up at the airport and I had a station wagon and I think we probably took the chickens up to my place to spend the night in the cages that he had brought them in. And he needed a place to stay. He was a really unassuming, very conservative, laid-back guy. Well, I put him up in the Tropicana. And I went down and picked him up in the morning and took him up to my place, and we shot for the day. And at the end of the day, he said, 'Peter, I didn't get a wink of sleep last night — the sirens, the women screaming and yelling all night long at that motel — can you get me someplace else?' And I took him into my guest room in my house and said, 'How'd you like to stay here with me and my girlfriend.' He said, 'Oh, I'd love it.' So Billy spent the night with us in Laurel Canyon. He brought the chickens with him. And anything about Roger's barber is somebody's fantasy.

When I tell him that Roger himself told me this, he shrugs: "Oh, well it's possible that his barber knew Billy Abbott before we knew Billy Abbott — that that could have been the connection."

I had a hard time believing Hellman wouldn't be upset by an editor he had brought on to the project shooting entirely new images and cutting them into his film. But Teague maintains that Monte knew the score and was unruffled by it. "It was just the action footage with the chickens," he says, "And that was what I'd been sort of relegated to edit anyway. I didn't change the dramatic structure and I didn't touch anything having to do with actors. So I don't think it mattered to Monte — in my opinion, it didn't make any difference." Like others who have worked with Corman, Teague felt that there were just certain things to be expected. "Roger had a specific pattern that he followed," says Teague,

> He was very organised kind of guy and my experience both as an editor and as a director, once he gave the director the script and told him how much money he had and who was going to play the leads, once that was settled, Roger left me and all the other directors I observed alone until the first day of shooting. He let the directors cast it, pick the locations, he did not micromanage any of that stuff. And then he would show up on the first day of shooting to make sure everything was together, that it was off to a good start. Then he would disappear until the director finished his first edit, which usually took about three, four weeks depending on the schedule. And then Roger would give the director prolific notes, lots of notes. And he was pretty good and clear in his note-giving. And that seemed to be my experience, and it was basically the way he dealt with Monte on *Cockfighter*, to the best of my memory. But I learned later that

105 **Billy Abbott had definitely been on a plane before — he had fought in championships in the Philippines.**

> Roger was unhappy with the film and the ending, and he was probably having private conversations with Monte during that time. And that's why Monte took off at a certain point because Monte wasn't around when I shot those scenes, I wouldn't have reshot them on my own if he hadn't disappeared.

Hellman later complained that in service of these inserts, Corman doused the chickens with fake blood — because according to the director, "there's no blood in a real cockfight." This however, is not true. The birds definitely bleed. Still, in order to emphasise the injuries of Frank's white bird, the prop man sprayed him with "Hollywood blood" from a squeeze bottle.

Despite his increasing arms-length relationship to the film, it was Hellman who got in trouble with the DGA when they realised the film's assistant director Don Walters and production manager Peter Cornberg were not members of a union — which they needn't be as Georgia is a right-to-work state, but in cases where they couldn't lean on the production company, the guilds often tried to punish their members for participation. As Hellman explained to me, directors are responsible for making sure they are not working on a set where certain colleagues are not guild members. He claimed he was taken to court and threatened with removal from the DGA for life. Because he was being paid DGA rates, he admitted that he assumed it was a DGA production and was let off with a warning.[106] When asked if this created friction with Corman, he said, "Roger's response was that he never claimed it was a DGA production, and that's true, he didn't." Hellman sighed. "Roger just doesn't care about those kinds of things."

Interestingly, Don Walters said the only way the DGA would even have tracked that Hellman had violated guild rules was if the film had been "submitted for an Academy Award or something" which, of course, it had. Though no one has owned up to submitting it for Best Screenplay, the record of submission for Oscar consideration is right there in the Margaret Herrick Library. Walters speculated that it was probably Monte himself who submitted it, recalling an anecdote from the set: "I remember we were in Atlanta during the shoot and it was Academy Awards time," he says, "And that night we all went to dinner, one of the really nice barbecue places, and Monte was just twitchy. And I was like, 'What's the matter with you?' 'Well the Academy Awards is on and I have to get there.' I guess he couldn't go in person 'cause he couldn't leave the shoot. So we had to get back to his motel and see the Academy Awards." I questioned this memory at first, since in my lifetime the Oscars have always been in February or March, but as it happens, in 1974 the awards were held on April 2, when the crew would have been in Atlanta for prep. However, since Monte's major beef with the film was the script, I have a hard time believing he would have submitted it for Oscar consideration. Who knows, maybe Charles Willeford wasn't so humble after all.

106 **I did contact the DGA about this but they no longer had records going back as far as 1974.**

The film had its world premiere on July 30, 1974 in Roswell, Georgia, with Oates, Willeford and producer Sam Gelfman in person (Corman was supposed to be there but was called to London on business). The screening was held at the Roswell Village Twins Cinema, whose two 300-seat auditoriums hosted three staggered screenings to accommodate audience numbers, with the $2.50 tickets partially benefiting the Roswell Booster's Club (who had provided extras for the film's final cockfight).[107]

The original trailer and TV spots were cut by Joe Dante and Allan Arkush, who — along with Jon Davison, who would become Head of Publicity at New World — had moved out to LA specifically to work for Corman. Arkush and Davison had met at NYU Film School and later both worked at the Fillmore. Dante, then living in Philadelphia and already a film collector, would provide film prints to run between the bands. Jon was the first to work for Corman and Dante and Arkush followed soon after. "I came out here and it was apparent that there was too much work for me," explains Dante. "What Jon was doing was he was trying to talk Roger into creating a trailer department instead of hiring piecemeal, a new editor for every trailer, and then having to explain to them what he wanted. Jon said, 'Look, why don't you just get some people, tell them once and they'll know it, and then they can make trailers.'" With so many pictures coming in, Allan Arkush soon joined the team. "And so we became the defacto trailer department."

"It was a very felicitous set of circumstances," says Arkush, "because Joe and Jon were huge Corman fans. So now Roger had people working for him who really understood all of his work, his entire catalogue. And as much as one could understand his psyche and taste from being a fan, and I was introduced to it by them. So I was learning this, and we're all crazy film lovers. We were full of ideas and we were trying to do justice to his sensibility."

New World's makeshift post-production facilities became a chaotic breeding ground for a motley crew of emerging filmmakers who were rising through the ranks of the Corman School.

Joe Dante: It was the back room of a guy named Jack Raven, who was a special effects guy.

Allan Arkush: He started working with Max Fleischer.

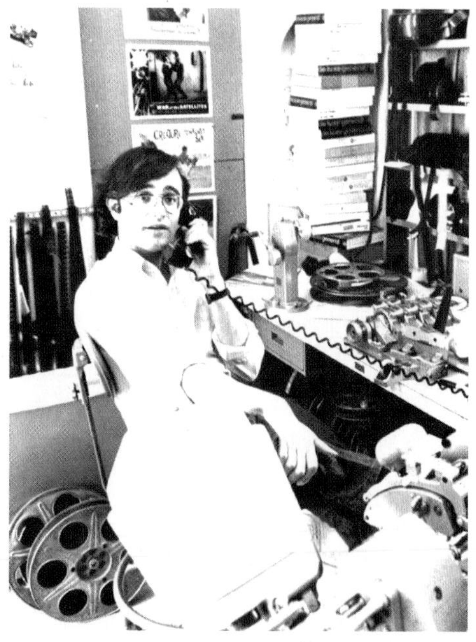

107 *Box Office Magazine*, Aug 5, 1974.

Above: Joe Dante in the New World post-production offices.

Joe Dante: And he was quite a character. And he worked on a lot of Roger's pictures and he did the special effects for *Night of the Hunter*, I mean, a lot of different kinds of things. And he was a bit of a shyster, but he was a really interesting guy. And he had a little post-production unit. And there was a back area which was let out to various movies. Somebody would rent it for three months and edit a whole picture there. We ended up just sort of moving into it. And it was great because now we could do the trailers and the effects and plan the wipes and all that kind of stuff, all in one place.

Allan Arkush: And the other rooms would fill up with the other New World pictures.

Joe Dante: Which we would usually be doing the trailers for.

Allan Arkush: So now you had Jonathan Demme there, and Lewis Teague and Paul Bartel, Tina Hirsch and everyone. And every day we'd go out to lunch together, we'd hang out. So it was this hotbed of movie fanatics and, and Jack kind of took on the role of our benevolent uncle who thought we were all a little crazy.

But they found the task of cutting a trailer for *Cockfighter* challenging, for a number of reasons. "The movie, as beautifully photographed as it is," says Arkush, "could not be cut into an effective trailer, just playing it like it was. Because you couldn't say that Warren Oates didn't speak." "That was the

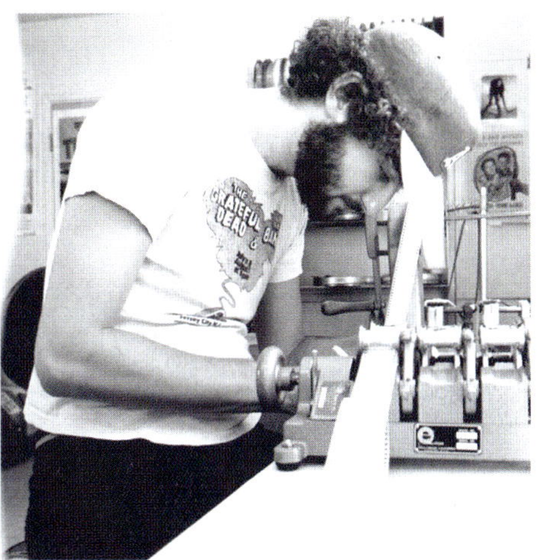

trick," adds Dante. "We had to hide the fact that he didn't speak. But we did what I actually thought was a pretty darn good trailer for it," asserts Dante. "It was pretty dramatic."

"What you are about to see is illegal in 47 states," the trailer begins, "Cockfighting — the dirtiest sport in the world!"

Allan Arkush: It's almost like a chorus — it's like a two-shot of the two chickens, the roosters. And they kind of go at each other and we slowed it down and put "Cockfighter!" with this interesting sound that happens like two or three times in the trailer. Like we're saying, this is Epic. This is about COCKFIGHTING!

It's an exploitation film trailer that, while effective, does not convey either the protagonist's stoic conviction or the meditative quality of the film's documentary minutia (it also contains a homophobic slur that makes it difficult to use in promotions

Above: Allan Arkush in the New World post-production offices.

today). As with many exploitation trailers that emphasise the film's most sensational images, it's a bait and switch.

> Joe Dante: The thing about the trailer was that, times being what they were, and us being young men, there was a lot of laughter about the title *Cockfighter*. And so one of the things we had to do with these trailers, we had to get them cleared by the MPAA. So we have to take the rough cut of the trailer to the MPAA and have them approve it.

> Allan Arkush: You have to understand that we were not the most sophisticated people.

> Joe Dante: We were just kids making trailers.

When the New World crew would bring trailers to the MPAA they would often only have a black and white rough cut with a crude recording of the voiceover — if not providing the voiceover live, which they sometimes did — which contrasted with other companies who showed up with a colour print and a fully mixed track. One day, as they ambled up to the MPAA offices, they ran into Ernie Anderson — best known to genre fans as horror host Ghoulardi, and to normie cinephiles as the father of Paul Thomas Anderson. "He had a great sonorous voice," recounts Dante. "We thought we would do something funny. So we had him record different dialogue for the trailer. "Frank Mansfield had the biggest cock in town and what he did with it was illegal in 47 States! With his cock in his hand, he took on the man..." and all that kind of stuff. So we only got a couple of lines into it and the MPAA guy — his name was Dick McKay — he's a very sweet guy, but he was always close to a heart attack. And when those lines came on...

> Allan Arkush: And Jon [Davison] was there and we were trying not to laugh.

> Joe Dante: And we had to say, it's a joke, we're not really gonna do this. But I guess he'd been getting flack from above about our trailers anyway. We got away with a lot of things because they would foolishly allow us to see other trailers that were being shown that day. And we would see what they got away with. And I remember seeing the *Texas Chain Saw Massacre* trailer and thinking, Holy Christ, they got away with this? Then we should get away with it. After a while they figured out it was better if we didn't see the other trailers.

> Allan Arkush: But we still were pretty smarmy though.

> Joe Dante: We got to a point where the movies were so silly that we just basically did parody trailers for the movies. Like *Covergirl Models*, which has no actually intrinsic merit at all. But the ad line is...

> Allan Arkush: "They don't need clothes to strike a pose."

> Both: "They may be overexposed, but they're never underdeveloped!"

After its official premiere in Roswell on July 30, the film opened the next day across the Atlanta Exchange (courtesy of sub-distributors Atco Gibraltar Pictures[108]). There were 100 prints struck for the release, 20 of which were booked for the five-county Atlanta region. "We didn't do national releases," says Jon Davison, "Everything was regional. New World basically was organised around a group of sub-distributors. I think we had 13 around the country. So, we may go 50 to 100 prints on a title and they would open territory by territory." By the first week of August, *Cockfighter* had rolled out through various sub-distributors to neighbouring Alabama, Florida and Tennessee (Atco Gibraltar) and Louisiana (Masterpiece Pictures), and by mid-August it had opened in Kentucky (JMG Films), North and South Carolina (Galaxy Film Exchange), and even Guam (which New World handled itself).

The Atlanta Journal-Constitution's review was headlined "A Fowl Film Orgy" and praised Oates' performance, as well as those of the many cockfighters-turned-amateur-actors: "Its portrayal of the seamier side of the South is chock full of a kind of verisimilitude rarely seen in a Hollywood movie… For once, the South looks like the South. The real Georgia on film is much more colorful and picturesque than any of the facsimiles Hollywood has used over the years."

But that was as good as it was going to get; the filmmakers knew from the first Friday night that the movie was going to fall on its face.

When the film premiered, Corman was in Europe. "He was out there for vacation," Allan Arkush says. "And he learned that the grosses were not there," adds Dante. "It was like $300," Arkush continues. "I mean, it was some insane amount like that."

Warren Oates Avoided 'One-Villain Style'

'He has a great face; he may have been cast as the heavy but you can have sympathy for him.'

—Filmmaker Stanley Colbert

In 'Cockfighter,' Warren Oates Plays a Braggart

The boredom is fatal in 'Born to Kill'

By DAVID COOPER
Courier-Journal Staff Writer

"Born to Kill" is bound to kill you with boredom.

This yawn-evoking potboiler, now playing at the Preston and Lakewood Drive-Ins, stars ex-Louisvillian Warren Oates and Patricia Pearcy, who has had several roles this season with Actors Theatre of Louisville.

Oates plays a man who owns fighting cocks (the original title of the film was "The Cockfighter") who is bent on winning the cockfight of the year medal. But our hero has a problem: He talks too much, brags too much, and ends up getting his best fighting cocks killed in "unofficial" contests.

Finally, he loses his last cock and all his money. After the fight, the winner tells Oates he could have been champion if he had kept his mouth closed.

So Oates vows not to talk to anyone until he wins the medal. And he keeps his promise. He doesn't even talk to his fiancee (Miss Pearcy).

REVIEW

'Cockfighter' a Fowl Film Orgy

By JOHN HUEY

If [illegible] chicken cooked, stay away from the "Cockfighter," a fowl film orgy of feathers and blood shot almost entirely in the remote wilds of exotic Georgia.

But if you want to see some well photographed scenes (some in slow motion) of brilliantly heed roosters spurring … the $400,000 film was shot in four weeks all over Georgia.

Yes, from Roswell to Mansfield to Toccoa to Lawrenceville to Klondike to Lithonia, the feathers and the bets fly.

Not to mention tempers. In one scene, for instance, Ed Begley, Jr. tries to chop up Oates with an ax because an involved "good old boy" fan simultaneously cheering [illegible] tearing the meat off a fried chicken leg.

The unquestionable highlight of the film is the cinematography of Nestor Almendros. And this is where the Georgians who attend the 194 "World Premieres" at …

The Society for the Prevention of Cruelty to Animals has criticized the film for its [illegible] chickens.

But as the producers point out, cockfighting is a reality in Georgia and throughout the South. If people like it live, why not on film? Besides, they say, we eat chicken don't we?

Anyway, the film has its good points and its bad points.

If you're interested in the [illegible] fighting, it's all there. If you want to see what little Georgia towns and their inhabitants look like on film, that's there too.

But if weak acting and lots of chicken blood easily offends you, that's all there too.

108 Atco Gibraltar Pictures covered the Atlanta and Jacksonville territories until late '74 when Corman and Atco's Jack Rigg became partners in New World Pictures of Atlanta.

Filmed, premiered in Georgia

by STEVE MYERS

The New World release "The Cockfighter," as the title indicates, concerns the modern illegal sport of fighting roosters for gambling purposes. The film is described as its director's version of "The Hustler." The film stars Warren Oates as the title character who believes he has a chance of winning in national competition with his rooster. The script is by Charles Willeford from his novel of the same name and is set in Georgia and northern Florida. The movie also stars Harry Dean Stanton ("Dillinger" and "Where the Lillies Bloom"), Millie Perkins ("The Diary of Anne Frank"), Patricia Pearcy, and Troy Donahue.

When I learned that parts of the film were being shot near Atlanta, I called the Public Relations office at the state capitol in an attempt to locate and interview the movie's director, star, and cinematographer. I finally ended up calling New World Pictures in Los Angeles. I was given the name of the associate producer and his last known telephone number in Georgia. After I contacted Samuel Gelfman, he gave me the day and time which would be most convenient for me to conduct my interviews. Without his gracious cooperation, the following article and photographs would not have been possible.

I arrived at the Sandy Springs Squire Inn at 8 a.m. on May 3. It was the next to the last day of shooting and the crew was preparing a hotel room for a scene near the end of the story. While these preparations were being made, Mr. Gelfman "rounded up" director Monte Hellman and cinematographer Nestor Almendros for my brief interviews. I talked to actor Warren Oates after the lunch break.

The producer of "The Cockfighter" is Roger Corman. Corman is perhaps, in a given span of time, the most prolific director since Allan Dwan. He is best known for his series of films based on stories by Edgar Allan Poe ("The House of Usher," "Pit and the Pendulum," "Masque of the Red Death," and "Tomb of Ligeia"), as well as gangster films such as "Machine Gun Kelly," "The St. Valentine's Day Massacre" and "Bloody Mama." He has financed the first efforts of the best young directors in America including Irving Kirschner, Francis Ford Coppola, Peter Bogdanovich, and Martin Scorsese.

Prompted by studio interference and the high cost of productions with large union crews, Corman formed his own independent company, New World Pictures, in 1971. Admittedly New World is mostly responsible for exploitation

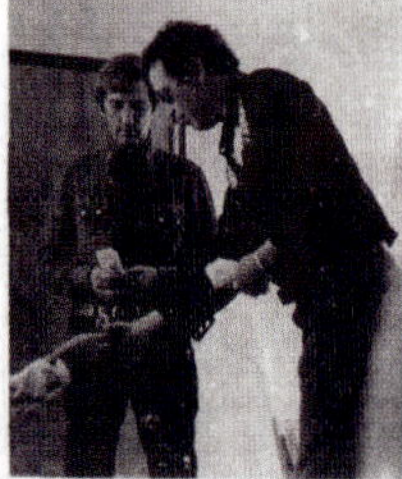

Photo by STEVE MYERS

FILMING OF 'THE COCKFIGHTERS' IN ATLANTA
Warren Oates (R) and Harry Stanton rehearse a scene

drive-in films. At the same time, the company's great success has allowed New World to become the U.S. and Canadian distributors of Ingmar Bergman's "Cries and Whispers" and the highly imaginative animated science-fiction feature "Fantastic Planet." For the past three years Corman's time has been occupied with the new company. Hopefully he will soon return to directing.

Monte Hellman has been associated with Roger Corman since 1959 when he directed the Corman-produced "Beast from Haunted Cave." In 1965 Hellman directed two war-adventure stories, "Flight to Fury" and "Back Door to Hell," both of which starred the then-unknown Jack Nicholson (who also scripted "Flight to Fury"). Two years later Hellman directed Nicholson again in two westerns, "The Shooting and "Ride in the Whirlwind." "The Shooting" was written by Adrien Joyce (writer of "Five Easy Pieces") and "Ride in the Whirlwind" was written by Nicholson. The westerns were well received in France where they were exhibited at film festivals.

"Two-Lane Blacktop" was Hellman's next effort. The film starred Warren Oates, James Taylor, and Dennis (Beach Boys) Wilson as drifters involved in a cross-country car race. The movie did not fare well with American critics, but the French appreciated its "New Wave" style. It is possible that the "The Cockfighter" will prove to be more appealing to American tastes.

Warren Oates has had important roles in "In the Heat of the Night," Peckinpah's "The Wild Bunch," and "Kid Blue." He has worked with Monte Hellman before in "The Shooting" and "Two-Lane Blacktop." Recently he had the starring role in John Milius' "Dillinger." Oates had travelled to the shooting locations of "The Cockfighter" in his Open Road camper. I talked to him in his room at the Squire Inn while his German shepherd gnawed on bones left over from the lunch break. Oates told me that his most challenging role had been in "Two-Lane Blacktop" and that he had been working on the script of a film he hopes to direct himself.

The cinematographer, Nestor Almendros, is an expatriate Spaniard whose most famous work has been in France. His films for Francois Truffaut include "The Wild Child" and "Two English Girls;" and with Claude Chabrol, "Claire's Knee." Almendros is one of the most respected cinematographers in the world owing to his intelligence and the excellence of his work. Of the three interviews, the one with Almendros was the easiest because he offered suggestions and gave more complete answers than I could have expected.

I asked Almendros if he agreed with Truffaut's controversial auteur theory — the idea that the director is the primary artistic force in filmmaking. He replied, "Yeah, I think so. Even directors who are not like Truffaut, who is a master, a genius. I notice that even the smallest director ends by imposing his point of view by some miracle, osmosis, or something."

"The Cockfighter" had its world premier on July 30 in Roswell, Ga., where much of the film was shot. It went into general release all over Georgia yesterday, and is now showing at the Alps Drive-In.

Photo by STEVE MYERS

'COCKFIGHTERS' DIRECTOR MONTE HELLMAN
Crew sets up on location in motel

Different accounts have the LA preview being held at either the Paramount (whose original name, the El Capitan, was restored in 1991) or the World Theatre, both on Hollywood Boulevard. "The World Theater was a triple-bill theatre," says Joe Dante. "That's where we ran *Rock n' Roll High School*. That was the go-to place because it was a grindhouse audience."

"Dave Garroway was sitting behind us in the audience," recalls Miller Drake, whose own New World history began in the trailer department before he moved on to a celebrated career as a visual FX artist on films like *The Abyss*, *Terminator 2* and more. Garroway was a well-known television presenter who had first risen to fame as the founding host of *NBC Today* from 1962-1951, and is known as one of the pioneers of the television talk show — although he long battled with depression and died of a self-inflicted gunshot wound in 1982. "As soon as the movie came on, when you saw the shots of those metal things ripping into the chickens and all that kind of stuff, he got up and walked out of the theater." Lewis Teague recounts another awkward moment at the screening:

> I went to the bathroom and I'm in the bathroom doing my thing at the row of urinals, and another guy came in whose name I'm not going to reveal. He's standing there and then Monte came in. So the three of us are standing there and the other guy turned to Monte and said "Well, Monte, you did it again!" And Monte smiled, taking that as a compliment. I bit my tongue and didn't laugh. And so Monte's films are appreciated, but a lot of people find them very puzzling.

"I do remember that after this screening of *Cockfighter* we were all dragged to the Hamburger Hamlet across the street to discuss the film's reception," recalls Jon Davison. "Roger didn't do previews like the studios do, where they have guys writing things down and asking questions and stuff," says Joe Dante. "You'd just go to the movie and see if it played, you can tell. Filmmakers can tell when their film is playing and when it is not." And *Cockfighter* was most assuredly *not*.

Stephen Hooker recalls not caring much for the film at first. "In 1974, I was most likely watching the movie from a technical point of view and may have seen it at the British Film Institute," he says, "At the time, I was an assistant film editor and DP wannabe. Later, when I saw it on TV, I realised how much better it played on a small screen. Finally, when I viewed it from the ambiance of a drive-in it was perfect."

Contemporaneous drive-in audiences did not seem to agree.

"As soon as it opened, it was obvious that the picture was underperforming," confirms Davison. "So I think what happened is immediately, probably Friday night, we knew that it wasn't happening. And so I think Saturday, I got the call from Roger that we need to change the title of the picture and do a new campaign." Within days of opening, an entirely new campaign was in the works — one that attempted to de-emphasise that the film was about cockfighting.

I-77 DRIVE-IN • 873-3082
At US 70 Exit
A COCKY MAN OF ALL-ACTION AND FEW WORDS . . . IF ANY!!!
WARREN OATES IS THE COCKFIGHTER
From Governors' Mansions to Cheap Hotels!
The Big Money Sport... Dirty, Violent And Outside The Law
Filmed In The Cockpits Of The South
OPEN 7:30 STARTS DUSK
Adm. Adult $1.50 Child 4-11 50c Open 7:30 Starts Dusk
IN COLOR R
6 BIG DAYS Tonight-Tuesday
ALSO Rated R "Student Teachers"
THE SOUTH'S MOST MODERN DRIVE-IN CINEMA

"Corman had once told me, Lewis, I will never lose money if I have the right title and a low enough budget," recalls Teague,

> And that was his philosophy. Now what happened was that we had just finished editing the film — we would work right up until the day the film was going to be released in those days, within a few days. So the film was released on a weekend. And then the following Monday, I was in the editing room, cleaning up, putting away trims, putting everything into storage. When I got a call from Roger. "Lewis, I was wrong." A rare admission from Roger!

In a now-infamous move, Corman attempted to further commercialise the film with inserts from other New World films that they could then use in a new trailer.

> Joe Dante: Never to be outdone, Roger decided that there was a way to save the picture by getting rid of that awful title and sort of disguising the fact that it was about cockfighting at all.

> Lewis Teague: Roger said, 'I want you to get all the footage of sex and violence that you have from the film and give it to Joe. So I said to Roger, 'But Monte didn't shoot any sex or violence!' And he said, 'I don't care where you get it. I just want you get some and give it to Joe.' So I went to Roger's library and

he had made a whole bunch of student nurse films. And I found car chases and shots of student nurses unbuttoning their blouses and all that kind of stuff. And I gave them all to Joe per Roger's instructions. Then I called Roger back. I said, 'Roger, I don't think it's right to use footage in a trailer that's not gonna be in the movie. Not only is it not right, but the audience will be disappointed.' Roger said, 'You're right, Lewis. Put it in the movie.'

Joe Dante: So he called us up in the editing room from Europe and he said, I have an idea. I want you to change the name of the of the picture to *Born to Kill*. And what I want you to do is I want you to go into *Night Call Nurses*, and I want you to take the dynamite truck chase out. And then I want you to go into, I can't remember, some other movie, and get the sex scene. And then there was some other picture that had a bunch of violence and guns and stuff. And he said, I want you to cut all that stuff together into a one-and-a-half minute montage. And then Warren Oates goes to sleep and turns the light out. I want you to put that in as a dream sequence, then all the new trailers for the picture can be made around this footage.

Allan Arkush: Literally, we thought he was kidding.

Joe Dante: He was not kidding.

But Corman denied that he did anything to significantly alter the film: "It wasn't much," he said,

> I would say there was maybe 30 seconds cut into it, or something like that. It was put in just to be able to put something in the TV ads. I wasn't interested in changing the film, I was just interested in trying to find a different

Above and opposite: the respective title treatments in the trailers for *Cockfighter* and *Born to Kill*.

> way to sell the film. I can't remember what [the footage] was. We had a meeting with all the guys — Joe Dante, Jon Davison and Allan Arkush were sort of our young braintrust at the time, and we all sat around trying to figure out what to do. And we decided the thing to do — because we thought we had a good picture and that somehow we had just failed to connect with the audience — so we did something to the TV spots and the trailers, and then to justify that we put a couple of shots in. But they were just there to legitimise the TV spots and the trailers.

By the end of August, the film was being explored in "test-sites" as *Wild Drifter*, and in October the name *Gamblin' Man* came into the mix. "We made up new title sections," recalls Miller Drake, "so we could drop them into prints and literally take the same print and time it, and have the optical track printed in, so we can physically go in and splice these new titles into the existing print, so you didn't have to make new prints."

Corman insisted the film was never actually released under those titles. As he explained, "We were only interested in titles. What we would do is we would send people out to theatres where a picture was playing that might appeal to the people we'd like to see this picture. And we would just present cards with three or four titles written down and say, which of these titles would you be more likely to see, and *Born to Kill* won that type of test. There was no actual test of the picture itself because the picture was what it was. We were just testing titles." Dante and Arkush can corroborate this practice because they were among the people recruited to go around conducting such polls. "For the testing of titles, I would go to Hollywood High School and ask everybody, but which one they like more, and mark it on a piece of paper," says Dante. "And this was sometimes before the movies were even made."

But the notion that *Wild Drifter* and *Gamblin' Man* were merely unused ideas is belied by existing advertisements confirming that the film was released in Mississippi and Louisiana under the title *Wild Drifter* starting Aug 30, 1974, and in Kansas and Missouri as *Gambin' Man* in October of that year. This was actually before the film had its second push as *Born to Kill* starting in March 1975.

But *Born to Kill* was the title that stuck. "We used to joke about that," Monte said. "We used to call it *Hatched to Kill*." A new trailer was cut with the new title, proclaiming it, "The macho movie that ricochets off the screen with a double-barrel action blast!" The new posters had reconfigured the original John Solie artwork to show Warren Oates now wielding an axe, standing up in the passenger seat of a muscle car being driven by a young blonde. Below that, a pair of illustrations from another movie entirely. Jon Davison, who was in charge of many of New World's promotional campaigns at the time, came up with a million taglines (including the infamous "He came to town with his cock in his hand and what he did with it was illegal in 47 states") and reissued press books to accompany the various retitlings. "I kept saying that we ought to call it *Naked under Feathers*!" remembers Beverly Gray.

On its *Born to Kill* release — a much wider release that saw it hitting screens in Texas, Kentucky, Nebraska, Iowa, Ohio, Illinois, Michigan, Wisconsin, Maryland, Oregon, Hawaii and California — *Variety* compared its cockfighting scenes favorably to those in *Day of the Locust* but said the script "supplies lots of technical info about the weird sport but is thin on dramatic values."

Hellman wasn't a part of the decisions made in the film's retitling and the inserts that came with it. "I don't think Monte was consulted on the idea of adding the dream sequence," says Dante. "I think he probably found out about it and there was nothing he could do about it. I mean, he may have been 'consulted,' but I've been consulted, that means nothing. I've been shown ads for pictures that I did that I thought were just abominable. And they said, so what, we don't care, this is how we're doing it. And that just comes with the territory."

"What I remember very vividly was people seemed to approach working on *Cockfighter* as outsiders from the artistic mission that Monte had," Steven Gaydos comments,

> And I learned probably for the first time that I saw people who looked at moviemaking as work and Monte never looked at it as anything but art, right? I mean, Monte was always very professional and very focused on the work, and he may deny what I'm saying. But when you're young and you see the two different approaches — there were people like Joe Dante and Lewis Teague and others who were, I thought, cynical and they were not friends of Monte. They were not friends of *Cockfighter*. They were not advocates of *Cockfighter* in my memory. They were working people. They were hired by Roger Corman to get a job done. It wasn't their baby.

Whether *Cockfighter* was *anyone*'s baby remains contentious. After researching it for eight years, I am compelled to think its authorship is not so cut and dried. Many people, including Monte Hellman himself, have referred to the film as Roger's, while others see it as a Hellman picture through and through. But there are just as many indications that the film was orphaned early on and only reclaimed with its belated cult status.

Right: New World press booklet for *Born to Kill*.

Rebel fury—the law can't touch him!

WARREN OATES

in

BORN TO KILL

A New World Pictures Release INC.

8831 SUNSET BLVD. / LOS ANGELES, CALIFORNIA 90069 / (213) 657-2201

It didn't occur to Hellman while he was making the film that it would be a hard sell. Still, Monte did his part in trying to reconfigure its placement once that proved to be the case; as explained on the Anchor Bay commentary, Hellman and Gaydos created ads for *Cockfighter* that tried to sell it as an arthouse film. It's a still of Oates flanked by puzzle pieces bearing the words "Love," 'Courage," "Manhood," and "Heart" — and then *He's Trying to Put it All Together* written vertically down one side. "Yeah. He's trying to put it all together," Gaydos remembers, "That was my very intellectual approach to making *Cockfighter* a story of a romance, and a man who's kind of coming to grips with himself."

"Look, it's an art film," shrugs Dante. "Monte made an art film. I think Roger was not expecting an art film. And we couldn't sell it as an art film, we had to sell it as an exploitation film. But luckily Nestor Almendros' photography is gorgeous and it's somehow all done at sundown. How they did that, I don't know." But why wouldn't Corman expect an art film? Hellman's track record as a director was obvious. *Two-Lane Blacktop* had been an existential road movie that was set up with high expectations and died at the box office. And Corman himself had sunk money into *The Shooting*, which took him two years to sell, and even then, just barely. "I can't imagine he was that shocked that it came out as a sort of a studious, stately kind of a movie," Dante muses. "I think he may have just banked on the idea that the subject itself was so sensational, that that was going to sell the picture."

In 1976 the film hit even more screens as the second feature with *Jackson County Jail*, notably bigger markets like LA and New York, along with Philadelphia, Boston, Tucson, Minneapolis, Salt Lake City and more.

August
1977

MONTHLY FILM BULLETIN

VOL. 44 NO. 523

FEATURE FILMS

RETROSPECTIVE

SHORT FILMS

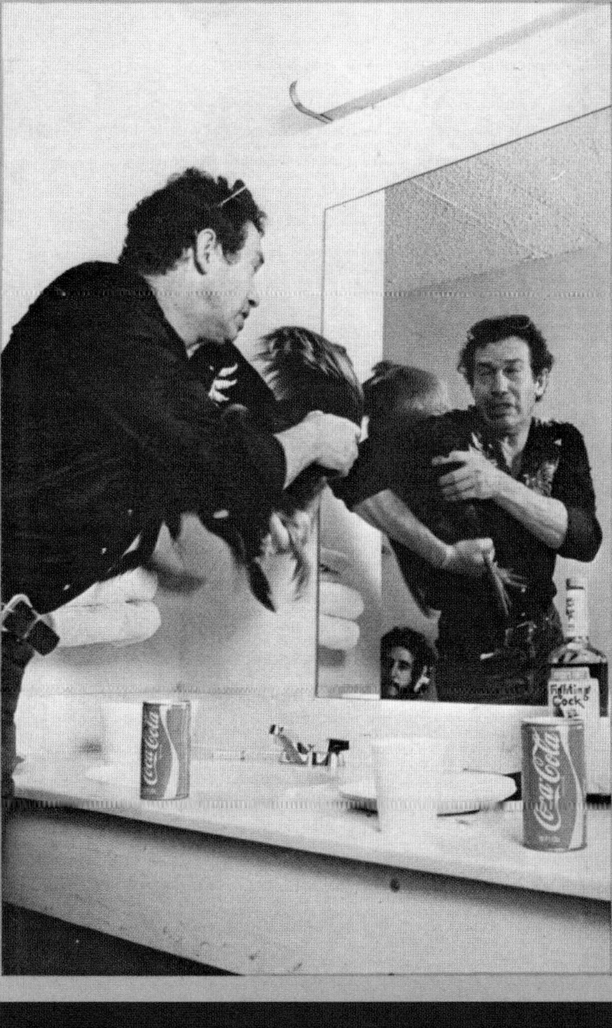

35p

The film played under its original title (and in its original cut) at the Edinburgh and London Film festivals, and in the 1987 coda to *Cockfighter Journal*, Willeford corroborates that the film did well "especially in England," with *Sight and Sound* naming it one of the top ten foreign films to play the UK in 1974. Willeford claims that in light of the positive review in *Sight & Sound*, he was so happy he "went out and drank without economy."[109] In her review of the film in *The Times*, Penelope Houston (longtime editor of *Sight & Sound*) says "cockfighting is not only a brutish sport but on the face of it a very monotonous one, in itself a kind of *reduction ad absurdum* of the impulse to bet on anything that moves or fights." Since the film remains unreleased in the UK to this day (despite the BFI's *Monthly Film Bulletin* putting it on the cover of their August 1977 issue), it's worth delving into the specifics surrounding its potential for distribution. According to Craig Lapper, the erstwhile director of compliance at the British Board of Film Classification (BBFC), *Cockfighter* has never actually been banned in the UK — because it has never been submitted for a certificate.

The UK, unlike the US, has an obligatory rating system — however festivals exhibiting films to the public which may or may not get distribution within the UK often come under the purview of local authorities, who do have the right to override BBFC classifications or lack thereof. That said, the issues surrounding *Cockfighter* are due to a law separate from the BBFC. As Lapper explained to me,

> The Cinematograph Films (Animals) Act 1937 makes it illegal 'to exhibit to the public, or supply to any person for public exhibition (whether by him or by another person), any cinematograph film (whether produced in Great Britain or elsewhere) if in connection with the production of the film any scene represented in the film was organised or directed in such a way as to involve the cruel infliction of pain or terror on any animal or the cruel goading of any animal to fury'. So, if the film contains any sequences of cockfighting that were set up by Monte Hellman and his crew for the purposes of making the film, then it is likely we would have to require cuts to those scenes as a condition of classification. The BBFC's view has always been that real cockfighting does involve the cruel infliction of pain and terror on the animals involved. Furthermore, even in cases where precautions have been taken to protect the animals from actual physical harm (for example, by fitting them with beak guards and rubber spurs), the mere act of placing them together and making them simulate 'fighting' amounts to a cruel goading of the animals to fury. It is worth noting that these tests are not tests set by the BBFC but tests laid out by UK law. It is also worth noting that the 1937 Act applies regardless of BBFC classification and applies equally to screenings of films without BBFC classifications. While local authorities undoubtedly have the right to permit the screening of films that have not been classified by the BBFC, they do not have the right to give permission for a film to be shown that is in breach of UK law. If a film breaches the 1937 Act then it cannot legally be publicly exhibited in the UK. While we don't know the circumstances that led to the film being screened in Edinburgh in the mid-1970s, we are aware that a more recent attempted retrospective screening of *Cockfighter* at Edinburgh in 2006 was cancelled after the Scottish Society for the Prevention

109 **Willeford, Charles. "From Cockfighter to Born to Kill" in *Film Quarterly*, Vol. XXIV, No. 1, Fall 1975. pp 20-24.**

of Cruelty to Animals intervened and threatened a prosecution under the 1937 Act.

Nonetheless, London newspaper listings show it playing at Screen on the Green (a 111-year old neighbourhood theatre now famous for several historical Sex Pistols gigs) as a "members-only premiere" on Feb 11, 1977, and again the next night on a double bill with *Macon County Line*. All films in the newspaper listing are rated X, likely as a means of satisfying local councils for screening approval on uncertified films.

"I know it was banned in a number of countries," said Corman, "It was never banned in the United States though, we never had any problems like that." He maintains that the film's problems were never legal ones, but purely box office-related. "We had a good advertising campaign, we had good TV spots, the picture I thought was a good picture, and it just didn't do any business. That was the only problem with the picture." Even on the Southern drive-in circuit it did nothing. "I expected to do very well in the South," Corman says, "and I think we did a little bit better in the South than other parts of the country, but not appreciably so." That didn't stop Corman from trying to push it in packages; it continued to play theatres and drive-ins, often paired with other Corman-produced Southern fare like *Black Oak Conspiracy* or *The Great Texas Dynamite Chase*, until 1980. In this scenario, "Cockfighter would have been booked as either a flat fee or no fee at all," explains Joe Dante. "And it's just to have another movie. And that's only because the prints hadn't fallen apart. That didn't play very many places, so the prints weren't beat up." Though sometimes drama would ensue when theatrical bookers realised they had booked both *Cockfighter* and *Born to Kill*, unaware that it was the same film. "Roger would never take the old one out of circulation." Says Dante, laughing. "It was all fancy footwork." Its March 1977 small screen debut on HBO (under the title *Born to Kill*) likewise didn't make much of a ripple.[110]

In December 1980, *Variety* reported that an 18-year-old had been stabbed in the Summit Drive-In theatre outside Akron, Ohio at a double bill of *The Exterminator* and *Born to Kill*. The victim's mother claimed the violent imagery in the films was to blame and sued both the theatre and sub-distributor Avco for $800,000 and the equivalent in punitive damages. The movie just couldn't get a break.

"It was an awfully big comedown for Monte," remembers Steven Gaydos. "I think that's the other thing you have to realise, you know, before he made *Two-Lane Blacktop* he was the hottest director in Hollywood. Afterwards he was so fricking cold as ice that the only movie he could get was this little $300,000 movie about cockfighting nobody wanted to touch. So he was as far into director hell in Hollywood, he was as much outcast from the top perch to the bottom as you could be. *Two-Lane Blacktop* killed his career. Now *think about that*. A movie that is now in the National Registry and regarded, I think universally, certainly everyone from the *New York Times* to every cinematheque on earth considers it an American masterpiece. It destroyed him. Because the town doesn't want soft-hearted gunfighters."

As Corman himself said, the film had everything going for it: a visionary director, an award-winning cinematographer, a sensational subculture, and a whole-hearted promotional push with a national network of sub-distributors and multiple ad campaigns. So why didn't it work?

110 **In a 1988 interview with Kris Gilpin, Hellman says Z Channel insisted that they broadcast the film uncut, and that this subsequently became the version that cable channels aired. However HBO's 1977 listings show the film as *Born to Kill*.**

Chapter Seventeen.

One Dead Game Chicken

There are a few reasons *Cockfighter* may have failed to find its footing, and many of them have to do with the changing face of the South in the 1970s. One could say that the social changes that paved the way for *Cockfighter* to be filmed on-location in Georgia were the very changes that ultimately strangled it, like Frank Mansfield wringing the neck of his own prize-winning cock.

As we've seen in an earlier chapter, the shooting of John Boorman's backwoods horror classic *Deliverance* in Georgia invited a mixed response: it was clear that the South had untapped potential as a shooting location, but it also drew attention to aspects of the South that many Southerners were trying to move away from. Over the course of the decade they would carefully dance around various "Southern" topics, characteristics and stereotypes with varying degrees of experimentation, trying to find a comfortable place to stand. The image of the Southerner was constantly wavering during this period.

The adaptation of *Cockfighter* to the screen coincided with what scholar Derek Nystrom described as a profound shift in the nation's economy and a period of aesthetic and industrial change in Hollywood that signified a "vivid sense of class difference not seen since the 1930s" (it seems fitting then that a cycle of Depression-era films such as *They Shoot Horses, Don't They?* (1969), *Bloody Mama* (1970), *Boxcar Bertha* (1972), *Dillinger* (1973), *The Sting* (1973), *Paper Moon* (1973), *Big Bad Mama* (1974) and others proliferated in this context). It was during this period, he argues, that "the 'redneck' character became an object of fascination for middle-class filmmakers, critics and audiences." Like the Depression, this was another era of great economic uncertainty; masculinity was in crisis, and artworks frequently sought to reestablish its traditional imagery and ideals in ways that were reacting to their post-civil rights, post-sexual revolution context.

After a brief spate of nihilistic Westerns in the late 1960s that responded to the racism and genocide spotlighted by the hugely unpopular Vietnam War, the Western started to cycle out. But as many critics noted, by the beginning of the 1970s, a new breed of rural film was emerging: one that borrowed heavily from the Western's emphasis on scrappy individuality, vigilante justice, and the fight against a wealthy, unjust establishment. Films that, according to critic James Monaco, "celebrate small-town self-

Right: ***Walking Tall*** **(1973).**

reliance, everyday working-class life, and the ongoing struggle with 'the Man'" — films that were "most often shot in the South and earn most of [their] income there."[111]

Walking Tall hit theatres a year before *Cockfighter* and introduced the concept of the specialty Southern audience. The film flopped in urban centres, but had a second life in small rural towns. The film's revised ad campaign compared it to *Billy Jack* and "foregrounded *Walking Tall*'s populist politics."[112] And so other Southern films followed this marketing and exhibition model of seeing the South as a self-sufficient target market, where the bulk of the film's revenues would come from.

But this changing perception of the South's viability was also connected to a shift in demographics towards a more upwardly mobile population. Not only was there an unprecedented economic elevation — it was the first time since before the Civil War that people were emigrating to the South for work — but as a new social class emerged, the "New South" wanted a new image along with it, aimed at keeping its pre-civil rights history at arm's length. "The South emerged from the dangerous days of the 1960s better than it entered, and it has been in a frenzy of self-congratulation ever since," wrote Fred Hobson in a 1985 essay on "The Savage South":

> It now looks disdainfully on the old and decaying cities of the once-superior North — now dismissed as the Rust Belt, the Frost Belt. All the derisive belts once belonged to Dixie — the Bible Belt, the Hookworm Belt, the Chastity Belt, all products of Mencken's imagination — but now Dixie is in the sun. The South, its numerous champions hold, is the place where America might finally work: an unspoiled land of success, optimism, harmonious race relations and shining new cities.

So the first step in shifting public perception of the South was to neuter its dominant character-type: the redneck.

"In Georgia it turns out that cockfighting is an embarrassment," said Joe Dante in Christopher Koetting's New World biography *Mind Warp!*. "It's like *child molesting*." He later elaborated to me that "Roger, I think felt that, it being of an outlaw persuasion, he thought, well, this is a popular sport, even though it's underground, that makes it even more exciting. And so I'll bet there's a big audience for that. And then unfortunately the reaction of a movie about cockfighting in that area — it was roundly condemned and business was very bad."

I always thought the film's failure was connected to what was known as the 'Rural Purge' of early 1970s television — in which provincial characters were seen as out of step with the changing times, resulting in the successive cancellation of all rural shows (basically any show mentioned in Gil Scott-Heron's "The Revolution Will Not Be Televised"). But this just didn't make sense when you consider the massive success of things like *Smokey and the Bandit* and *The Dukes of Hazzard* toward the end of the decade (and even other Corman-produced Southern films in between). Audiences' love-hate relationship with the South in that decade was enough to give you whiplash.

---

111 Qtd in Nystrom, Derek. *Hard Hats, Rednecks and Macho Men: Class in 1970s American Cinema*. New York: Oxford University Press, 2009.
112 Nystrom, Derek. *Hard Hats, Rednecks and Macho Men: Class in 1970s American Cinema*. New York: Oxford University Press, 2009.

I think the best articulation of what happened between the release of *Deliverance* in 1972 (and by extension television's 'Rural Purge') and the subsequent popularity of *Smokey and the Bandit* and *The Dukes of Hazzard* comes from scholar Derek Nystrom. Nystrom refers to *Deliverance* — with its story of city businessmen who come to face a raging river before the building of a dam obliterates the film's "atavistic backwoods spaces" — as "an allegory of the Sun Belt's

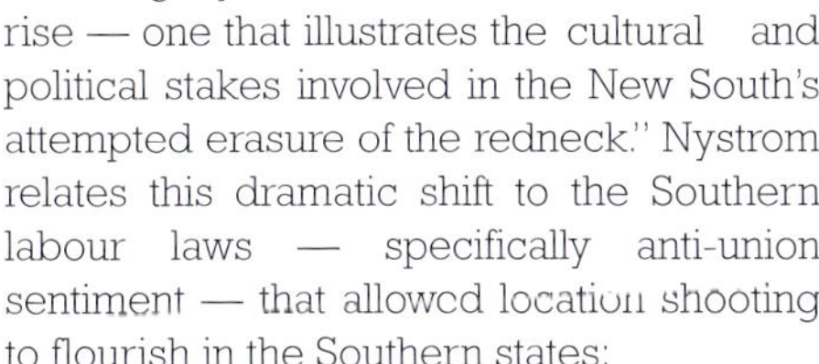

rise — one that illustrates the cultural and political stakes involved in the New South's attempted erasure of the redneck." Nystrom relates this dramatic shift to the Southern labour laws — specifically anti-union sentiment — that allowed location shooting to flourish in the Southern states:

If the obstinate and hostile 'rust belt' workers of *Joe* are to be understood as the product, in part, of the New Hollywood's confrontations with the aging, exclusionist film unions, then we can take the affable, easy-going blue-collar men of the Southern cycle to be partially generated by the right-to-work, employer-friendly labor context of Sunbelt location shooting. (Here, too, we might find another determinant for the good ole boy's consistently anti-union identity in the Southern cycle.) Add to these conditions of production the fact that most of these films considered southern audiences to be their initial (and sometimes only) target market, as well as the fact that many filmmakers negotiated film

Above: Good ol' boys in *Smoky and the Bandit* (1977) and *The Dukes of Hazzard* (1979-1985).

content with local residents (as was the case with *Walking Tall* and *Buster and Billie*, among others), and the reasons behind the Southern cycle's shift from the murderous, degenerate rednecks of *Deliverance* to the playful, fast-driving good ole boys of *Smokey and the Bandit* come into sharper relief.

If, as scholar Charles P. Roland wrote in 1983, the South is the "willful, delinquent child" of the American community, nowhere could this be illustrated more plainly than in the yee-hawing moonshiners and truckers of the Southern cycle, who countered the region's racial history with their insistence that they were, ahem, "never meanin' no harm."

Cockfighter differed from many of the Southern films in that its central imagery is not automotive — very few scenes are set in or around automobiles, and in fact at one point, Frank has to take the bus — whereas the car and the rig are key to most films of the Southern cycle. And while evading the law is also a key element of these films, in *Cockfighter* the sport's illegality is referenced but not activated in the plot. On the contrary — the final tournament that the entire film has been building to takes place at a Senator's mansion. Frank isn't an anti- hero pitted against the Establishment; he is indifferent to the Establishment. The film's central conflict is centred within the psyche of the main character. So in many ways *Cockfighter* deconstructs not only 1970s ideals of masculinity but the emerging subgenre it was part of — a subgenre that was constantly reconfiguring the identity of the Southerner.

Ultimately, as Fred Hobson notes, what changed wasn't the South, but the image of the South. "It is not the loss of Southern distinctiveness I am talking about," he wrote, "but rather the demise of one powerful image, the savage or benighted." He goes on to elaborate that the New South is actually *imported*, and thus can't actually replace the underlying image of the benighted South. As a film, *Cockfighter* came in that period between what was known as 'The Benighted South' (think *Deliverance*) and 'The Vanishing South' (think *Stay Hungry*, or even *Dallas*) and there is an ambivalence in *Cockfighter* about the redneck/good 'ole boy distinction that many Southern films prop up, and this surely contributed to its inability to enjoy the financial success experienced by other films in the cycle — including others produced or distributed by Roger Corman himself, like *Nashville Girl* (1976),

Above: ***Moonshine County Express*** **(1977).**

had been a moonshiner or a trucker, it likely would have made out okay — unlike cockfighting, the trucker craze had infiltrated mainstream culture.

The trucker mini-cycle of films had its basis in an incident that had seized the public imagination — namely, a series of dramatic nationwide trucker shutdowns in late 1973 and early 1974 prompted by rising diesel prices and lower speed limits. The national scale of the event, which included convoys and the blocking of interstate highways, was facilitated by CB radios. Quickly, CB radios and CB lingo became an obsession for middle-class viewers who sought to fashion anonymous alter-egos (the very plot of Jonathan Demme's *Citizen's Band*) — one such alter ego being that of ad man Bill Fries, who changed his name to C.W. McCall and had a hit song with "Convoy," which inspired the film of the same name — not to mention toys and games for kids. But the CB craze also served to hammer a certain point home, the very same point Monte Hellman had honed in on years earlier with Warren Oates' character GTO in *Two-Lane Blacktop*: that middle-class men were "motivated by the familiar, homosocial impulse to remasculinize themselves through an affective connection with laboring bodies."[113] Like many men suddenly buying CB radio kits in the mid-70s, GTO tried to buy his way into a subculture.

Jackson County Jail (1976), *The Great Texas Dynamite Chase* (1976), *Moonshine County Express* (1977) or *Black Oak Conspiracy* (1977). "Through these opposing characterizations," says Nystrom, "the Southern film acknowledges the historical baggage that this classed masculinity had to overcome and then predicts a reconstructed version of this identity." So certain aspects of the Southerner were made 'abject' by the transition to the Southern cycle — the corrupt, racist elements were assigned to the 'redneck' and the independence, integrity and southern manners and hospitality were shifted to the 'good 'ole boy'. And this may be why *Cockfighter* would seem to be primed for box office success and yet ultimately fail — because there was a reconstruction of Southern identity happening and the sport of cockfighting — however widely practiced it may have been — was part of the redneck rejection. It was not what the New South envisioned for itself. That's why it was seen as "an embarrassment," as Joe Dante called it. If Frank Mansfield

Above: *Jackson County Jail* **(1976).**

113 **Nystrom, Derek.** ***Hard Hats, Rednecks and Macho Men: Class in 1970s American Cinema*****. New York: Oxford University Press, 2009.**

But there was no way a subculture that involved the spectacular death of animals was going to go mainstream in the decade that gave us the modern animal liberation movement, prompted by influential books like Peter Singer's *Animal Liberation* (1975) and eventually resulting in the founding of PETA in 1980. There was not going to be a *Cockfighter* playset or boardgame or a Frank Mansfield Barbie doll.

Throughout the decade there was increasing controversy over animal violence in films. "*Cockfighter*... is still around," reported *Box Office Magazine* on July 7, 1975, "A storm of protest from state humane societies did not stop shooting on the picture, but it failed to draw in this territory and has made no appreciable dent in the box office." As Christopher Koetting discusses in *Mind Warp!*, both the *New York Times* and the *Chicago Tribune* featured articles that summer denouncing animal cruelty in films such as *Day of the Locust*. *Variety* called *Cockfighter* "an offbeat slice of grotesque Americana... too slowly and cryptically developed to have much appeal" while Kevin Thomas said that "the grisly sport itself is off-putting in the extreme, and there is finally not enough substance to sustain Hellman's relentlessly austere style and strong existentialist vision."[114] But a year after Oates' death in 1982, Thomas championed the film as a vehicle for Oates, saying "*Cockfighter* depicts an authentic American subculture, and it is a tribute to Oates that he could find some scrappy, bedrock dignity in his cockfighter, just as he did in so many men living on the margin of existence."

"Well it was the first time the sport, or whatever you want to call it, was depicted

---

114 **Nystrom, Derek.** ***Hard Hats, Rednecks and Macho Men: Class in 1970s American Cinema.***

on film," offers Steve Railsback. "And there's always gonna be critics who won't like it until someone else does it, and someone else does it after that."

As Railsback surmised, the film's failure to make an impact at the box office didn't stop other exploitation filmmakers from exploring the subject in *Cockfighter*'s wake. Interestingly, two such examples moved the sport out of the South into other locations.

As noted previously, no nation has invested more in cockfighting than the Philippines — it is the country's oldest spectator sport after boxing. It's so popular in fact, that boxing matches are held in cockfighting arenas, and not the other way around: in 1975 it was a 23,000-seat cockfighting arena that served as the site of the "Thrilla in Manila," the famous boxing match between Muhammad Ali and Joe Frazier for the title of World Heavyweight Champion.

The Philippines provided the backdrop of Gus Trikonis' *Supercock* (1975) starring Ross Hagen, who also produced the film (often working alongside his wife Claire Polan). It was a behind-the-camera role first formed for Trikonis' 1969 film *Sidehackers*; Hagen reteamed with Trikonis (also the director of personal fave *Nashville Girl*) and headed for the Philippines for the PG-rated *Supercock*. "We opened the film in Louisville Kentucky, and the *Louisville Times* wouldn't take the ad," said Hagen in an interview with Brian Albright, for his book *Wild Beyond Belief!*,

> I walked into their offices and said, 'I hope you guys don't have your dicks confused with a chicken. Look it up. Look it up in the dictionary.' They finally gave in and put it in the paper.

> The review came out and said this was the most pornographic film we've ever seen, good for locker room trash only. There wasn't a cuss word in it. The cockfighters, when they get together, they talk about how they feed their cocks. My cock's name was Friendly and Nancy Kwan stole my cock. I ran around the whole movie looking for my lost cock... So we never had to do anything except choose real dialogue from the actual cockfighters... The film is hysterical. Gus and I had a lot of fun making that film.

Charles Willeford had similar concerns that the audience would be snickering during *Cockfighter*, but then resigned himself to it, saying, "If the audience is going to laugh every time the word is mentioned, my undeserved reputation as a comedy writer will be enhanced."

YOU'RE 18, YOUR DAD'S A LOSER.
YOU'VE GOT TO WIN YOUR SPURS.
I NEVER GET KISSED ANYMORE
Rooster
WarBick Productions Present
"ROOSTER"
Starring VINCENT VAN PATTEN · RUTA LEE · KRISTINE DeBELL
TY HARDIN · JEFF COREY · and introducing O. GENE BICKNELL as "STOKE"
Produced by THOMAS K. WARFORD • Directed by BRICE MACK • Music by ROBERT O. RAGLAND
Title Song by "COTTON" WESTHOFF and O. GENE BICKNELL • Original Screenplay by JOHN F. EASTMAN
PG PARENTAL GUIDANCE SUGGESTED
SOME MATERIAL MAY NOT BE SUITABLE FOR CHILDREN
©1977 WarBick Productions
Color by CFI

The next American film to address the sport was Brice Mack's *Rooster: Spurs of Death* (1977), which overtly articulates a lot of *Cockfighter*'s allusions in the dialogue (as one contemporary review stated, "the characters don't have dialogue — they *orate*") as well as in its mute African-American cock handler, Billy, who adopts a Buford-like role in the film. Director Mack himself had been born in the Philippines (which may explain an interest in the sport) but was best known as a longtime Disney background animator, working on everything from *Snow White and the Seven Dwarfs* (1937) to *Song of the South* (1946) and *Lady and the Tramp* (1955). *Rooster* stars Vincent Van Patton, who was then best known for his role on TV's *Apple's Way* (and yet to have his most memorable role in Allan Arkush's *Rock n' Roll High School*), as a hereditary cocker-in-training about to debut in his first public match at the behest of his longtime loser father (played by the film's co-producer Gene Bicknell). The film is set in the Midwest and makes sure you know it; aside from frequent references to its geographical setting, the referee (veteran character player Jeff Corey, who also appeared in Brice Mack's *Jennifer* the same year)[115] announces that the fights abide by Midwestern Derby Rules (as distinct from Wortham's rules, standard in the South).[116]

While posing as a coming-of-age story, the film's left-turn violent climax — "a double murder committed by a sex-crazed dwarf," [117] wrote one reviewer, incredulously — *Rooster* seemed to have an even worse time at the box office than *Cockfighter*. "The good news is that *Rooster* is the best film ever made in Pittsburgh, Kansas," wrote the Kansas City Times in March 1978, "The bad news is that it should have been called 'Turkey'."

While both *Supercock* and *Rooster* employ the kind of balletic, slow-motion cockfighting scenes that characterise Hellman's film, they are distinctly more concerned with corruption among those who gamble on the sport, with the protagonist foiling the criminal element in one (*Supercock*), and joining them in the other (*Rooster*). But in both, the stakes are played out more traditionally than in the introspective *Cockfighter*, which doesn't rely on the triumphant ending typical of most films based on sporting competition. Exploitation films may carry all kinds of subversive messages but their success is dependent on providing simple pleasures. One of those pleasures is the spectacle of the win and the subsequent adulation of the hero. Instead, Frank leaves the pit and follows Mary Elizabeth to the parking lot. We never see him win the medal. Everything the story has been building up to, we don't get to actually witness and celebrate. This defiant withholding is one of the reasons I like it, but it's not the yee-haw ending that drive-in audiences probably expected.

"I was very sorry, especially for [Willeford's] sake, that the movie was such a flop, such a disaster," says Frances Doel. Charles Willeford felt the final film foregrounded the cockfighting too much, at the expense of character. Not only Frank's character, but those of the complex cockers in his milieu. Nonetheless, the prominence of *Cockfighter*-related materials in Willeford's papers show how proud he was of it. He later worked for Corman again, getting roped into location scouting in the Everglades for *Thunder and Lightning* (1977), a moonshiner road movie in which he again had a small role — an experience that later became the subject of a humorous profile Willeford wrote on Corman called "Roger Corman's Little House of Horrors" (retitled "Hollywood's Wild Angel"

115 Many sources claim that Rooster sat unreleased until 1983 but newspaper ads show it screened throughout March 1978 in Kansas and Missouri and Florida — former Florida Governor Claude Kirk has a small role as a corrupt senator.
116 Shooting location Pittsburgh, Kansas is also home to the famous fried chicken feud between competing female-founded restaurants Chicken Annie's and Chicken Mary's. But that's another story.
117 Butler, Robert W. "'Rooster' a Time Waster" in *Kansas City Times*. Wed March 1, 1978. Pg 21.

for its appearance in *The Miami Herald*). The author's Hollywood experience swirled around in his imagination in other ways too; the year after *Cockfighter's* release, Willeford shopped around a new novel called *The Shark-Infested Custard* — which would remain unpublished until 1993 — in which four men who live in a Miami singles high rise have a discussion about drive-in movies that zeroes in on *Two-Lane Blacktop* in particular. "I read the script when it came out in *Esquire* and really wanted to see the movie," one of the men says. Another counters: "Except for Warren Oates as GTO, none of the other people in the movie can act." Willeford goes on to praise the script further, presumably having gained a recent appreciation for this particular skill. When one of the men shows up with a dead teenager in his car, special attention is given to her outfit — including a patch over the crotch of her Daisy Dukes depicting a muscle-flexing rooster and the words, "I'M A MEAN FIGHTING COCK."

According to Willeford's biographer Don Herron, Willeford had another "lost" memoir called *Remembering Warren Oates; or the Demise of the First Five in Line*, a chronicle of a road trip he and Oates took between locations during the *Cockfighter* shoot ("The First Five in Line" being a reference to an aborted novel of the same name, which was meant to depict a TV game show in which contestants sacrifice body parts for prizes). "Charles liked Warren Oates for the reasons so many people did," offers Betsy Willeford, "and he was disconsolate when Warren Oates died, as many people were."

Despite all the issues hampering its release, Nestor Almendros was proud of his work on the film. "I still hope this curious and original film will be discovered one day by true movie lovers," he wrote in his autobiography.

"Well, I'm proud to have worked on it too," says Lewis Teague. "I just didn't understand it fully. I mean I understood basically what it was about, but whatever that was supposed to mean on a metaphysical level escaped me. But I've grown a lot — what was that, 1974? In the 43 or so years since, my insights into what goes on on the planet I think have improved. So it's probably worth another look."

Variety VP Steven Gaydos, then a 22 year-old PA working on his first movie, credits *Cockfighter* with directly shaping the trajectory of his career; afterwards, he even briefly became the personal assistant of *Cockfighter* co-star Richard B. Shull. "I think I did not perform that duty well and was dismissed, probably just for being such a chowder-headed kid," he says, "But what happens is you have an entry point into a life and into a world, and the river starts, and you start flowing with it... and here I am."

Many people asked Monte Hellman why he didn't like the film. "It felt dramatically incomplete," was his standard explanation. But let me return to Siegfried Kracauer, who addresses the suspect nature of pat conclusions in the novel-to-film chapter of his *Theory of Film*: "The novelist naturally wants to bring his story to a conclusion which will put the seal on its wholeness," he writes. "But in genuine novels, it is precisely this conclusion that makes the reader feel uneasy; it strikes him as an arbitrary intervention, cutting short developments that might, or indeed should, be carried on and on."

And that's kind of fitting, because the story of *Cockfighter* never really ended — Willeford knew that. And through its various recuts, re-titlings and re-releases it keeps sticking its head up above the rubble to take another jab at life. After 50 years, that sucker is still pecking. That's what you call a dead-game chicken.

Afterword.

Cockfighter Aspires to Endlessness

They say that you can't change the past. But you can change what the past *means*. You can change the past by attributing significance to different things, by shifting the hierarchy of memories. After all, what is the past but a conglomeration of memories, which are intangible anyway?

Cockfighter is a footnote in the memories of most people who worked on it. It came out, it flopped. In dollars and cents, the film meant nothing to anyone.

"It was one of the few movies I did that I hardly remember anything about," concedes Millie Perkins. "I remember Monte, but Monte was who he was. And we kept in touch kind of, but he was his own person so much that it's not as if he admired people and loved them. He respected people and wanted the best that he could get from them to enhance *his* project. I don't know exactly how to say it. That's how we all felt about Monte… I didn't stay in close contact with Monte, but we always liked each other and we're happy to see each other, which was not often at all. And it was not a social life. He was not a social person and neither was I, I was raising family, you know? So it was not something that we had."

This surprised me to hear. When I stayed at Monte's AirBnB, and during the subsequent times I interviewed him, he spoke of Millie as though they were close friends. And it made me wonder whether he was such an insular person that he could feel close to someone without them knowing it, without them understanding how much of himself he was actually sharing with them; that it could be so hard for a person to express closeness that it is almost imperceptible. It was sad to think about.

Laurie Bird had a tragic end; after being briefly married to Hellman — as he told it, getting married was the death knell for their love affair and they split less than a year later — she embarked on a five-year relationship with Art Garfunkel, and lensed the cover for his 1977 album *Watermark*. In 1979, she overdosed on valium in the New York penthouse they shared (despite Willeford's remark in *Cockfighter Journal* that she "defenestrated herself"[118]). Her death was officially ruled a suicide, though Hellman maintained it was an accidental overdose, timed with the hope of a dramatic intervention. Garfunkel mourned her loss with a dedication and partial photo of her on the back cover of his 1981 album *Scissors Cut*, and in a series of poems entitled *Still Water* in 1989. His 2020 stream-of-

118 Willeford, Charles. *Cockfighter Journal: The Story of a Shooting*. Santa Barbara: Neville Press, 1989. Pg 90. It should be noted that although Monte Hellman told me he never read Willeford's set diary, he took issue with this description of Laurie Bird's death at the 1999 SXSW Film Festival, where he was presenting a screening of *Cockfighter* alongside the film adaptation of Willeford's *The Woman Chaser*. "So he either read the Journal or somebody sent along that reference to him," said Betsy Willeford. "Not sure that it matters, except that it obviously mattered to him. Understandably."

ARRIFLEX

consciousness autobiography *What is it all but Luminous* mentions Bird's death multiple times, but with no factual or emotional detail. Instead, a breakout passage in bold:

Here a silent pause to honor private pain.

By 1980 when Garfunkel was promoting his role in Nicolas Roeg's *Bad Timing*, the coincidence of the film being about an obsessive love that results in a suicide attempt was too juicy for the papers not to mention it, and Garfunkel was forced to relive and recount his grief publicly.

Hellman likewise remained haunted by his time with Bird. In the press notes to his 2010 film *Road to Nowhere* — which he dedicated to her — he said "She memorized every line from every movie or play I ever directed. This was the truest act of love I've ever experienced." A lingering mythology surrounds Laurie Bird; she remains a fascinating enigma for many.

In 2014, musician Tim Kinsella fashioned a strange alternate biography of Laurie Bird called *Let Go and Go On and On*, a fictional narrative assembled out of her film roles and what little was known about her life. It reads lyrically but if you've seen the films you recognise much of the prose as refashioned plot synopses, including actual dialogue. It is a strange experiment.

Hellman never read Kinsella's book, but its central conceit — to uncover a person's real essence through the fictions they created — was not a foreign notion to him. "I think you have to lie to tell the truth," Hellman said in

'Bad Timing' like bridge over troubled waters

From Wire Reports

NEW YORK — After a year mourning the death of his girlfriend, actor-singer Art Garfunkel says he is finally ready to get back to work, promoting his new Nicholas Roeg film, "Bad Timing," and recording a new album.

Last year, while Garfunkel was in Austria making "Bad Timing," a film about an obsessive relationship and an attempted suicide, his girlfriend, Laureen Bird, killed herself. Garfunkel finished the film, then withdrew to spend time with close friends.

"I'm only just now finding myself in the mood to get back to work," he said. "The most important thing in my life is getting a better fix on the question, 'What's the point? What's the point of tomorrow, next year, next decade? What am I alive for?'

"When my lover took her life, I was exposed to suicide for the first time as someone else's choice," he said. "As much as I've never

See Garfunkel, Page 56

1986, "The only real truth is in poetry and in fiction. If you want to tell the truth in non-fiction, it's never gonna be quite as true as the truth of poetry."

A 1983 screening of *Cockfighter* paired with *The Shooting*, hosted by Jack Nicholson and Monte Hellman in honour of Warren Oates (who had died of a heart attack in April of the previous year) sparked the first rumblings of reappraisal for the film, which would develop into firmly entrenched cult status by the following decade. As Charles Willeford passed away in 1988 — less than a month after the release of the last Hoke Moseley novel, *The Way We Die Now* — he never got to witness the numerous special editions of the film, or even really experience his own canonization as an author. *Cockfighter* is widely spoken of as his masterpiece, as well as an integral document of the machinations and values of a subculture that — in the US, anyway — has since been driven deeply underground. *Cockfighter* has been included in many Hellman retrospectives over the years, with several taking place at the American Cinematheque where Hellman's devoted friend and fan Dennis Bartok was a longtime programmer. But outside of such retrospectives it remains rarely celebrated on the big screen, possibly due to its protest-baiting subject matter.

"It will never be my favourite," Hellman told me in our last interview, softening somewhat from his earlier assertion that it was "the worst picture I ever made." I suppose I'll have to live with that.

There are layers of mythology baked into this film: whether that's mythology concerning the noble history of the violent sport at its heart; mythology about the 'auteur' and exactly what constitutes authorship of a film; mythology around rising stars who disappeared from view too soon; mythology about The South — what it means and who it belongs to. Some mythologies I have projected onto the film myself.

Like many movie pilgrims, much of my travel is determined by proximity to film locations, and in March of 2018, with the help of fellow movie fanatic Mike Malloy (a historian of 'tough-guy' cinema of the 1970s), the time had come to visit Mansfield, Georgia. The people in Mansfield will be quick to tell you that *My Cousin Vinny* was filmed there in the '90s, but few of them remember *Cockfighter*. All of the film's cockfighting consultants are dead, but an old timer in Mansfield pointed us to a remote out-of-town spot where he thought there was a disused cockpit that had featured in *Cockfighter*. We drove out to find it, getting deeper into rural Georgia, passing "no trespassing" signs and trying to ignore the gunshots we were hearing out in the woods. Eventually we came upon some kind of strange, half-collapsed structure, not far from what can only be described as a shanty village and a tiny graveyard. We ventured inside, but it was far too small for any regulation cockpit. If it was a cockpit at all, it must have served some pretty desperate amateur cockfighters.

We subsequently went to Bulloch Hall in Roswell, the former plantation house that served as Senator Foxhall's mansion, the setting for the film's conclusion. Though there remains no sign of the bespoke cockpit fashioned for the film, I sat on the rocking chair on the porch, like I was Ed Middleton waiting to tell Frank he'd broken

his promise to stay out of the cockfighting racket. It probably wasn't the same chair, but sometimes an imperfect recreation is as good as those of us who live in our imaginations can muster in this life.

In 2018, former New World PR man-turned-film-producer Jon Davison (*Airplane!*, *Starship Troopers*) and Roger Corman worked with the Academy Film Archive to create a new 35mm preservation print of *Cockfighter* from the original camera negative. It was one of many Corman-produced New World and AIP films being re-struck as part of an ongoing collaboration between Davison — who co-owns an extensive film archive with Joe Dante[119] — and the Academy Film Archive. Davison organised a screening on April 10, 2018 at Fotokem in Burbank and invited me to come out for it. Both Corman and Monte Hellman were there, the latter with his new sheepdog puppy in tow (his longtime companion Kona, a bumbling sheepdog who seemed to love all the attention from guests at Monte's AirBnB, had passed away not long before). After a new 35mm trailer for Corman's *The Trip* played, *Cockfighter* began, and I had never seen it look better.

Monte was quiet as usual, and the presence of the puppy meant that he had to skip out on lunch with the rest of us, who went to famous Rat Pack haunt The Smoke House for a belated birthday celebration for Roger, who'd just turned 92 a few days before on April 5th — 45 years to the day he touched down in Atlanta for the filming of *Cockfighter*.

I remain envious of Frank Mansfield's silence. The writing of this book was hampered by far too much noise. Like Frank, there were times I couldn't shut up, to my own detriment.

On April 20, 2021, as I thought I was nearing the end of this manuscript, Monte died while resting in the backyard of his Palm Springs home. He was 91.

When I saw the news, casually scrolling through Twitter, all the air went out of my body and I just deflated and shook. I cried for hours. Not that Monte and I were close, far from it. In fact he was quite unimpressed by my obsessive interest in a film he considered so disappointing. But my primary drive in writing a book about the film — when I started it, anyway — was to prove to him that he was wrong about it. That his film meant something. And now he would never hold that book in his hands. I am pretty sure I felt how Frank Mansfield felt when he lost his prize bird in that ill-calculated hack right before the big tournament. I blew it.

Dennis Bartok offered me a record from Monte's personal collection as a consolation. He rattled off some of the titles: "If you're into Ronee Blakley from *Nashville*, he gave me two of her albums (I'm guessing they

119 Davison was one of the print collectors profiled in Dennis Bartok and Jeff Joseph's epic book *A Thousand Cuts* (2016).

were friends); James Taylor's *Mud Slide Slim* (sealed!); the soundtrack to Resnais's *Stavisky* by Sondheim; Albert Camus reading in French; piano rags by Scott Joplin; the cast album to T.S. Eliot's *The Cocktail Party* featuring Alec Guinness. This also gives you some idea of Monte's eclectic tastes!" I chose the Ronee Blakley. I listened to it incessantly as I was finishing this book.

But in tribute to Monte let me conjure a Beckett catchphrase — "fail better" — and writer Terence Killeen's poignant summation of what that really means: "Failing better is not a failure to create something, to achieve something, but rather a failure to *de-create* something, to undo something that stubbornly refuses to be undone." *Cockfighter* had no great ambitions, as a book or a film, and yet it is the one that remains untamable and abiding. It is the one that dominates Willeford's archive, that had tendrils stretching from one end of his career to the other. Whether the film failed is irrelevant. Because *this is something you don't conquer.*

About a month before my print deadline, Roger Corman, the indefatigable, seemingly immortal titan of the B-picture and arguably the most important movie producer of the 20th century — passed away, two years shy of his centennial.

I was struck by the realization that this book now had the same ending as my last book. A missed chance, a broken promise, people dying and me not making it in time. The book ending with the completion of the book itself. Well, I guess there are worse endings.

Oh — it also ended with a tattoo.

As Frank Mansfield says, "There is no such thing as a passive interest in cockfighting."

Bibliography

All interviews not credited to third party sources in the text were conducted by the author.

Ackerman, Bill. "Episode 31: Molly Haskell" on *Supporting Characters Podcast*, Dec. 12, 2017.

Albright, Brian. *Wild Beyond Belief! Interviews with the Exploitation Filmmakers of the 1960s and 1970s.* Jefferson: McFarland & Company, Inc., 2008.

Alexander, Chris. *Corman/Poe.* Oxford: Headpress, 2023.

Allen, Frederick. "End to Cockfights for Film Demanded" in *Atlanta Constitution*, April 18, 1974.

Almendros, Nestor. *Man with a Camera.* New York: Farrar-Strauss-Giroux, 1984.

Anderson, Eric Gary, Taylor Hagood and Daniel Cross Turner. *Undead Souths: The Gothic and Beyond in Southern Literature and Culture.* Baton Rouge: Louisiana State University Press, 2015.

Germani Greg. "Cockfighter" in *Atlanta Time Machine.* Accessed online at http://www.atlantatimemachine.com/cockfighter/05.htm

Barolsky, Paul. "The Fable of Failure in Modern Art" in *The Virginia Quarterly Review* 73, no. 3 (1997): 395-404.

Becker, Ernest. *The Denial of Death.* New York: Free Press, 1973.

Begley, Ed. Jr. *To the Temple of Tranquility.... And Step on it!* New York: Hachette Books, 2023. Kindle.

Black, Louis. "Cinematexas Program Notes" Vol. 19, No. 2 (Oct. 28, 1980)

Bleich, Joshua and Lawrence Webb. *Hollywood on Location: An Industry History.* New Brunswick: Rutgers University Press, 2019.

Boetticher, Budd. *When in Disgrace.* Santa Barbara: Neville Press, 1989.

Box Office Magazine, May 20, 1974

Box Office Magazine, Aug 5, 1974

Bruce, Dixon B., Jr. *Violence and Culture in the Antebellum South.* Austin: University of Texas Press, 1979. Kindle.

Burkert, Walter. *Creation of the Sacred: Tracks of Biology in Early Religions.* Cambridge: Harvard University Press, 1966.

Burkert, Walter, René Girard and Jonathan Z. Smith. *Violent Origins: Ritual Killing and Cultural Formation.* Stanford: Stanford University Press, 1987.

Butler, Robert W. "'Rooster' a Time Waster" in *Kansas City Times.* Weds, March 1, 1978.

Caldwell, Erskine. *The Bastard.* New York: Novel Selections, 1958.

Carpenter, Brian and Tom Franklin. *Grit Lit: A Rough South Reader.* Columbia: University of South Carolina Press, 2012.

Cash, W.J. *The Mind of the South.* New York: Vintage Books edition, 1991.

Christol, Florent. "Christmas Evil and the Cultural Myth of the Fool-Killer" in *Yuletide Terror: Christmas Horror on Film and Television.* Eds. Paul Corupe and Kier-La Janisse. Toronto: Spectacular Optical, 2017.

Compo, Susan. *Warren Oates: A Wild Life.* Lexington: University Press of Kentucky, 2009. Kindle.

Cooper, David. "The Boredom is Fatal in 'Born to Kill'" in *The Courier Journal*, April 26, 1975.

Corman, Roger with Jim Jerome. *How I Made a Hundred Movies in Hollywood and Never Lost a Dime*. London: Muller, 1990.

Corman, Roger. "Working with Young Directors" in *Roger Corman: Interviews*. Ed. Constantine Nasr. Jackson: University Press of Mississippi, 2011.

Crane, Robert and Christopher Fryer. *Jack Nicholson: The Early Years*. (Originally published in 1975 as *Jack Nicholson: Face to Face*) Lexington: University Press of Kentucky, 2012.

Crayon, Porte. "North Carolina Illustrated" in *Harpers New Monthly Magazine* (May 1857): 741-775. Accessed April 29, 2024 at https://babel.hathitrust.org/cgi/pt?id=uc1.b000541560&seq=9

Crews, Harry. *The Hawk is Dying*. New York: Alfred A. Knopf, 1973.

Crews, Harry. *A Childhood: The Biography of a Place*. New York: Harper & Row, 1978.

Crews, Harry "The Violence that Finds Us" *Playboy* 31.4 (April 1984): 98-99, 186, 188, 190-192.

Crews, Harry. "Cockfighting: An Unfashionable View" in *Florida Frenzy*. Gainesville: University of Florida Press, 1992.

Crews, Harry. "A Day at the Dogfights" in *Florida Frenzy*. Gainesville: University of Florida Press, 1992.

Curtwright, Bob. "Kansas Cockfighting Film Tosses in Violent Ending" in *The Wichita Eagle*, Weds. March 1, 1978.

Cutter, Robert Joe. "Brocade and Blood: The Cockfight in Chinese and English Poetry" in *Journal of the American Oriental Society*, Vol. 109, No. 1 (Jan-Mar 1989): 1-16.

Davis, Lennard J. *Obsession: A History*. Chicago: University of Chicago Press, 2009. Kindle.

Dell, Floyd. "Hallelujah, I'm a Bum" in *The Century Magazine* (June 1925): 137-151.

Dempsey, Ralph. "Cockfighting in Louisiana" in *New Histories* (Feb 2, 2011): Accessed Feb 23, 2017 at http://newhistories.group.shef.ac.uk/wordpress/wordpress/cockfighting-in-louisiana/

Donlon, Jon Griffin. "Cajun Cock Pits" in *Material Culture*, Vol. 25, No. 2 (SUMMER 1993): Pgs. 25-36.

Donlon, Jon Griffin. *Bayou Country Bloodsport: The Culture of Cockfighting in Southern Louisiana*. Jefferson: McFarland & Company, Inc., 2014. Kindle.

Doss, Erika. "Toward an Iconography of American Labor: Work, Workers, and the Work Ethic in American Art, 1930-1945" in *Design Issues*, Vol 13, No. 1 (Spring 1997) MIT Press.

Drinkwater, Ouida. "Acting Comes Second (An Interview with Patty Shaw)" in *The Delta Democrat Times*, Sunday, July 27, 1975.

Duina, Francesco. *Winning: Reflections on an American Obsession*. Princeton: Princeton University Press, 2010.

Dundes, Alan. "Gallus as Phallus: A Psychoanalytic Cross-Cultural Consideration of the Cockfight as Fowl Play" in *The Cockfight: A Casebook*. Madison: University of Wisconsin Press, 1994.

Eamon, Willliam. "Drunk with the Cup of Liberty" in *Southwest Review*, Vol. 70, No. 4 (AUTUMN 1985): 534-541.

Fay, Tim. "Farmer Keeps Tradition of Breeding

Gamecocks" in Atlanta Journal-Constitution, Feb 3, 1994.

Feathered Warrior. Various issues, 1973-1997

Foroutan, Aida. "Why the Fighting Cock? The Significance of the Imagery of the Khorus Jangi and its Manifesto 'The Slaughterer of the Nightingale,'" *Iran Namag*, Volume 1, Number 1 (Spring 2016): 28-69.

Forsyth, Craig J. "A Pecking Disorder: Cockfighting in Louisiana" in *International Review of Modern Sociology*, Vol. 26, No. 1 (Spring 1996): 15-25.

Forter, Greg. *Murdering Mas culinities: Fantasies of Gender and Violence in the American Crime Novel.* New York: New York University Press, 2000.

Freud, Sigmund. *Civilization and its Discontents.* New York: W.W. Norton & Co, 1961.

Gallup, P.W. "The Ceremony of the White Cock in Winchester" in *Folklore*, Vol. 96, No. 1 (1985): 112-114.

Garner, Phil. "Blood and Feathers in the Gallant South" in *Atlanta Journal-Constitution*. June 9,1974

Geertz, Clifford. "Deep Play: Notes on the Balinese Cockfight" in *The Cockfight: A Casebook.* Madison: University of Wisconsin Press, 1994.

Geltner, Ted. *Blood Bone and Marrow: A Biography of Harry Crews.* Athens: University of Georgia Press, 2016. Kindle.

Gilpin, Kris. "Monte Hellman: The Lost Interview" in *Cinema Retro* (Dec. 28, 2009): Accessed online at: https://cinemaretro.com/index.php?/archives/4108-CINEMA-RETRO-PRESENTS-MONTE-HELLMAN,-THE-LOST-INTERVIEW-FINAL-PART.html#extended

Girard, René. *Violence and the Sacred.* Baltimore: John Hopkins University Press, 1979.

Goldberg, Lee. "Interview with Earl Mac Rauch" in *Starlog*, No 84 (July 1984): 66-68.

Golsan, Richard J. "Interview with James Lee Burke" in *South Central Review*, Vol. 27, No. 1/2, Hard-Boiled (Spring/Summer 2010): 167-170.

Goodell, Jeff. *The Heat Will Kill You First.* New York: Hachette Book Group, 2023. Kindle.

Gorns, Elliot. "Gouge and Bite, Pull Hair and Scratch" in *The American Historical Review*, Vol. 90, (February to December 1985): 18-43.

Gould, Thomas. *Silence in Modern Literature and Philosophy.* New York: Springer Books, 2018.

Gow, Gordon. "Moving Along with Love and Obsession" in *Films and Filming*, Vol 21, No 1 (October 1974): 61.

Gray, Beverly. *Roger Corman: Blood-Sucking Vampires, Flesh-Eating Cockroaches, and Driller Killers.* AZ Ferris Publications, 3rd Edition, 2012. Kindle.

Gray, Farnum. "'Poor Pretty Eddie' Repugnant Film" in *The Atlanta Constitution*, August 14, 1974.

Grit & Steel, Various issues, 1906-1982.

Grosjean, Pauline. "A History of Violence: The Culture of Honor and Homicide In The US South" in *Journal of the European Economic Association* 12, no. 5 (2014)

Harmetz, Aljean. "Monte's Turn for the Big Time?" in *The New York Times*, May 16, 1971.

Hartzog, L. T. "Mrs. McMillan Wins S.C. Press Awards" in *The Gaffney Ledger*, Feb. 14, 1968.

Haut, Woody. *Neon Noir: Contemporary American Crime Fiction.* London: Serpent's Tail, 1999.

Haley, Alex. "Researching the Unknown" in *Writer's Yearbook*, no 44 (Feb 1973): 26-30/106.

Haley, Alex. *Roots: The Saga of an American Family.* Philadelphia: Da Capo Press, 2014. Kindle.

Haskell, Molly. *From Reverence to Rape: The Treatment of Women in the Movies.* New York: Penguin Books, 1974

Hawley, Fred. "The Moral and Conceptual Universe of Cockfighters: Symbolism and Rationalization" in *Society and Animals*, Vol 1, No 2 (1993): Pgs. 159-168.

Herron, Don. *Willeford.* Tucson: Dennis McMillan Publications, 1997.

Herzog, Harold A. Jr. "Hackfights and Derbies" in *Appalachian Journal*, Vol. 12, No. 2 (WINTER 1985): Pgs. 114-126.

Hill, Thomas E. "Symbolic Protest and Calculated Silence" in *Philosophy & Public Affairs*, Vol. 9, No. 1 (Autumn, 1979): Pgs 83-102.

Hobson, Fred. "The Savage South: An Inquiry into the Origins, Endurance, and Presumed Demise of an Image" in *The Virginia Quarterly Review*, Vol. 61,No. 3 (Summer 1985): Pgs 392-393.

Hogan, William. "Roots, Routes, and Langston Hughes's Hybrid Sense of Place." in *Langston Hughes* ed. Harold Bloom. New York: Blooms Literary Criticism, 2006. Pg. 188.

Hollywood Reporter, April 1974.

Hooven, F. Vallentine. *BeefCake: The Muscle Magazines of America, 1950-1970.* Cologne: Taschen Books, 1995.

Houston, Penelope. "Corralling the Non-Conformists" in *The Times*, Aug 16, 1974.

Huddy, John. "Wild Oates" in *Miami Herald*, Sunday Sept. 20, 1974.

Huey, John. "Cockfighter a Fowl Film Orgy" in *Atlanta Constitution*, Weds July 31, 1974.

Hughes, Langston. *The Collected Poems of Langston Hughes.* New York: Alfred A. Knopf, 1994.

Hundley, Daniel. *Social Relations in our Southern States.* Hardpress, 2018. Kindle.

Isenberg, Nancy. *White Trash: The 400-Year Untold History of Class in America.* New York: Penguin Books, 2016.

Jones, Joseph R. "Out of Sight, Out of Mind: Recovering the History of Cockfighting in Kentucky" in *The Kentucky Review*, Vol. 13, No. 3 (1997): Pgs. 3-48.

Jones, Kent. "The Cylinders Were Whispering My Name: Monte Hellman" in *The Last Great American Picture Show.* Amsterdam: Amsterdam University Press, 2021. Kindle.

Kinsella, Tim. *Let Go and Go On and On.* Chicago: Curbside Splendor Publishing, 2014. Kindle.

Kleinberg-Levin, D.M. *Before the Voice of Reason: Echoes of Responsibility in Merleau-Ponty's Ecology and Levinas's Ethics.* Albany, New York: SUNY Press, 2008.

Koetting, Christopher. *Mind Warp! The Fantastic True Story of Roger Corman's New World Pictures.* Hailsham: Hemlock Books Limited, 2000.

Kracauer, Siegfried. *Theory of Film: The Redemption of Physical Reality.* Princeton: Princeton University Press,1960.

Lawler, Andrew. *Why Did the Chicken Cross the World?: The Epic Saga of the Bird that Powers Civilization.* New York: Atria Books, 2014. Kindle.

Laxness, Halldor. *Independent People.* New York: Knopf Doubleday Publishing Group, 1997.

Loughborough, William B. Personal website, accessed online at: http://w3.gorge.net/love26/GAME.htm

Love, Damien. *Supporting Features: Writing and Interviews on Movies and Moviemakers.* CreateSpace, 2016. Kindle.

Mailer, Norman. *Why Are We in Vietnam?* New York: Random House, 1967. Kindle.

Marrs, Daniel J. "Ineluctable Mystery and Sacramentality in Flannery O'Connor's *Wise Blood*" Baylor University Paper, 2010.

Maunula, Marko. "Of Chickens and Men: Cockfighting and Equality in the South" in *Southern Cultures*, Vol. 13, No. 4, The Global South (WINTER 2007): 67-85.

McMillan, Ruth De Camp. "Gaffney Strangler Indicted on Four Counts of Murder" in *Grit & Steel.* April 1968.

Means, George W. *The Game Cock: From the Shell to the Pit.* Cookhill: Read Country Books, 1911. Kindle.

Michaud, Michael Gregg. *Inventing Troy Donahue: The Making of a Movie Star.* Orlando: BearManor Media, 2023.

Milne, Tom. "Cockfighter Review" in *BFI Monthly Film Bulletin*, Vol. 44, No. 523 (August 1977): 165-166.

Miner, Sara. "Cockfighting in the American Midwest During the Mid-Twentieth Century: Women's Participation in the Practice" in *UCLA: Center for the Study of Women* (2012) Retrieved from https://escholarship.org/uc/item/4771c7p1

Mortley, Raoul. "The Theme of Silence in Clement of Alexandria" in *Journal of Theological Studies.* Vol. 24, No. 1. (1973) Pgs. 197-202.

Munro, Richard. "Letter From the Publisher" in *Sports Illustrated* (May 22, 1972): Pg 5.

Murphy, Bernice. *The California Gothic in Fiction and Film.* Edinburgh: Edinburgh University Press, 2022.

Murphy, Kathleen. "The Color of Home" in *Film Comment*, Vol. 28, No. 5 (SEPTEMBER–OCTOBER 1992): Pgs. 62-63.

Murray, Gabrielle. *This Wounded Cinema, This Wounded Life: Violence and Utopia in the Films of Sam Peckinpah.* Westport: Praeger, 2004.

Myers, Steve. "Filmed, Premiered in Georgia" in *The Red and Black*, Nov 7, 1974.

Naficy, Hamid. *A Social History of Iranian Cinema Vol 2: The Industrializing Years, 1941-1978.* Durham: Duke University Press, 2011.

Nashawaty, Chris. *Crab Monsters, Teenage Cavemen and Candy Stripe Nurses: Roger Corman: King of the B Movie.* New York: Abrams Books, 2013. Kindle.

Nette, Andrew and Iain McIntyre. *Dangerous Visions and New Worlds: Radical Science Fiction, 1950-1985.* Binghamton: PM Press, 2021

Nilsen, Lars. *Warped & Faded: Weird Wednesday and the Birth of the American Genre Film Archive.* Austin: Mondo Books, 2021.

Nystrom, Derek. *Hard Hats, Rednecks and Macho Men: Class in 1970s American Cinema*. New York: Oxford University Press, 2009.

O'Connor, Flannery. *Wise Blood*. Toronto: Harper Perennial Classics, 2015. Kindle.

Pasquariello, Nicholas. "Monte Hellman on Corman and Cockfighter" in *Jump Cut: A Review of Contemporary Media* No 10-11 (1976): 17-18.

Pearson, Jesse. "A Man's Field" at http://jesse-pearson.com/writing/a-mans-field/

Percy, Walker. *The Moviegoer*. New York: Noonday Press, 1960.

Photinos, Christine. "The Tramp in American Literature, 1873-1939" in *AmeriQuests* Vol. 5, No. 1 (2008) Accessed online at: https://ejournals.library.vanderbilt.edu/index.php/ameriquests/article/view/62

Pinkerton, Nick. "Fowl Play: Charles Willeford's Cult Chicken Novel" in *Book Forum*. July 20, 2011. Accessed online at http://www.bookforum.com/pubdates/8073

Poggiali, Chris. "The Truth About Eddie: Remembering Poor Pretty Eddie" in *Temple of Schlock*. Sept 10, 2011. Accessed online at http://templeofschlock.blogspot.com/2011/09/truth-about-eddie-remembering-poor.html

Poller, Betsy. "Rape in the Kitchen: Food Used as Weapon" in *Miami Herald*. May 31, 1972.

Pridgen, Tim. *Courage: The Story of Modern Cockfighting*. Boston: Little, Brown and Company, 1938.

Publisher's Weekly "Rights & Permissions" column, Jan 7, 1974

Publishers Weekly "Rights & Permissions" column, June 3, 1974.

Rader, Richard. "The Fate of Humanism in Greek Tragedy" in *Philosophy and Literature* 33, no. 2 (2009): 442-454. doi:10.1353/phl.0.0063.

Rauch, Earl Mac. *Arkansas Adios*. New York: Alfred A Knopf, 1971.

Remes, Justin. *Absence in Cinema: The Art of Showing Nothing*. New York: Columbia University Press, 2020.

Roland, Charles P. "The Ever-Vanishing South" in *The Journal of Southern History* 48, no. 1 (1982): 3-20. Accessed July 17, 2021. doi:10.2307/2207294.

Rosenbaum, Jonathan. "Paris-London Review" in *Film Comment*, November/December 1974.

Shermer, Elizabeth Tandy. "Counter-Organizing the Sunbelt: Right-to-Work Campaigns and Anti-Union Conservatism, 1943–1958." in *Pacific Historical Review*, Vol. 78, No. 1 (February 2009): Pgs. 81-118.

Silver, Alan and James Ursini. *Roger Corman: Metaphysics on a Shoestring*. Los Angeles: Silman-James Press, 2006.

Snow, Ollie Tine. "The Functional Gothic of Flannery O'Connor" in *Southwest Review*, Vol. 50, No. 3 (SUMMER 1965): Pgs. 286-299.

Sontag, Susan. "The Aesthetics of Silence" in *Styles of Radical Will*. London: Picador Books, 2013. Kindle.

Spektor, Matthew. *Always Crashing in the Same Car: On Art, Crisis & Los Angeles, California*. Portland: Tin House, 2021. Kindle.

Spiegel, Alan. "A Theory of the Grotesque in Southern Fiction" in *The Georgia Review*, Vol. 26, No. 4 (Winter 1972): Pgs. 426-437.

Stevens, Brad. *Monte Hellman: His Life and Films.* Jefferson/London: McFarland & Company, 2003.

Stevens, Chuck. "Moebius Dragstrip" in *Film Comment*, Vol. 36, No. 2 (MAR/APR 2000): Pgs. 52-54, 57-60, 63-65.

Stubblefield, Paul. "Fightin' Roosters Now Stars" in *Kansas City Star*, Thursday June 9, 1977.

Stultz, Michael. "A Revisionist Reading of Existentialism in Flannery O'Connor's *Wise Blood*" Masters' Thesis. Indianapolis: Butler University Press, 2005.

Supporting Characters Podcast: Molly Haskell

Svinth, Joseph R. "Death Under the Spotlight: The Data" in *Journal of Combative Sport* (Nov 2007).

Tatum, Charles Jr. *Monte Hellman.* Amiens: Festival d'Amiens / Editions Yellow Now, 1988.

Taylor, Charles. *Opening Wednesday at a Theater or Drive-In Near You: The Shadow Cinema of the American '70s.* New York: Bloomsbury USA, 2017.

Thomas, Barbara. "$30 Million Fattens Economy" in *Atlanta Journal Constitution*, Sunday Jan 11, 1976.

Thomas, Kevin. "Warren Oates: Slices of Americana" in *Los Angeles Times*, Aug 31, 1983.

Townsend, Sylvia. *Bumpy Road: The Making, Flop, and Revival of Two Lane Blacktop.* Jackson: University of Mississippi Press, 2019. Kindle.

Unknown. "Cockfighter Review" in *Variety*, June 3, 1975.

Unknown. "Son slain, Mother Sues Theatre, Avco Over Violent Pix" in *Variety Daily*, Dec 19, 1980.

Various Authors. *Histories of Game Strains.* Cookhill: Read Country Books, 2005.

Vernon, Alex. "Staging Violence in West's "The Day of the Locust" and Shepard's "True West"" in *South Atlantic Review* 65, no. 1 (2000): 132-51.

Von Doviak, Scott. *Hick Flicks: The Rise and Fall of Redneck Cinema.* Jefferson: McFarland & Company, Inc., 2005.

West, Nathaniel. *The Day of the Locust.* Kaf Publishing, 2012. Kindle.

Wheatley, Catherine. "La Famille Denis" in *Intimacy on the Border: The Films of Claire Denis.* Ed. Marjorie Vecchio. London/New York: IB Taurus, 2014.

White, Mike. "Madness in the 20th Century" in *Cashiers du Cinemart*, No. 11 (2012).

Willeford, Charles. "The Alectryomancer" in *The Machine in Ward Eleven.* New York: Belmont Books, 1963.

Willeford, Charles. *Cockfighter.* Chicago: Chicago Paperback House, 1962.

Willeford, Charles. *Cockfighter.* New York: Overlook Press, 2011. Kindle.

Willeford, Charles. *Cockfighter Journal: The Story of a Shooting.* Santa Barbara: Neville Press, 1989.

Willeford, Charles. "From Cockfighter to Born to Kill" in *Film Quarterly*, Vol. XXIV, No. 1 (Fall 1975): 20-24.

Willeford, Charles. "Cockfighter: Novelist Turns His Book into Screenplay — And Learns Some Tricks in the Process" in *The Miami Herald*. Sunday July 21, 1974.

Willeford, Charles. "Introductory notes to *Cockfighter* original screenplay" in personal papers at the Dianne and Michael Bienes Special Collections and Rare Book Library, Bienes Museum of the Modern Book, Broward County Library.

Willeford, Charles. "A Perspective on Nathaniel West" in personal papers at the Dianne and Michael Bienes Special Collections and Rare Book Library, Bienes Museum of the Modern Book, Broward County Library.

Willeford, Charles. "The Gambler and the Guitar" date unknown. In personal papers at the Dianne and Michael Bienes Special Collections and Rare Book Library, Bienes Museum of the Modern Book, Broward County Library.

Willeford, Charles. Letter to the editor in *Hollywood Reporter*, Dec 27, 1972.

Willeford, Charles. "New Forms of Ugly: The Immobilized Hero in Modern Fiction" in *Writing and Other Bloodsports*. Audible Studios, 2021. Audiobook.

Willeford Charles. *The Black Mass of Brother Springer*. Wit's End Publishing, 2004. Kindle.

Willeford, Charles. *The Woman Chaser*. Chicago: Newsstand Library, 1960.

Willeford, Charles. *The Burnt Orange Heresy*. New York: Vintage Crime/Black Lizard, 1990.

Willeford, Charles. *The Shark-Infested Custard*. New York: Vintage Crime/Black Lizard, 2009. Kindle.

Willeford, Charles. *Miami Blues*. New York: Ballantine Books, 1985.

Willeford, Charles. "Rolling With the Punches at 14" in *The Miami Herald*. Sunday Oct 20, 1974.

Willeford, Charles. *Sideswipe*. New York: Vintage Crime/Black Lizard, 2009. Kindle.

Willeford, Charles. *Something About a Soldier*. New York, Ballantine Books, 1988.

Willeford, Charles. *I Was Looking for a Street*. Brooklyn/Los Angeles: Picturebox and Family, 2010.

Wood, Amy Louise, Ed. *The New Encyclopedia of Southern Culture, Vol 19: Violence*. Chapel Hill: University of North Carolina Press, 2011.

Wright, Tom F. "Edgar Allan Poe and the Southern Gothic" in *The Palgrave Handbook of the Southern Gothic*. Eds. Susan Castillo Street and Charles L. Crow. London: Palgrave Macmillan, 2016.

Wurlitzer, Rudolph and Will Corry. "Two-Lane Blacktop: A Screenplay" in *Esquire*, Vol. LXXV, No 4 (April 1971): Pgs. 104-114 / 142-144.

Wurlitzer, Rudolph. *Nog*. Columbus: Two Dollar Radio, 2009.

Wyatt-Brown, Bertram. *Southern Honor: Ethics and Behavior in the Old South*. New York: Oxford University Press, 25th Anniversary Edition, 2007. Kindle.

FAB Press presents a Spectacular Optical book
COCKFIGHT: A FABLE OF FAILURE

This first pressing of the FAB Press edition published April 2025
The first edition of this book was originally published July 2024 by Spectacular Optical

FAB Press Ltd., 2 Farleigh, Ramsden Road, Godalming, Surrey, GU7 1QE, England, UK

www.fabpress.com

Layout/Design: Luke Insect

Cover Design: Adam Juresko

Additional Editing: Sean Hogan and Naben Ruthnum

Research Assistance: Chris Poggiali and Bill Ackerman

Special Thanks to:
Allan Arkush, Jasmine Baker, Dennis Bartok, Wayne Blackwell, Cassie Blake, Brian Block, Jim Branscombe, Cindy Brown, Kelly A. Brown, Heather Buckley, Michael Chinich, King-Wei Chu, Susan Compo, Julie Corman, Roger Corman, Peter Cornberg, Carl Daft, Frank Daft, Joe Dante, Mitch Davis, Jon Davison, Steve De Jarnatt, Lee Demarbre, Jim Demoruelle, JT Dockery, Melissa Eastin, Jeff Field, Andrew Furtado, Jarret Gahan, Jeannie from Mansfield City Hall, Lee Gambin, Steven Gaydos, Beverly Gray, David Gregory, Harry Guerro, Mark Hartley, Monte Hellman, Ben Hellwig, Norm Hill, Foster Hirsch, Stephen Hooker, Gillian Wallace Horvat, Felix Hubble, David Hyman, Craig Lapper, Tim and Karrie League, Andrew Leavold, Jeff Lieberman, Mike Malloy, Chandra Mayor, Jimmy McDonough, Deanne Mencher, The Mustarinda Association, Cherry Pearcy, Millie Perkins, Don Phillips, Rochelle Pienn, Ed Polgardy, Steve Railsback, Earl Mac Rauch, Larry Richardson, Kimmy Robertson, Naben Ruthnum, Amy Voorhees Searles, Noah Segan, Josh Stafford, Lewis Teague, Valerie Torres, Deborah Van Valkenburgh, Don Walters, Mike White, Betsy Willeford, and all the Indiegogo Supporters.

Printed in India

A CIP catalogue record for this book
is available from the British Library

ISBN 978-1-913051-40-2

GPSR Compliance
Publisher:
FAB Press Ltd, Surrey, United Kingdom
Authorised Representative:
Easy Access System Europe –
Mustamäe tee 50, 10621 Tallinn, Estonia,
gpsr.requests@easproject.com